The Ecumenical Movement

Recent Titles in
Contributions to the Study of Religion

Noble Daughters: Unheralded Women in Western Christianity, 13th to 18th Centuries
Marie A. Conn

Confessing Christ in a Post-Holocaust World: A Midrashic Experiment
Henry F. Knight

Learning from History: A Black Christian's Perspective on the Holocaust
Hubert Locke

History, Religion, and Meaning: American Reflections on the Holocaust and Israel
Julius Simon, editor

Religious Fundamentalism in Developing Countries
Santosh C. Saha and Thomas K. Carr

Between Man and God: Issues in Judaic Thought
Martin Sicker

Through the Name of God: A New Road to the Original of Judaism and Christianity
Joel T. Klein

Gods of Our Fathers: The Memory of Egypt in Judaism and Christianity
Richard A. Gabriel

Human Dignity and the Common Good: The Great Papal Social Encyclicals from Leo XIII to John Paul II
Richard W. Rousseau, S.J.

Searching for Meaning in the Holocaust
Sidney M. Bolkosky

Christianity, the Other, and the Holocaust
Michael R. Steele

Return: Holocaust Survivors and Dutch Anti-Semitism
Dienke Hondius
David Colmer, translator

The Ecumenical Movement

An Introductory History

THOMAS E. FITZGERALD

CONTRIBUTIONS TO THE STUDY OF RELIGION, NUMBER 72

Westport, Connecticut
London

Library of Congress Cataloging-in-Publication Data

FitzGerald, Thomas E., 1947–
The ecumenical movement : an introductory history / Thomas E. FitzGerald.
p. cm.—(Contributions to the study of religion, ISSN 0196–7053 ; no. 72)
Includes bibliographical references (p.) and index.
ISBN 0–313–30606–0 (alk. paper)
1. Ecumenical movement—History. I. Title. II. Series.
BX6.5.F58 2004
280′.042′09—dc22 2003058159

British Library Cataloguing in Publication Data is available.

Library of Congress Catalog Card Number: 2003058159
ISBN: 0–313–30606–0
ISSN: 0196–7053

First published in 2004

Praeger Publishers, 88 Post Road West, Westport, CT 06881
An imprint of Greenwood Publishing Group, Inc.
www.praeger.com

Printed in the United States of America

The paper used in this book complies with the Permanent Paper Standard issued by the National Information Standards Organization (Z39.48–1984).

10 9 8 7 6 5 4 3 2 1

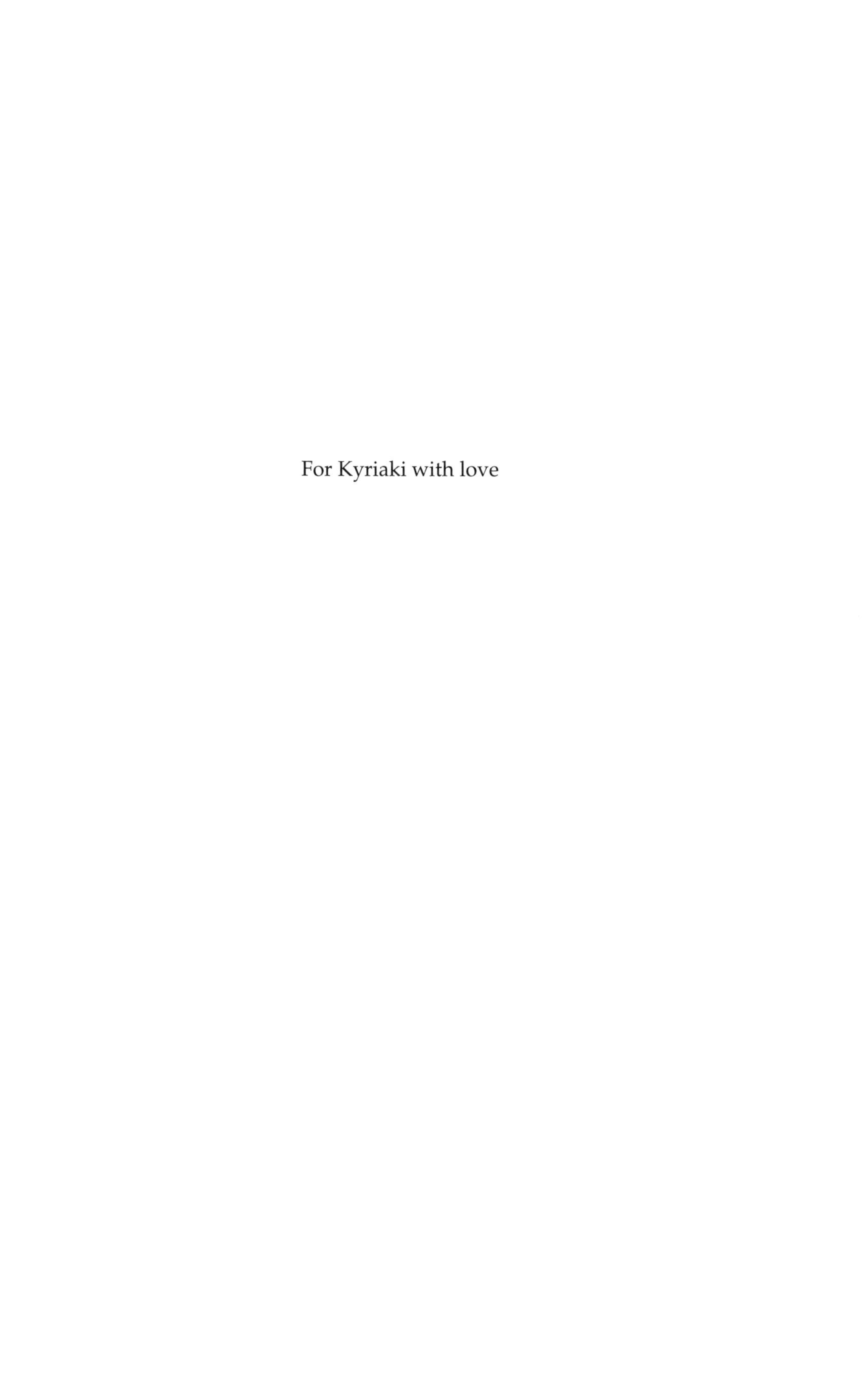

For Kyriaki with love

Our movement towards the visible unity of the churches is one filled with great joy and some sorrow. We know that the road to reconciliation is not an easy one. Yet, we also know that Our Lord is truly with us. He is our way. He is our life. He travels with us as he walked with his disciples on the road to Emmaus. In calling us to be His disciples, Christ calls us to join with Him in His ministry of reconciliation and renewal. Let us lift the veil of division from our face that we might move together from glory to glory. To Christ be all glory, honor, and worship together with the eternal Father and the life-giving Spirit, now and forever, and unto ages of ages. Amen.

Ecumenical Patriarch Bartholomew of Constantinople
Service of Prayer
National Council of Churches of Christ
New York
October 27, 1997

Contents

Preface

The ecumenical movement has been a part of my life as long as I can remember. I was raised in a family that appreciated both the tradition of Eastern and Western Christianity and in a neighborhood where good friends belonged to different churches. As I walked to elementary school and later to high school, I passed many church buildings. Eventually, my curiosity got the best of me and I explored them. Often, I experienced the worship and met with the pastors of these communities of faith. As an undergraduate and graduate student, the issue of church divisions and unity was a thread uniting many of my academic and vocational interests. As a theologian, teacher, and pastor, I have been a part of many prayer services, dialogues, and expressions of social concern reflecting the ecumenical commitment of the churches. With friends, colleagues, and parishioners, I have experienced the tragic consequences of church divisions and the joyous appreciation of church unity.

This book has a very modest intention. It is designed to introduce the topic of the ecumenical movement to a wider audience, especially those studying the Christian Church and Christianity in the past century. The ecumenical movement is a process through which many of the Christian churches are seeking to overcome past divisions and to be visibly united in common faith, worship, and service. Throughout the twentieth century, the many expressions of the ecumenical movement have affected all aspects of church life, its worship, theology, mission, and service in every part of the world. The movement has touched the lives of most Christians wherever the church is present. It is a movement of reconciliation that has by no means been completed.

I fully realize that all aspects of this historic movement cannot be adequately captured in a single volume. Many of my friends and colleagues, who are truly experts in this area of study and activity, will be disappointed that some personalities, topics, documents, and events do not receive sufficient attention in this introductory work. I apologize for this. I do hope, however, that this introductory study will provide many others with an appreciation of the essential elements of the ecumenical movement and its centrality to Christian life and thought. The ecumenical movement has been a major characteristic of the life of the Christian churches for over a century. It is a remarkable story.

Acknowledgments

I am deeply conscious of the influence others have had on my research, reflection, and writing. While space does not permit me to acknowledge all, I believe that some deserve particular mention.

My wife, Kyriaki, has been a constant source of wisdom and inspiration. I have benefited greatly from her own insights into the events and themes discussed in this book. She has not only read the story but also has contributed to the story as a theologian.

I continue to remember with thanksgiving my teachers. I am especially grateful to my major professors: Metropolitan Maximos Aghiorgoussis, Professor Anthony-Emil Tachiaos, and Professor Angelos Philips. Together with their ongoing support, I also appreciate the guidance of Metropolitan John Zizioulas, Bishop Kallistos Ware, and Father Laurence of New Skete Monastery.

I am thankful that leaders of the Orthodox Church have supported my work and have given me many opportunities to be active in ecumenical dialogues. I am especially grateful to Ecumenical Patriarch Bartholomew of Constantinople for his paternal support and for the opportunity to serve the Patriarchate and to represent it.

Likewise, I appreciate the encouragement of Archbishop Demetrios of America, Archbishop Iakovos, Metropolitan Methodios of Boston, Metropolitan Emilianos of Sylibrias, Bishop Dimitrios of Xanthos, Bishop Athanasios of Achaea, Bishop Joseph of Katana, and Bishop Ilia of Philomelion. Each of these distinguished bishops has represented the Orthodox Church in ecumenical dialogues with other churches.

During my research and writing, I have had the opportunity to be associated with a number of communities and ecumenical bodies. I appreciate the encouragement of Father Nicholas Triantafilou, the President of Hellenic College and Holy Cross School of Theology, as well as my colleagues and my students there. I also appreciate the support of many colleagues at the World Council of Churches in Geneva, on the North American Orthodox-Roman Catholic Theological Consultation, in the National Council of Churches, in the Massachusetts Council of Churches and in the Boston Theological Institute.

As I prepared this study, I especially appreciated the helpful assistance from: Nicholas Apostola, Thomas Bird, Paul A. Crow Jr., Brian E. Daley, James Dutko, Michael A. Fahey, Peter Galadza, Dan Gerhard, Robert Haddad, Gregory Havrilak, Alexander Karloutsos, Diane Kessler, Leonid Kishkovsky, Elpidophoros Lambriniadis, Mary Ann Lundy, John Maheras, Tarek Mitri, Christine Nelson, Despina Prassas, Vito Nicastro, Rodney Petersen, John Pobee, Marina Risk, Ronald Roberson, Todor Sabev, Ioan Sauca, Robert Stephanopoulos, Mary Tanner, and the late Luke Arakelian, Ion Bria, Jan Kok, Jean-Marie Tillard, and Marlin Van Elderen. The guidance of the librarians Pierre Beffa and Timothy Andrews is gratefully recognized. Likewise, I have benefited from the assistance of Béatrice Bengtsson, my administrative assistant in Geneva, and Nikki Stournaras as well as my teaching assistants, Iulia Corduneanu, Constantine Sinos, and Austin Reno. As part of a seminar on the ecumenical movement, portions of this text were discussed with my students, Hilary Chala, Iulian Damian, and Gift Makwasha.

I also want to express my appreciation to Gerald FitzGerald, to Michael and Tula Karidoyanes, and to John and Carol Van Osdol for their continued support.

This is my second book published by Praeger. I am grateful for the thoughtful assistance of the editorial staff, especially the senior editor, Suzanne I. Staszak-Silva. I also appreciate the valuable contributions of the staff of Impressions Book and Journal Services that prepared the text for publication.

CHAPTER 1

An Introduction to the Ecumenical Movement

> The unity to which the followers of Jesus Christ are called is not something created by them. Rather, it is Christ's will for them that they manifest their unity, given in Christ, before the world so that the world may believe. It is a unity grounded in and reflects the communion which exists between the Father and the Son and the Holy Spirit. Thus, the ecumenical imperative and mission of the Church are inextricably intertwined, and this for the sake of the salvation of all. The eschatological vision of the transformation and unity of humankind is the fundamental inspiration of ecumenical action.
>
> —The Joint Working Group, World Council of Churches-Roman Catholic Church[1]

INTRODUCTION

The ecumenical movement is the quest of Orthodox, Roman Catholic, Anglican, Old Catholic, and most Protestant churches for reconciliation, and the restoration of their visible unity in faith, sacramental life, and witness in the world. Over the past century especially, this quest has dramatically altered the relationship of these divided churches to each other. The isolation, condemnations and mistrust, which characterized their relationship for centuries, have given way in many places to new encounters. These are characterized by opportunities for prayers together, for theological reflection together, and for witness together for the well-being of the society. A number of the churches have clearly affirmed that the goal of this process is the restoration of full communion. This means a full unity of churches in the common profession of the Christian faith and expressed in the sharing together in the Eucharist, the most important act of Christian worship.

Most observers date the beginning of this process from the early decades of the twentieth century. The World Missionary Conference in Edinburgh in 1910 opened the eyes of many to the tragedy of disunity and competition among many churches. The establishment of the Faith and Order movement and the Life and Work movement in the 1920s began to bring Anglican, Protestant, Old Catholic, and Orthodox theologians into contact with each other. These early organizations eventually contributed to the establishment of the World Council of Churches in 1948. Yet important expressions of concern for reconciliation and unity can be found among church leaders and in some church families in the late nineteenth century. One of the earliest expressions bringing together members from a number of divided churches was the Association for the Promotion of the Unity of Christendom founded in 1857. This organization advocated prayers for the unity of the churches.

Over the past hundred years, the relationships among the separated Christian churches have gone through remarkable developments. Today, the quest for reconciliation and the visible unity of the churches has reached a point that could not have been foreseen only 50 years ago. A number of Orthodox, Anglican, Old Catholic, and most Protestant churches have been involved in contacts for over a century. Yet the formal entrance into the ecumenical movement of the Roman Catholic Church in the 1960s contributed to unprecedented theological dialogues, common witness, and united prayers for unity.

The historic divisions of the various churches reaching back centuries are being addressed in significant and dramatic ways at the local, regional, and global levels. There has been a profound desire to understand the reasons behind the historic differences between the Christian churches and traditions. There has been a desire to overcome mutual misunderstanding and prejudice. There has been a desire to bear witness together in the society and to care for the needy together. There has been a desire to pray together for reconciliation and the unity of the churches. There has been a desire to find the means to restore the visible unity of the Christian churches in the profession of the apostolic faith and celebrated in the Eucharist.

Clearly, this process of Christian reconciliation is not easy. Especially during the past 40 years, the Orthodox, the Anglican, the Old Catholic, the Roman Catholic, and most Protestant churches have made a firm commitment to the quest for reconciliation and the restoration of their visible unity. However, this does not mean that there is full agreement on methodology of even the expressions of this visible unity.

At the same time, not all Christian communities and traditions have been able to commit themselves to the formal process of reconciliation.

There are a sizeable number of Protestant communities, especially in the Baptist, the Evangelical, and the Fundamentalist traditions, that have generally avoided ecumenical engagement. Many have consciously chosen to avoid cooperation and theological dialogue with other Protestants, as well as with Roman Catholics and Orthodox. The reasons for this avoidance vary. In addition to this, there are also other Christian movements and groups that have not been able to accept the essential perspectives of the ecumenical movement because of their own particular teachings.

TERMINOLOGY

There is a need to make some important distinctions regarding the use of certain words. First of all, the term ecumenical requires further elaboration.[2] The word comes from the ancient Greek word *ekoumeni,* that means "the whole world." It is used in this sense in the New Testament in Matthew 24:14 and Acts 17:31. In other instances, such as in Acts 17:16, the word can refer more specifically to the Roman Empire of the first century. In the use of the term by early Christian writers both meanings can be detected. By the fourth century, the church uses the word to speak about the Ecumenical Councils. These were the councils of bishops and other theologians who gathered together in particular cities and at certain times to address issues of Christian faith that were being questioned and to find the means of reconciliation of divided parties. Unlike local or regional councils, the Ecumenical Councils addressed issues affecting all the regional churches within the entire Roman-Byzantine Empire and beyond. The term gradually came to refer to the entire church throughout the world. From the sixth century, the patriarch and archbishop of Constantinople was also referred to as the "Ecumenical Patriarch."

The term ecumenical began to be used in the late nineteenth and early twentieth centuries with reference to new Christian organizations or new international church organizations. By 1919 in both Europe and the United States, there were calls to form an "ecumenical council of churches" or an "ecumenical conference of churches."[3] The use of the term became more standardized from 1937. In that year, the Oxford Conference on Life and Work said: "The term 'ecumenical' refers to the expression within history of the given unity of the Church. The thought and action of the Church are ecumenical, in so far as they attempt to realize the *Una Sancta,* the fellowship of Christians who acknowledge the one Lord."[4] From that time onward, ecumenical began to describe meetings bringing together representatives from a variety of separated Christian churches. It also was used to describe perspectives on Christian teachings that took into account views of the divided churches. In more recent times, ecumenical has been more properly used to describe those meetings and councils bringing together the representatives of Orthodox, Roman Catholic, Anglican, Old

Catholic, and most Protestant churches. Thus, the phrase ecumenical movement points to the process of reconciliation and the restoration of visible unity to which these churches are formally committed.

The term ecumenical is clearly distinguished from such terms as interdenominational or interconfessional. These have been used in the past to describe primarily relationships among Protestant churches. Since the sixteenth centuries, Protestants in Europe frequently spoke of their churches in relationship to particular confessional statements. Likewise, in the United States Protestant churches frequently used the word denomination to describe a large church family or tradition. More recently, some churches, such as the worldwide Anglican Church, have used the term communion to describe the association of its regional churches. In some Protestant circles, it is not uncommon to see references to nondenominational congregations. This generally refers to a local Protestant parish community or associations that are not a formal part of any historical Protestant church. Often, the popular term "mainline" is used to describe historic churches of the Protestant Reformation.

The word church also has a variety of interrelated meanings.[5] From the time of the New Testament, the Greek word for church, *ekklesia,* referred broadly to the called and gathered People of God as in Matthew 16:18, 18:17, in Acts 5:11, and 1 Corinthians 12:28. However, St. Paul also uses the same word to refer to the community of Christians in a particular place such as the churches in Galatia (Gal. 1:2) and the church of the Thessalonians (1 Thes. 1:1). From the earliest days, therefore, the word church could refer to the entire people who followed Christ or it could refer to a specific community of Christians in a given place. These two uses have continued throughout Christian history. Following the major divisions, however, the term church could also be used to refer to a particular church family that was distinguished by its teachings from another. Thus, one can speak of the Orthodox Church, the Roman Catholic Church, or the Lutheran Church. Throughout this study, the terms denomination and confession generally have been avoided. The term church is used in a variety of ways according to the context. At times, church is used in its broadest sense to describe those who claim to be part of the one Church of Christ through the ages, sometimes referred to in Latin as the *Una Sancta.* This phrase comes from the historic Nicene-Constantinopolitan Creed of 381, which speaks of the "one, holy, catholic and apostolic Church." At other times, the word church is used to refer to a particular historical or regional expression of a community of Christians. The context of the use of the word will indicate the meaning of the usage.

Finally, there is a clear distinction between the ecumenical movement and interfaith relations. When understood properly, the ecumenical movement strictly refers to the quest for Christian reconciliation and the restoration of the visible unity of the Christian churches in shared Christian faith, in the sacraments, and in witness. Interfaith relationships refer to those contacts between Christians and members of other living religions such as Judaism and Islam. Certainly, these contacts are important in their own right and have also increased in recent decades. These contacts have led to greater mutual understanding and respect between religions and their followers. In some parts of the world, they have led to a common concern for human rights and for the well-being of society. Yet there are essential differences in beliefs between historic Christianity and other religions. The Christian faith is rooted in the person and work of Jesus Christ and his teachings. The Christian churches, which are engaged in the ecumenical movement, do so because of their essential understanding of the Christ and the Christian faith.

THE ECUMENICAL IMPERATIVE

Throughout the past century, most Christian churches at the highest levels of authority have affirmed theological principles on reconciliation and the challenge of seeking reconciliation and visible unity. These principles are really not new at all. Rather, they represent a rediscovery of perspectives rooted in the heart of the Christian message. Yet they are theological principles that have often been neglected because of the polemics of divisions as well as by cultural and political forces. Once viewed as normative, the historic divisions of the Christian churches are now called into question. The historic divisions are now seen as factors that also have contributed to divisions among peoples and nations. Indeed, they are seen as a scandal and an impediment to the Christian message. The differences in teachings, which are rooted in the animosities of the past, are now being reexamined in a new light. In many parts of the world, Christians from the divided churches are coming together to pray for reconciliation and to engage in common witness with a new sense of the demands of the Christian message.

All of this reflects a number of profound theological principles regarding unity and reconciliation that have been affirmed by the Orthodox, the Roman Catholic, the Anglican, the Old Catholic, and most Protestant churches.[6] They are principles that find expression in the various levels of church life today. These principles point to the fact that the churches are seeking much more than mutual toleration of differences or voluntary cooperation in certain activities. Rather, they are seeking to overcome their divisions and to find ways of expressing a genuine unity in faith, worship, and service. Such a unity does not mean absolute uniformity in all things. But it does mean that acceptable diversity does not hinder their expression of unity.[7]

First, these churches reaffirm their conviction that the Christian gospel is essentially a message of unity and reconciliation. Both separately and in their common affirmations, the churches point to the coming of Jesus Christ as the great event of reconciliation. He has come into human history in order to restore humanity and all of creation to communion with God. The churches declare that this was expressed in Christ's teachings about God and the human person as well as in his healings, miracles and especially through his death and resurrection. The words of St. Paul are often repeated: "All this is from God, who reconciled us to himself through Christ, and has given us the ministry of reconciliation; that is, in Christ God was reconciling the world to himself, not counting their trespasses against them, and entrusting the message of reconciliation to us. So we are ambassadors for Christ, since God is making his appeal through us" (2 Cor. 5:17–20).

The churches see a gospel imperative for the unity of Christ's followers. In their renewed interest in reconciliation and unity, the churches have together reaffirmed the reconciling message of the Christian gospel. The churches are concerned with the restoration of their visible unity because they believe that the Triune God is a God of reconciliation and unity. The life of the church and of Christians must bear witness to the reconciling activities of God. Likewise, the churches have affirmed the critical importance of making visible their unity. It cannot be expressed simply in idealistic terms or even in occasional acts of cooperation. True unity must be expressed in visible ways. The Anglican-Roman Catholic Commission affirms this saying: "Christ's will and prayer are that his disciples should be one. Those who have received the same word of God and have been baptized in the same Spirit cannot, without disobedience, acquiesce in a state of separation. Unity is of the essence of the Church, and since the Church is visible its unity also must be visible."[8]

The World Council of Churches's Canberra Assembly also affirms the relationship between God's actions and the visible unity of the churches saying: "The purpose of God according to the holy scripture is to gather the whole of creation under the Lordship of Jesus Christ in whom by the power of the Holy Spirit all are brought into communion with God (Eph. 1). The church is the foretaste of this communion with God and with one another. The grace of our Lord Jesus Christ, the love of God, and the communion of the Holy Spirit enable the one church to live as sign of the reign of God and servant of the reconciliation with God, promised and provided for the whole creation."[9]

Second, these churches reaffirm their conviction that the church of Christ is meant to proclaim the message of reconciliation in Christ and to be a sign of that reconciliation in the world. If Christ is the expression of God's healing love and reconciliation, then the church of Christ must also be a sign of divine love and reconciliation. The church does this through its worship, its teachings, and its witness. There is an intimate relationship between Christ and his church, which is described by St. Paul as the "body of Christ" (Eph. 1:23). As the Joint Working Group between the World

Council of Churches and the Roman Catholic Church says: "Ecumenism is not an option for the churches. In obedience to Christ and for the sake of the world the churches are called to be an effective sign of God's presence and compassion before all nations. For the churches to come divided to a broken world is to undermine their credibility when they claim to have a ministry of universal unity and reconciliation. The ecumenical imperative must be heard and responded to everywhere."[10]

Third, the churches recognize anew the desire and prayer of their Lord for the unity of his followers. As the bearer of God's reconciliation, Christ directed his followers to be people of reconciliation whose lives are characterized by unselfish love, healing, and peace. In praying for his followers, Jesus likened their unity with the bond of love existing between him and God the Father. He says: "As you Father, are in me and I am in you, may they also be one in us, so that the world may believe that you have sent me. The glory that you have given me I have given them, so that they may be one as we are one, I in them and you in me, that they may be completely one, so that the world may know that you have sent me and have loved them even as you have loved me" (John 17:22–23).

From the earliest days of the ecumenical movement, this prayer of Christ for the unity of his followers has resounded again and again in the prayers of Christians and in their theological discussions. "We remain restless," says the Canberra Assembly, "until we grow together according to the wish and prayer of Christ that those who believe in him may be one (Jn. 17:21). In the process praying, working, and struggling for unity, the Holy Spirit comforts us in pain, disturbs us when we are satisfied to remain in our division, leads us to repentance, and grants us joy when our communion flourishes."[11]

Fourth, the churches recognize that their historic divisions have had consequences upon their own appreciation of the apostolic faith in all its breath and depth. In the wake of the various divisions in Christian history, the divided churches sought to emphasize their particular perspectives in opposition to the other. This frequently led to an emphasis upon one aspect of the Christian faith and to a de-emphasis upon others. Thus, within each church, its teachings, worship, and witness were affected either directly or indirectly by the divisions and the polemics that usually accompanied them. The tragic wounds of alienation and division have touched each church by the loss of unity. Already at the first Assembly of the World Council of Churches in 1948, this important principle was affirmed. "Within our divided churches," the assembly said, "there is much which we confess with penitence before the Lord of the Church, for it is in our estrangement from him that all our sin has its origin.... Within our divided churches, it is to our shame that we have so often lived in preoccupation with our internal affairs, looking inward upon our own concerns in stead of forgetting ourselves in outgoing love and service."[12]

The concern for reconciliation has led to numerous multilateral and bilateral dialogues between representatives of the divided churches at the local, regional, and global levels. There has been a clear recognition that the great divisions of the churches are rooted in historic differences in doctrines and teachings. The churches have affirmed that these historic differences must be resolved in order for genuine reconciliation to take place. The churches of Europe have said together: "Fundamental differences in faith are still barriers to visible unity. There are different views of church and its oneness, of the sacraments and ministries. We must not be satisfied with this situation. Jesus Christ revealed to us on the cross his love and the mystery of reconciliation; as his followers, we intend to do our utmost to overcome the problems and obstacles that still divide the churches."[13]

Fifth, the churches recognize the tragic consequences of their own divisions for the world. The disunity of the churches and of Christians is a counter witness to the gospel of reconciliation. It is a scandal that impedes the message of the gospel in the world. The divisions are tragic because they also contribute to further divisions in families, societies, and nations. In recent times, this has been seen most especially in Northern Ireland, Lebanon, and Rwanda, and in the Balkans. The Canberra Assembly says "the churches are painfully divided within themselves and among each other. The scandalous divisions damage the credibility of their witness to the world in worship and service. Moreover, they contradict not only the church's witness but also its very nature."[14]

Sixth, the churches see their ecumenical engagement not only as a means to reestablishing visible unity but also as a means of renewal. As the great divisions had a negative impact upon the churches and their life, the movement toward reconciliation is also having a positive influence upon their life and witness today. The new encounter of the churches has sparked common approaches to Scripture study and translations, has inspired a common liturgical renewal, has contributed to common theological reflections, and has opened up common avenues of service to the society. The encounters between the churches and their members are providing fresh opportunities to see old issues of division in a new light. As the Canberra Assembly declares: "Churches have reached agreements in bilateral and multilateral dialogues which are already bearing fruit, renewing their liturgical and spiritual life and their theology. In taking specific steps together the churches express and encourage the enrichment and renewal of Christian life, as they learn from one another, work together for justice and peace, and care together for God's creation."[15]

Seventh, the churches reaffirm the need to be open to the promptings of the Holy Spirit. In seeking to heal the difficult wounds of division, the churches are involved in a process that brings them into new and uncharted territory. Yes, there are important examples from the early church that can be instructive. However, a number of factors today, such as the prevalence of a strong secular spirit in some regions, place the churches in a very unique situation as they relate to each other. The churches engage in the process of reconciliation with the conviction that it is not only the will of Christ but also nurtured by the Holy Spirit. As the World Council of Churches Assembly at New Delhi (1961) says: "We all confess that sinful self-will operates to keep us separated and that in our human ignorance we can not discern clearly the lines of God's design for the future. But it is our firm hope that through the Holy Spirit God's will as it is witnessed to in the Holy Scripture will be more and more disclosed to us. The achievement of unity will involve nothing less than a death and rebirth of many forms of church life as we have known them."[16]

Eighth, the churches recognize that the movement toward reconciliation and visible unity must be nurtured and supported by prayer. From the very beginning of the ecumenical movement, there has been a strong emphasis upon the importance of prayer for unity and for finding opportunities when the Christians from the divided churches can pray together for unity.[17] The tragic expressions of church disunity are often reflected in the maintenance of painful memories, in bigotry, and in discrimination. "Our progress towards unity" says Kyriaki FitzGerald, "will ultimately lead us nowhere, if we let the walls of our hearts remain as they are."[18] Prayer for reconciliation and unity seeks the healing of those affected by the sins of divisions and seeks to open all Christians up to the reconciling actions of God. As a Faith and Order Consultation says: "In our present divided state, visible unity can not be restored unless each church becomes aware of the painful situation of our divisions and takes decisions to overcome our disobedience to the will of Christ expressed in his prayer for unity (John 17:1–26). These decisions will be genuine only to the extent to which they imply a resolve to do what the reestablishment of communion demands: conversion through a constant return to the source which is God as revealed in Jesus Christ through the Holy Spirit."[19]

At a time when emphasis is often placed upon the activities of the ecumenical movement, the churches have affirmed also the value of what has come to be called "spiritual ecumenism."[20] The fundamental features of this were expressed by the Roman Catholic Second Vatican Council. It said: "There can be no ecumenism worthy of its name without a change of heart. For it is from newness of attitude... from self denial and unstinted love, that yearnings for unity take rise and grow to maturity... This change of heart and holiness of life, along with public and private prayer for the unity of Christians, should be regarded as the soul of the whole ecumenical movement."[21]

Finally, the churches recognize that their divisions do not honor the God they worship. The Orthodox-Roman Catholic Consultation in North America says: "Church divisions reflecting divergent teachings do not honor God or help to proclaim the Gospel to all nations" (Matt. 28:19).[22]

The churches believe that their quest for reconciliation and visible unity is a witness to the message of Christ and the Christian gospel.[23] Their acts of reconciliation express the conviction that Christians and their churches must "live together in harmony so that together with one voice they may glorify God" (cf. Romans 15:5–6).[24]

THE PROCESS OF RECONCILIATION AND UNITY

The movement toward Christian reconciliation and the visible unity of the churches is a process. It is a dramatic process through which these theological principles of reconciliation and unity have slowly emerged as the churches have moved out of isolation and have engaged each other. The theological principles of reconciliation and unity of the churches are normally expressed through the dialogues and statements of the churches, through opportunities for common prayer, and in joint expression of witness in the society. The principles are expressed when church leaders from different churches gather in meetings. They are also expressed when members of local parishes of different church families meet together for a prayer group or bible study. Depending upon the geographical setting, a new relationship among the divided churches has been growing and deepening for decades. Indeed, those with no direct knowledge of the preecumenical days may not even be aware of the dramatic changes that have already occurred. While all the churches have not as yet restored their unity, there have been significant changes in their relationships that express the process of reconciliation. The ecumenical movement is a process that is not complete.

The chapters of this book that follow trace this process and identify the essential characteristics of each stage in the development of the ecumenical movement.

Chapter 2 deals with the relationship of Jesus Christ and the early church. Here, we identify some aspects of Christ's teachings and the life of the early Christian community that have a direct bearing upon the contemporary ecumenical movement. All the major Christian churches trace their existence and their teachings back to Christ and the early apostolic community.

Chapter 3 identifies four significant divisions that divided the Christian churches and that continue to persist to this day. These are: the divisions following the Council of Ephesus in 431, the division following the Council of Chalcedon in 451; the division between the church of Rome and the church of the Constantinople and other Eastern churches during the Middle Ages, and the division between the church of Rome and the churches of the Reformation as well as divisions among the Reformation churches of the sixteenth century.

Chapter 4 examines trends and associations that began to challenge the divisions of Christians and their churches during the nineteenth century.

This was a time when a number of new Christian organizations came into existence seeking to bring together Christians for prayer, fellowship, or service in spite of their church affiliation. It was also a time when some churches began to establish contacts and dialogues with one another.

Chapter 5 looks at the fledgling ecumenical movement of the early twentieth century. Particular attention is given to the development of the Faith and Order movement, the Life and Work movement, and the movement calling for prayer for Christian unity. Through each of these, the churches slowly began to be drawn out of their isolation. Their representatives began to meet to pray together and to discuss the historic differences among the churches, and the ways in which they could work together in the area of humanitarian concern.

Chapter 6 traces the development of the World Council of Churches, founded in 1948, chiefly through a review of the themes and characteristics of its seven Assemblies. During the first 20 years of its existence especially, the WCC was the focal point of the global ecumenical movement and became the model for councils developed at the regional and local levels.

Chapter 7 discusses the formal entrance of the Roman Catholic Church into the ecumenical movement in the 1960s. Prior to this time the Roman Catholic Church had formally avoided ecumenical discussions and had called other Christians to return to its care. Under the leadership of Pope John XXIII, the Second Vatican Council dramatically chartered a new course. From that time, the Roman Catholic Church became fully committed to the quest for visible unity and gradually became a partner in ecumenical dialogues and in a number of councils or conferences of churches.

Chapter 8 examines the concerns and contributions of the Orthodox Church. Involved in the ecumenical movement from its beginning, Orthodox representatives have made substantial contributions to the dialogues. In so doing they offered the rich theological and liturgical perspectives of the Christian East to a movement that had been dominated by Western Christian perspectives. This occurred despite challenges to ecumenical dialogue from within the Orthodox Church and despite concerns over recent directions in the World Council as well as tense relationships in some places with Roman Catholic and Protestant churches.

Chapter 9 reviews the tensions within Reformation churches, especially related to the fundamentalist and modernist controversy of the early twentieth centuries, and the more recent development of Evangelical Protestant church families and institutions. The chapter also identifies the significant agreements that have formally established new relationships among many Anglican and Protestant churches in Europe and in the United States.

Chapter 10 discusses the contributions of the multilateral and bilateral dialogues that developed from the 1960s. These dialogues, that exist both at the global and the regional levels, bring together representatives of two churches to study more particular theological issues of division and to propose areas of consensus or agreement.

Chapter 11 looks at some aspects of regional and local ecumenism in the context of the United States.

NOTES

1. "Ecumenical Formation: Ecumenical Reflections and Suggestions," *Joint Working Group between the Roman Catholic Church and the World Council of Churches Seventh Report* (Geneva: WCC Publications, 1998), p. 53.

2. For a more complete discussion, see Willem Visser 't Hooft, "The Word 'Ecumenical'—Its History and Use," in *A History of the Ecumenical Movement, 1517–1948,* ed. Ruth Rouse and Stephen Charles Neill (Philadelphia: The Westminster Press, 1967), pp. 735–40.

3. Ibid., p. 737.

4. Ibid., p. 740.

5. See F.L. Cross et al., *The Oxford Dictionary of the Christian Church* (Oxford: Oxford University Press, revised edition, 1983), pp. 286–88.

6. I acknowledge the valuable insights offered by Günther Gassmann in his "Retrospective of an Ecumenical Century," in *Agapè, Études en l'honneur de Mgr. Pierre Duprey,* ed. Jean-Marie Roger Tillard (Geneva: Centre Orthodoxe de Patriarcat Ecuménique, 2000), pp. 63–86.

7. "The Unity of the Church as Koinonia: Gift and Calling," Günther Gassmann, *Documentary History of Faith and Order 1963–1993* (Geneva: WCC Publications, 1993), p. 4.

8. "Final Report, 1981," in *Growth in Agreement Reports and Statements of Ecumenical Conversations on a World Level,* ed. Harding Meyer and Lukas Vischer (New York: Paulist Press, 1984), pp. 66–67.

9. "The Unity of the Church as Koinonia: Gift and Calling," in *Documentary History of Faith and Order 1963–1993,* ed. Gassmann, p. 3.

10. "Ecumenical Formation: Ecumenical Reflections and Suggestions," *Joint Working Group between the Roman Catholic Church and the World Council of Churches Seventh Report,* p. 59.

11. "The Unity of the Church as Koinonia: Gift and Calling," in *Documentary History of Faith and Order 1963–1993,* ed. Gassmann, p. 5.

12. "The Message of the Assembly (Amsterdam, 1948)," in *A Documentary History of the Faith and Order Movement 1927–1963,* ed. Lucas Vischer (St. Louis: The Bethany Press, 1963), p. 81.

13. *Charta Oecumenica: Guidelines for Growing Cooperation among the Churches in Europe* (Geneva, St. Galen: Conference of European Churches, Council of European Bishops' Conference, 2001), p. 3.

14. "The Unity of the Church as Koinonia: Gift and Calling," in *A Documentary History of Faith and Order 1963–1993,* ed. Gassmann, p. 5.

15. Ibid., p. 4.

16. "Report on the Section on Unity (New Delhi, 1961)," in *A Documentary History of the Faith and Order Movement 1927–1963,* ed. Lucas Vischer, p. 145.

17. See Dianne C. Kessler, "Ecumenical Spirituality, The Quest for Wholeness of Vision," in *The Vision of Christian Unity Essays in Honor of Paul A. Crow, Jr.*, ed. Thomas F. Best and Theodore J. Nottingham (Indianapolis: Oekoumene Publications, 1997), pp. 91–103.

18. Kyriaki FitzGerald, "The Fifth World Conference and Walls of the Heart, " *Ecumenical Trends* 22:4 (1993), p. 14.

19. "Towards the Common Expression of the Apostolic Faith Today (1982)," in *Documentary History of Faith and Order 1963–1993*, ed. Gassmann, p. 191.

20. Paul A. Crow, Jr., *Christian Unity: Matrix for Mission* (New York: Friendship Press, 1982), pp. 77–79.

21. "Decree on Ecumenism," cited in Walter M. Abbott, ed., *The Documents of Vatican II* (New York: The America Press, 1960), pp. 351–52.

22. "Sharing the Ministry of Reconciliation (June 1, 2000)," *Origins* 30:5 (June 15, 2000), p. 80.

23. Geoffrey Wainwright, "Ut Unum Sint, ut Mundis Credat: Classic Ecumenism from John R. Mott to John Paul II," in *Agapè: Études en l'honneur de Mgr. Pierre Duprey*, ed. Jean-Marie Roger Tillard (Chambésy: Centre Orthodoxe, 2002), p. 44.

24. Ibid., p. 48.

CHAPTER 2

Jesus Christ and the Beginning of the Church

> As you Father, are in me and I am in you, may they also be one in us, so that the world may believe that you have sent me. The glory that you have given me I have given them, so that they may be one as we are one, I in them and you in me, that they may be completely one, so that the world may know that you have sent me and have loved them even as you have loved me.
>
> —Jesus Christ, The Gospel of John 17:22–23

INTRODUCTION

The ecumenical movement is the quest for the visible unity of the various Christian churches and the reconciliation of Christians today. This process inevitably leads back to Jesus Christ and to the early church. Regardless of their particular tradition, most Christians would affirm that there is an intimate relationship between Jesus Christ and the Church. Most would affirm that Jesus Christ established the Church in an embryonic manner with the call of the first apostles and disciples. There is an intimate relationship between Christ's coming and his teachings, and the growth of the early church. Likewise, there is an historic connection between developments in the early church and the various Christian churches today. The Orthodox Church, the Roman Catholic Church, the Anglican Church, the Old Catholic Church, and most Protestant churches affirm an historical connection with the early Christian Church and with its earliest development. This connection is reflected in the basic faith affirmations as well as in the practice of baptism and the celebration of the Eucharist. It is also expressed in use of the New Testament, in the tradition of ministry, in ethical standards, and in a concern for mission. This chapter provides a brief introduction to the essential features of the early Christian Church prior to the major divisions that afflict it today.

GOD'S OWN PEOPLE

The Christian Church owes its origin to the person, ministry, and teachings of Jesus Christ in the land of Palestine over two thousand years ago. According to our present method of calculation, Jesus was born in the town of Bethlehem about 6 or 7 B.C. He did much of his three years of teaching in the province of Galilee and was put to death by Roman authorities in the capital city of Jerusalem about the year A.D. 33. While the Jews of Palestine had some measure of religious and political freedom, the land was then under the ultimate political control of the Roman Empire. At that time, the majority, but certainly not all, of the residents of Palestine were Jews. Many were deeply troubled by the Roman control. While there were serious religious and political differences among them, the Jews were a distinctive people because they acknowledged one God in a world where polytheism was the norm.[1]

Jesus did not leave any written record of his life or teachings. He did call to a number of men and women to be his followers. Those who responded to his call recognized him to be the long awaited Messiah of Ancient Israel. In the words of the Apostle Peter, they acknowledged him to be "the Messiah (Christ), the Son of the living God" (Matthew 16:16). They treasured his teachings about the loving and merciful God, and the value and dignity of the human person. They experienced his healings and signs of divine blessing. Through their association with him, the early followers came to believe that he was truly God who came to earth for the purpose of reconciling humankind. After Christ's betrayal and brutal death on the cross, these same followers affirmed that he rose from the dead.[2] Believing that he was present with them, they honored him as their Lord and Savior (Col. 1:15–20).

Many of the first followers, especially the Twelve Apostles, traveled with Jesus during his public ministry. Following Christ's death and resurrection, these apostles and disciples were responsible for bearing witness to his continuing presence, teaching others about Jesus, and leading the church communities. A number of the disciples recorded some of his teachings and reflected upon the significance of his coming. The four Gospels of Matthew, Mark, Luke, and John, for example, began to circulate in the period between the years 55 and 90.[3] Coming from within this community of believers, the four Gospels provided a brief introduction to the events of Christ's life and to his essential teachings. At the center of each of the four books was the bold proclamation of Christ's resurrection.[4] About the year 90, the apostle John wrote to the newcomers to the Christian faith and said:

> We declare to you what was from the beginning, what we have heard, what we have seen with our own eyes and touched with our hands, concerning the word of life—this life was revealed, and we have seen it and testify to it, and declare to you the eternal life that was with the Father and was revealed to us—we declare to you what we have seen and heard so that you may also have fellowship with us and truly our fellowship is with the Father and with his son Jesus Christ. We are writing these things that your joy may be made complete. (1 John 1:1–4)

Centered upon Christ, this community of believers in various cities was in fact the church in its most basic expression. The members of the community believed that they were a special people called into being by God and united not by blood or race but by Christ and his teachings. They were bound together with Christ and with one another. Through these relationships, they claimed to truly know God as a loving Father and to be blessed with the fruit of the Holy Spirit. Their gospel spoke of God's gift of reconciliation through Christ. Their mission was to spread this message of divine love and reconciliation in Christ throughout the world. One of the first Christian teachers, St. Paul, described the message and the mission in these words:

> So if anyone is in Christ there is a new creation: everything old has passed away; see, everything has become new! All this is from God, who reconciled himself to us through Christ and has given us the ministry of reconciliation; that is, in Christ God was reconciling the world to himself not counting their trespasses against them, and entrusting the message of reconciliation to us. So we are ambassadors for Christ, since God is making his appeal through us; we entreat you on behalf of Christ be reconciled to God. (2 Cor. 5:17–20)

The early Christians believed that the great event of reconciliation had taken place through Christ. It was an event of healing, reconciliation and salvation initiated by God in his love. Mindful of this divine love, the followers of Christ sought to live their lives according to his Gospel. As faithful persons and as a community of believers, they felt called to bear witness to God's love in the world.

From the beginning, the earliest Christians described the church in rich images that related it to the very presence and actions of God in their midst. They spoke of the church as being "God's own people" (1 Peter 2:9–10), "the Body of Christ" (Eph. 1:23), and "the Household of God" (Gal. 6:10). It was in the community of the church where the Spirit of God revealed its gifts (1 Cor. 3:16f.). These and other images were used to affirm the intimate relationship between God and the church. The images also reflected the conviction that the church was a witness to the reconciling actions of God in Christ. As Maximos Aghiorgoussis says: "God reveals himself and his mighty works including salvation in Christ not to individuals only, but to a people, his chosen people, to a community, to a covenant community, both the old and the new."[5]

A PEOPLE OF FAITH

As members of the church, the first followers of Jesus Christ had profound convictions. These convictions were rooted in his coming and his teachings. Convinced that Jesus rose from the dead, the followers believed that God had acted in a decisive and unique way in him to manifest the reign of God. It was expressed through Christ's teachings, through his healings, his signs, and most especially through his victory over the power of death. Through the coming of Christ, the early Christians believed that God's reign, his Kingdom, had been revealed. They believed that Jesus was the risen Christ whom they honored as their Lord and Savior (Col. 1:15–20). They believed that he continued to be present with them.[6]

Because of this, they were convinced that Jesus was the divine "Son of God."[7] They believed that Jesus was not simply another teacher of virtue. But more, they honored him as the "Son of God" who became human in order to restore humanity to communion with God. He truly was the Savior who rescued humanity from the power of sin and death and restored them to communion with God. They believed that Jesus revealed the mysterious reality of the one God, who is Father, Son, and Holy Spirit. The early Christians believed that they had received an insight into the reality of the one God that was not based upon human speculation but upon divine revelation in Christ.[8]

Perhaps reflecting on early Christian hymns, the apostle Paul expresses the central faith affirmation of the early church when he says of Christ:

> Who though he was in the form of God, did not regard equality with God something to be exploited, but emptied himself, taking the form of a slave, being born in human likeness. And being found in human form, he humbled himself and became obedient even to the point of death—even death upon the cross. Therefore, God has highly exalted him and gave him the name that is above every other name, so that at the name of Jesus every knee should bend, in heaven and earth, and every tongue should confess that Jesus Christ is Lord, to the glory of God the Father. (Phil. 2:6–11)

The early Christians also believed that Jesus revealed the deepest truth about the human person. They believed that the human person is meant to live in harmony with God and one another in the midst of creation. Jesus' teaching about love of God and neighbor were central to his ministry. His prayers emphasized the immediacy of God who is like a loving father. His miracles manifest the ultimate power of God. Jesus' care for the sinners and outcasts of society bore witness to God's mercy and love for all. His love for the sick and crippled emphasized the profound value of each human person. Indeed, the followers of Christ preached a radical gospel that was truly good news for those who longed to know, love, and serve God.[9]

A UNIVERSAL MESSAGE AND MISSION

The first Christians believed that the message of Christ was not meant to be confined to Palestine or to the people of Israel.[10] Following his resurrection, Jesus had directed his disciples to gather in Jerusalem in order to await the coming of the Holy Spirit. He also said to them: "Go therefore and make disciples of all nations, baptizing them in the name of the Fathers, of the Son, and of the Holy Spirit, teaching them to observe all that I have commanded you. And remember I am with you always, to the end of the age" (Matt. 28: 19–20). While they may have felt ill prepared for their mission, the first apostles and disciples knew that they had to bear witness to Christ and his gospel in lands near and far. They remembered the words of Jesus: "You shall be my witnesses both in Jerusalem, and in all Judea and in Samaria and into the utter most parts of the earth" (Acts 1:8).

The early followers of Christ believed that God the Holy Spirit strengthened them for their missionary work. Gathered together in Jerusalem 50 days after Christ's resurrection, they experienced the presence of God the Holy Spirit and were strengthened for their mission. This day, which came to be known as Pentecost, marked the formal beginning of the church's mission in the world.[11] From the city of Jerusalem, the apostles and disciples set out along the roads of the Roman Empire to the cities and villages of the Mediterranean world and beyond. Within only a few years after the resurrection of Christ, Christian communities existed in the major cities of the Roman Empire and in other more distant regions. Some of the story of the church's development from Jerusalem to the city of Rome is contained in the Book of the Acts of the Apostles written about the year 63.[12]

Wherever the missionaries went, they established Christian communities that became local churches in their most basic expression. New Christians were taught about Christ and his gospel by the apostles or by the designated leaders of the community. The new Christians were normally integrated into the community through the rite of baptism. This meaningful rite identified them with Christ's death and resurrection (Rom. 6:3–5). It signified their new life in union with Christ and his followers in the church (Gal. 3:27–28). It was a sign of the washing away of sin and a new birth (1 Cor. 6:11; John 3:5). It expressed the presence of the Spirit of God (2 Cor. 1:21–22). In accordance with Christ's directive, the members of the community gathered at a common meal to pray and to offer their gifts of bread and wine in remembrance of all God's saving actions (1 Cor. 11:23–25). This gathering, which came to be known as the Lord's Supper and the Eucharist, became the principal act of Christian worship on the Lord's Day, which was the first day of the week. The Eucharist gathered together in each place the Christians of that area. At the same time the local observance of the Eucharist expressed a bond of faith and worship with other Christian communities. "There was a time," says John Meyendorff, "when the Church had no canon of scripture and no elaborate organization. However, there was never a time when it did not celebrate the Supper of the Lord."[13] This gathering for worship in obedience to Christ's command was the most basic expression of church life.

TRUTH AND UNITY

The early church also had to proclaim its faith and define itself in relationship to Judaism and to the various religious cults and philosophies of the regions about the Mediterranean as well as in more distant places such as Syria, Africa, Armenia, Persia, and India. Based upon Jesus' life, death, and resurrection, the early church presented a very distinctive view of God and reality, which could not be harmonized with the polytheistic religions and philosophies. These often had great acceptance and an air of antiquity. Very early on, the apostle Paul had recognized this challenge to the universality of the Christian faith when he said: "For Jews demand signs and Greeks desire wisdom, but we proclaim Christ crucified, a stumbling block to Jews and foolishness to Gentiles, but to those who are called both Jews and Greeks, Christ the power of God and the wisdom of God" (1 Cor. 1:22–24). For those nurtured in Judaism or in the philosophies of the ancient world, the teachings of the Christian faith were seen as novel and their truth was not always easy to perceive.[14]

From the time of the apostles, the church was intent both to proclaim the message of faith free from distortions and to maintain its unity as a sign of the God's gift of reconciliation in Christ. The ultimate concern of the church was for the salvation of the entire world. And authentic Christian teaching contributed to the process of salvation that was God's gift. Christians were concerned with professing their faith in a truthful and accurate manner. Distortions in Christian teachings were viewed as dangerous because they were not faithful to Christ's revelation. Moreover, distorted teachings could prevent believers from entering into a healthy relationship with God and from a gaining a proper understanding of the value of the human person. "The unity of the scattered Christian community," says Henry Chadwick, "depended upon two things—on a common faith and on a common way of ordering their life and worship. They called each other 'brother' or 'sister.' Whatever difference there might be or race or class or education, they felt bound together by their focus of loyalty to the person and teachings of Jesus."[15]

Divisions among Christians and between church communities contradicted their message of reconciliation between God and humanity that came through Christ. From the earliest days of the church, all forms of divisions among Christians and their churches were viewed as a tragedy that needed attention. Jesus had prayed for the unity of his disciples. He linked their unity both to his relationship with God the Father and to their mission in the world. The earliest Christians could not forget the prayer of Jesus that he said on the night before his death. Known as the "High Priestly Prayer," it contained a number of references to the unity of Christ's disciples. He said in part:

> As you Father, are in me and I am in you, may they also be one in us, so that the world may believe that you have sent me. The glory that you have given me I have given them, so that they may be one as we are one, I in them and you in me, that they may be completely one, so that the world may know that you have sent me and have loved them even as you have loved me. (John 17:22–23)

In this prayer, Jesus expresses he deep love for his disciples, as he is about to go to his own death. In praying for their unity, he links their oneness to the bond between himself and the Father. He also relates the unity of his disciples to their mission in the world.[16]

The theme of the unity of Christians is also found extensively in the writings of the apostle Paul. Through his letters, Paul frequently urges the early Christians both to maintain the faith and to avoid divisions. Indeed, he frequently criticizes those Christians who distorted the faith and those who introduced divisions into the church. Writing to the church in Corinth, Paul laments the internal quarrels there and says: "Now I appeal to you brothers and sisters, by the name of our Lord Jesus Christ, that all of you be in agreement and that there be no divisions among you, but that you be united in the same mind and same purpose" (1 Cor. 1:10).

In his letter to the Ephesians, Paul emphasizes the relationship between the authentic faith and the unity of the church. Both are important for the church. He calls upon them to make "every effort to maintain the unity of the Spirit in the bond of peace. There is one body and one Spirit, just as you were called to the one hope of your calling, one Lord, one faith, one baptism, one God and Father of all, who is above all and through all and in all" (Eph. 4:3–6).

To the early church in Rome, Paul has a similar message. He urged them to live in harmony as they praise God. He declares: "May the God of steadfastness and encouragement grant you to live in such harmony with one another in accord with Christ Jesus, that with one mind you may with one voice glorify the God and Father of our Lord Jesus Christ" (Rom. 15:5–6).

The strong admonition of St. Paul especially to the early churches in Corinth, Rome, and Ephesus pointed to the important relationship between teaching the faith properly and maintaining unity in the church. Both were necessary. The distortion of the faith and the disunity of the Christian community betrayed the reconciling message of Christ and did not give glory to God. Whereas, God is glorified, according to Paul, when the believers live in harmony and are of one mind and one voice. "The church," as Bruce Metzger says, "is the community of believers who constitute one body in Christ (Rom. 12:5). All members of the body—eyes, ears, hands, feet—need one another and the life-giving presence supplied to individual members of the church (1 Cor. 12: 12–31)."[17]

The early church was rapidly compelled to strengthen its internal life in the light of the teachings and practices of the apostles. This was the immediate consequence of its obligation to maintain unity and to teach the faith to newcomers in different cultural contexts. By the end of the first century, a number of interrelated characteristics are especially significant and present wherever churches were established. First, baptism marked the normative entrance into the community of believers. It signified a new life centered upon Christ and lived in relationship with other believers. Second, the celebration of the Eucharist, the Lord's Supper, was the center of the church's life and the central act of community worship. The church was a worshipping people. Third, a threefold order of ministerial leadership was gradually established. Following the Twelve Apostles, the bishops, presbyters, and deacons exercised particular responsibility for the worship, teaching, and missions of the church communities. Fourth, brief creedal affirmations expressing essential faith convictions became more formalized, especially within the context of baptism and in relationship to mission. And finally, the church began to develop a consensus on the collection of books that would comprise its scripture. This process, which was finalized by the early fourth century, ultimately led to the canon of the New Testament containing 27 books that were written approximately between 55 and 90.[18] Centered upon Christ and his teachings, the composition of these books was regarded as divinely inspired. All of these developments took place to enable the church to be the salutary community through which persons could grow in their relationship with God and others in the midst of creation.[19]

MAINTAINING THE FAITH AND UNITY OF THE CHURCHES

The rapid growth of the early church was phenomenal but not without other serious challenges. Within the confines of Palestine, the early Christians often experienced persecution from other Jews. The famous apostle Paul had in fact persecuted Christians before his own conversion from Judaism.[20] Between the year 58 and 312, the churches within the wider Roman Empire were subject to various degrees of persecution from one region to another. Because of their faith in Christ and the witness of the church, Christians refused to honor the pagan Roman emperor as God. As a consequence of this, the Christians were accused from time to time of blasphemy, atheism, sedition, and treason. During this period, thousands of Christians lost their lives at the hands of the pagan Roman government up to the early decades of the fourth century. It was truly an age of martyrs. In many places, the early Christian communities gathered as a catacomb church to pray, teach, and to celebrate the Eucharist.[21]

Despite the persecution, the church refused to be a secret sect. Christians could be found at all levels of society and in most occupations certainly by the second century. Some would claim that the Christians ultimately conquered the pagan empire from within through their faithful witness. Under the Roman Emperor Constantine, formal persecution of the church ceased in 311, and a new relationship between the church and government was developed after 313. Prior to his death, Constantine was baptized. Emperor Theodosius finally proclaimed Christianity the official faith of the Roman-Byzantine Empire in the year 380.

With the end of persecution and the dramatic growth of members throughout the fourth century, the church continued to structure its internal organizational life, to strengthen its missions, to develop its liturgical practices, and to deepen its theological witness.

During the first four centuries, the church rapidly moved beyond the confines of Palestine and the world of monotheistic Judaism.[22] In so doing, it entered into a pluralistic world with many belief systems. For the most part, a number of outstanding Christian teachers, later called Apologists, entered into a dialogue with Jewish and Pagan teachers. The Apologists sought to speak about the significance of Christ in terms that were understandable to those coming from radically different religious and philosophical traditions. As a result of the teachings of the Christian Apologists, many intellectuals in the Roman world were attracted to the church.[23]

The encounter with Judaism and the ancient philosophies, however, was not without challenges. As a consequence, the church had to face a number of threats to its teachings and to its unity. In this very significant period of development, there were a number of movements expressing teachings that the church judged to be inconsistent with its faith. Some, such as Ebionism, emphasized Jesus' humanity but failed to also affirm his divine nature. Some, such as the various types of Gnosticism, attempted to merge aspects of Christian faith with ancient philosophies. Others, such as Montanism and Marcianism, were viewed as distorting aspects of Christian teachings. A number of early Christian leaders, later called Apostolic Fathers, taught and guided the churches through this difficult period.[24]

When these and other views challenged the teachings of the church, bishops of a particular region would meet in council. Each bishop came as the leader, teacher, and representative of his diocese, which was the church in a given place. The bishops would often be joined by other clergy and laity who served as advisors. The practice of bishops meetings became quite common from the second century onward. These councils reflected especially the meeting of the apostles in Jerusalem as recorded in the Book of Acts. There, the apostles discussed issues related to the growth of the church in the Gentile world. Likewise, the councils of bishops deliberated upon the challenges to the Christian faith and unity of the church and sought to express with a common mind the truths of the faith. Those teachings that were viewed as distortions were formally repudiated as heresies, that is to say, distortions of the apostolic faith. This led to a break in relations between church communities. This schism was expressed chiefly as a break in sacramental communion. While the concern for teaching the faith accurately was very strong, a break in communion among churches also was viewed as tragic and contrary to the message of the gospel.

Every attempt was made to heal the wounds of divisions while maintaining the faith free from distortion. The church sought to reconcile those who had become associated with heresies through misunderstanding, ignorance, or deliberate choice. The church viewed these distortions as serious impediments for a person's growth in salvation. One cannot fully understand the profound concern that the church had for opposing false teachings apart from its deep concern over salvation. Salvation was considered to be union with God offered through Christ in the Spirit. Misunderstanding of the reality of God could affect one's salvation. It was not simply a matter of words and phrases to be debated. According to the early church, it was a matter of communion with God and his people.[25]

DIVERSITY IN UNITY

From the beginning, the one church was a communion of local churches. As such, it was not a monolithic community from the start. As has been noted, the church was concerned about preserving the authentic faith and its own unity within the context of a Eucharistic community. Yet there was a healthy diversity in the manner in which the churches expressed the one faith and celebrated that faith in worship. Unity in faith did not mean uniformity in expression. The Christian faith was expressed in churches containing a wide variety of peoples. The faith was expressed in a variety of languages and through various cultures. In the eastern portion of the Roman-Byzantine Empire, Greek was the preferred language of education and culture. In the western portion, Latin predominated. Beyond the borders of the empire, the local churches were composed of believers of a wide variety of cultures who used languages such as Aramaic, Syriac, and Armenian. Because of the various developments and characteristics in the early church, it has become common to speak broadly of Eastern and Western Christianity. These broad descriptive terms have their limitations. But they do help us to sense the diversity in unity that was reflected in early Christianity.[26]

Two points should be mentioned in this regard. First, the association of local dioceses in a particular geographical region became more pronounced from the second century onward. Each diocese continued to be seen as the local church in which there were a number of Eucharistic communities. Each diocese maintained its integrity under the leadership of its bishop who was the president of the Eucharistic assembly. Moreover, there was a regional association of dioceses that served to strengthen the unity of the churches in a particular area. These provinces were eventually structured along the lines of five regional patriarchates within the Roman-Byzantine Empire. By the fourth century, these patriarchates were associated with the great cities of Rome, Constantinople, Alexandria, Antioch, and Jerusalem. The bishops of these churches and cities, who came to be known as patriarchs, exercised certain primatial authority among the bishops of their region. The bishop of Rome, known as the Pope, was accorded a primacy of honor among the patriarchal bishops.[27]

With this perspective in mind, one can speak about both the one church and the many churches. From the apostolic period onward, this one church was viewed as teaching the authentic Christian faith in all places. Thus, from the first century, the church frequently referred to itself as the Catholic Church. In this way, the church sought to distinguish itself from heretical groups and sectarian movements that, it believed, had distorted the Christian message. The Catholic Church saw itself as the one church of all faithful clergy and laity who maintained their unity in the orthodox faith and gathered together in particular places to celebrate the Eucharist in accordance with Christ's directive.[28]

At the same time, therefore, the one church was in fact comprised of many regional churches that were united in the orthodox Christian faith and were in sacramental communion. By the fourth century, the five ancient patriarchates were a very prominent feature of the organization of the church in the Mediterranean world. Yet each of these patriarchates was in turn comprised of local dioceses that had their own identity and integrity. Led by a bishop, each of these dioceses contained the local Eucharistic communities where the faith was taught and celebrated. At that level, there was often diversity in language, in theological emphasis, and in liturgical customs.

Second, a number of theological perspectives on the Christian faith and schools of Christian thought became more pronounced, especially in the fourth and fifth centuries. Each of these sought to express the faith of the church within the different historical and cultural contexts. The church was active in different cultures with their own philosophical antecedents. Wherever the Christian gospel was preached, those teachers had to take seriously the existing religious and philosophical perspectives. In addition, different languages and different terms were being used to express the Christian faith. By the third century, important centers of Christian learning and thought could be found in the cities of Alexandria, Antioch, and Edessa, as well as in the regions of Cappadocia and North Africa.

Each of these centers of thought expressed distinctive, but not necessarily opposite, perspectives on the Christian faith.

THE CHALLENGE OF DIVISION

The theological debates of the fourth century centered on the heresies of Arianism, Apolinarianism, and Pneumatomachianism. Arianism raised questions about the full divinity of Christ and his relationship to God the Father.[29] Apolinarianism raised questions about the full humanity of Christ and his relationship to the rest of humanity.[30] Likewise, Pneumatomachianism raised questions about the divine nature of the Holy Spirit and the relationship to Christ and the Father.[31] In the face of these teachings, the church was obliged to reflect more deeply upon its understanding of the God the Trinity and to find words that could express this. The Scriptures and the tradition of the church had to be interpreted in a manner that was faithful to the faith of the first apostles.

These theological issues led to the convening of historic bishops' meetings in the city of Nicaea in 325 and the city of Constantinople in 381. There had been meetings of bishops in particular regions from the late first and early second century. The councils at Nicaea and Constantinople were in time considered to be the first and second ecumenical councils because, with imperial support, they gathered bishops not simply from one region but from throughout the Roman Empire. As a result of these councils and the theological reflection associated with them, general agreement was reached over the formal terminology to be used for describing the Trinity. And, at the same time, the church acted to reconcile the divided parties.[32]

In the period surrounding the Council of Nicaea, the church was challenged to reflect more deeply upon its understanding of Jesus Christ as being at once both a divine and a human reality. St. Athanasius of Alexandria opposed the teaching of Arius, a priest from the same city. The teaching of Arianism spoke about Jesus as being divine but not in the same way as God the Father. To the ears of many, Arius and his followers preached a Christ that was something of a demigod. Athanasius forcefully responded to this view and emphasized that Jesus was fully divine. For him, this was the key to the Christian understanding of salvation. God had freely and completely entered into communion with humanity in Christ. The Council of Nicaea in 325 affirmed this truth by saying that Christ is in his divinity the "same substance (*homoousios*)" as God the Father. In the wake of this council, church divisions continued especially over the understanding of the divinity and humanity of Christ as well as over the term that could be used to describe Christ.[33]

In an effort to clarify the church's teaching and to unite the divided churches, a number of outstanding theologians addressed both the various expressions of Arianism as well as those teachings, referred to as Apolinarianism, which questioned the full humanity of Christ. Chief among these teachers were St. Basil the Great, St. Gregory the Theologian, and St. Gregory of Nyssa. Known as the Cappadocian Fathers, they appeared to have been greatly assisted by St. Macrina, the sister of Basil and Gregory of Nyssa. Based upon the apostolic faith, these teachers proposed a theological solution, which made an important distinction between the three persons *(hypostasis)* of the Father Son, and Holy Spirit, and the one nature *(ousia)* of God. This perspective affirmed the Christian view that God is truly one and the three persons share fully in this divine reality while at the same time expressing their own distinctive integrity as divine persons. The Mystery of the Christian God is that God is both one and three.[34] As Kallistos Ware says: "While Athanasius emphasized the unity of God—Father, Son and Holy Spirit—the Cappadocians stressed God's threeness—Father, Son and Holy Spirit are three persons (hypostaseis). Preserving a delicate balance between the threeness and oneness in God, they gave full meaning to the classic summary of Trinitarian doctrine, three persons in one essence."[35]

The debate over Arianism, Apolinarianism, and Pneumatomachianism divided many of the local churches and their teachers. In some cases, there were profound differences of opinion over the deeper understanding of the divine persons of the Trinity. In other cases, there were differences over the terms used to describe the divine persons and their relations to each other. The Cappadocian teachers led the churches in affirming an understanding of God that was faithful to the Scripture and tradition. They also found the appropriate terminology to express that understanding. Indeed, the solution affirmed by the Cappadocian teachers did much not only to clarify the traditional faith but also to reconcile divided churches especially in the eastern portion of the Roman-Byzantine Empire by the Council of Constantinople in 381.

The Cappadocians were also deeply concerned with healing the divisions that afflicted the churches as a result of the controversies. St. Basil especially lamented the divisions that existed between the regional churches. He declared that schisms were "nothing less than a disaster."[36] Time and again, he called upon church leaders to seek reconciliation and the healing of wounds caused by the harsh theological debates and misunderstandings. In so doing, he consciously followed the example of earlier teachers such as St. Ignatius, St. Irenaeus, and St. Athanasius of Alexandria. They both defended forcefully the faith in the face of misunderstandings and distorted teachings. Yet they also sought reconciliation with those who had become alienated. Schism was an evil that these great teachers could not easily tolerate.[37] As St. Basil said: "The one great end of all who are really and truly serving the Lord ought to be to bring back to unity the churches which 'at sundry times and in diverse manner' (Heb.

1.1) are divided from one another,... for nothing is so characteristically Christian as being a peacemaker, and for this reason the Lord has promised us peacemakers a very high reward."[38]

The theological insights and reconciling spirit of the Cappadocian teachers stand behind the discussions at the Council of Constantinople in 381 and the important creed that is historically connected with it. This council bore witness to the church's faith. It also bore witness to the process that healed many of the divisions in the churches of the fourth century. The creed of the council built upon the creed of the earlier Council of Nicaea in 325 as well as even earlier baptismal creeds. Creedal statements were a part of the church's life since the apostolic period.[39] The creed of Constantinople expressed the faith of the church in a succinct manner. It also sought to be faithful to the divine revelation as expressed in the church's Scripture and tradition. In addition to this, the creed of Constantinople was also meant to be a statement of faith that could be a unifying element within and among the churches.

The Creed of the Council of Constantinople of 381 is as follows:

> We believe in one God,
> the Father, the Almighty,
> maker of heaven and earth,
> of all that is, seen and unseen.
>
> We believe in one Lord, Jesus Christ,
> the only Son of God,
> eternally begotten of the Father,
> God from God, Light from Light,
> true God from true God,
> begotten, not made,
> of one Being with the Father.
> Through him all things were made.
>
> For us all and for our salvation
> he came down from heaven:
> by the power of the Holy Spirit
> he became incarnate from the Virgin Mary,
> and was made man.
>
> For our sake he was crucified under Pontius Pilate;
> he suffered death and was buried.
> On the third day he rose again
> in accordance with the Scriptures;
> he ascended into heaven
> and is seated at the right hand of the Father.
> He will come again in glory to judge the living and the dead,
> and his kingdom will have no end.

We believe in the Holy Spirit, the Lord, the giver of life,
who proceeds from the Father.
Who, with the Father and the Son, he is worshiped and glorified,
who has spoken through the Prophets.

We believe in one holy catholic and apostolic Church.
We acknowledge one baptism for the forgiveness of sins.
We look for the resurrection of the dead,
and the life of the world to come. Amen.[40]

While the record is not entirely clear, this Creed began to circulate among the churches in the years following the Council of Constantinople in 381. Within less than 100 years, it appears to have become an important expression of faith and a sign of unity among the churches of the Roman-Byzantine Empire and beyond.

CONCLUSIONS

From the beginning the Christian Church was centered upon the life and teachings of Jesus Christ. He established the church in its most basic form with the call of the first apostles and disciples. The believers honored him as the promised Messiah. They viewed him as their Lord and Savior. They confessed him to be the Son of God who was the bearer of God's gift of salvation. As followers of Christ, they felt called to live their lives in a loving manner that reflected their Lord's life. After Christ's death and resurrection about the year 33 in Jerusalem, his followers began their mission to spread the message of Christ's coming and his teachings throughout the Mediterranean world and beyond.

The concern of the contemporary ecumenical movement is for the visible unity of the various Christian churches. Yet this concern cannot ignore the story of Christ's coming and the earliest development of the church. Regardless of their particular tradition, most Christian churches today would affirm that there is an historic connection between Jesus Christ and the early church. This connection is reflected in the basic faith affirmations as well as in the rites of Baptism and the Eucharist. It is also expressed in use of the New Testament, in the tradition of ministry, in ethical standards, and in a concern for mission.

As we shall see in the next chapter, however, divisions in the church frequently reflected different interpretations of early church's teachings and practices. Differences developed over the interpretations of both Scripture and tradition. These theological differences were frequently compounded by political and cultural factors. In subsequent chapters, we shall also see that the contemporary ecumenical movement is providing the churches today with opportunities to look together at the life of the early church with an eye toward overcoming doctrinal differences and affirming a common heritage.

NOTES

1. Bruce M. Metzger, *The New Testament: Its Background, Growth, and Content* (Nashville: Abington Press, 1965), pp. 17–31.
2. Ibid., pp. 126–27.
3. Ibid., pp. 79–88.
4. Ibid., p. 127.
5. Maximos Aghiorgoussis, *In the Image of God* (Brookline: Holy Cross Orthodox Press, 1999, p. 3.
6. Metzger, *The New Testament: Its Background, Growth, and Content,* pp. 130–32.
7. Ibid., p. 154.
8. Ibid., pp. 145–47.
9. Ibid., pp. 157–64.
10. Henry Chadwick, *The Early Church* (Middlesex, England: Penguin Books, 1967–1973), pp. 15–31.
11. Ibid., pp. 181–85.
12. Ibid., pp. 178–79.
13. John Meyendorff, "The Bishop in the Church," in *Ministers of Christ,* ed. Theodore O. Wedel (New York: The Seabury Press, 1964), p. 155.
14. See Henry Chadwick, *Early Christian Thought and the Classical Tradition* (New York, 1966).
15. Chadwick, *The Early Church,* p. 32.
16. Lesslie Newbigin, *Is Christ Divided?* (Grand Rapids, Mich.: Eerdmans Publishing Company, 1961), pp. 18–25.
17. Metzger, *The New Testament: Its Background, Growth, and Content,* pp. 243–44.
18. Ibid., pp. 273–76.
19. Chadwick, *The Early Church,* pp. 41–53.
20. Ibid., p. 185.
21. Ibid., pp. 61–72.
22. Jaroslav Pelikan, *The Christian Tradition 1* (Chicago: The University of Chicago Press, 1971), pp. 11–27.
23. Ibid., pp. 27–41.
24. Ibid., pp. 68–108.
25. A.J. Philippou, "The Mystery of Pentecost," in his *The Orthodox Ethos* (Oxford: Holywell, 1964), pp. 91–92.
26. Yves Congar, *Diversity and Communion* (Mystic, Conn.: Twenty-Third Publications, 1985), pp. 15–33.
27. The nature of this primacy has been discussed since at least the fourth century.
28. John D. Zizioulas, *Eucharist, Bishop, Church* (Brookline: Holy Cross Orthodox Press, 2002), pp. 128–35.
29. Jaroslav Pelikan, *The Christian Tradition: A History of the Development of Doctrine, Vol. 1,* pp. 191–200.
30. Ibid., pp. 239–40.

31. Ibid., pp. 211–14.
32. Ibid., pp. 228–29, 270.
33. Ibid., pp. 200–11.
34. Ibid., pp. 211–25.
35. Timothy Ware, *The Orthodox Church* (Baltimore: Penguin Books, revised edition, 1976), p. 30.
36. St. Basil the Great, *Epistle 203.*
37. Jean Danielou, S.J., "The Fathers and Christian Unity," *Eastern Churches Quarterly* 16:1 (1964), pp. 8–18.
38. St. Basil the Great, *Epistle to Kyriakos,* cited in The Nicene and Post Nicene Fathers, vol. 8 (Grand Rapids, Mich.: Eerdmans, reprint, 1971), p. 190.
39. Pelikan, *The Christian Tradition 1,* pp. 116–20.
40. This translation of the text is found in *Confessing the One Faith* (Geneva: WCC Publications).

CHAPTER 3

Historic Church Divisions

> The Lord has cut off the islands from the mainland by the sea, but he has united in love those who live on the islands with those who live on the mainland. We have but one Lord, one faith, one hope. Even if you consider yourself the head of the whole church, the head cannot say to the feet "I have no need of you ..." So far as we are concerned, in consideration of our own weakness, we are seeking to be united in a living union with you. We realize that even if you are not present in your body, yet the assistance you obtain for us by means of your prayers will, in these most difficult circumstances, be of the greatest use to us... How can we possibly be ashamed of keeping ourselves to ourselves, and how indeed can we fail to see our break in unity as nothing less than as disaster?
>
> —St. Basil the Great[1]

INTRODUCTION

The contemporary ecumenical movement is concerned with resolving the historic doctrinal differences that are at the root of the divisions between the Orthodox, Roman Catholic, Anglican, and the Reformation churches. These divisions go back centuries. In this chapter, we shall identify the four major divisions. The first is the division following the Council of Ephesus in 431. The second is the division following the Council of Chalcedon in 451. The third, commonly called the Great Schism, is the division between the Church of Rome and the Church of Constantinople and related churches in the Middle Ages. The fourth is the division between the Roman Catholic Church and the various Reformation Churches in the sixteenth century. As we shall see, each of these divisions reflected serious theological questions. At the same time, each was compounded by the political and cultural factors that frequently made the resolution of differences very difficult at the time.

DIVISIONS AFTER THE COUNCIL OF EPHESUS IN 431

Throughout the first four centuries, the church had to articulate its faith in response to philosophical and theological challenges. Distortions of the Christian faith deeply troubled church leaders. At the same time, the regional churches sought to maintain their unity in the apostolic faith as a salutary sign of God's unifying activity in Christ. Both of these concerns can be found side by side in the preaching, teaching, and writing of many of the great teachers of the church during this early period. The distortions of the apostolic faith could not be tolerated and the divisions of the churches were viewed as a tragedy that demanded resolution.

New questions regarding the relationship of the divinity and the humanity of Christ and the appropriate terminology to be used led to serious and unresolved divisions among the churches in the fifth century. Significant divisions came about following the Council of Ephesus in 431 and the Council of Chalcedon in 451. The division of the fifth century reflects primarily differences between the theological schools of Alexandria and Antioch over the understanding of the person of Christ and the terms to be used in describing properly the relationship between the divinity and humanity of Christ.

Raised in the Antiochian tradition, Patriarch Nestorius of Constantinople refused to speak of Mary as the Theotokos (Birth giver of God) and preferred to use the term Christotokos (Birth giver of Christ). While needing clarification, the term Theotokos had long been part of the church's understanding of the Virgin Mary and her relationship to Christ. To Nestorius' Antiochian ears, however, the term Theotokos was less preferable because it sounded as though the humanity of Christ was somehow lost. Following the lead of its great thinker, Theodore of Mopsuestia, the Antiochian tradition was concerned with safeguarding the integrity of the humanity and divinity of Christ. Not known for his theological abilities, however, Nestorius was unable to explain well how the humanity and divinity are related. He was accused of having taught that Christ was not only divine and human but also that Christ was two beings. In other words, there was no true connection between humanity and divinity in Christ.[2]

Patriarch Cyril of Alexandria, the chief opponent to Nestorius and his teachings, represented well the Alexandrian school. Cyril emphasized the union of humanity and divinity in Christ. In so doing, he used the phrase "One nature of the Incarnate Word." While not denying Christ's full humanity and divinity, Cyril clearly placed emphasis upon their union in the one reality of Christ. He also initially used the word nature *(physis)* to describe the concrete expression of the one Christ.[3]

When the Council of Ephesus in 431 began, not all the invited bishops had arrived, especially those from the region of Antioch. Under the guidance of Cyril, the council deposed Nestorius and affirmed Cyril's Christological perspectives. When the bishops from Antioch arrived, a rival council was held and they refused to accept the decision of Ephesus. They were concerned that the terminology of Cyril could be used to deny the integrity of the divinity and humanity in Christ. For some, the term nature *(physis)* was used to speak about the two realities of humanity and divinity. Simply stated, moderate Alexandrians emphasized the union of the divinity and humanity in Christ. Moderate Antiochian emphasized the integrity of both the humanity and divinity in Christ. "Either approach," says Kallistos Ware, "if pressed too far could lead to heresy, but the Church had need of both in order to form a balanced picture of the whole Christ. It was a tragedy for Christendom that the two schools, instead of balancing one another, entered into conflict."[4]

In the year 433, Patriarch Cyril and Patriarch John of Antioch came to an agreement that affirmed a common Christological teaching and that sought agreement on terminology. They spoke of Christ of being one person *(hypostasis)* and being of two natures *(physis).* This agreement eventually led many in the Antiochian tradition to accept the decision of the Council of Ephesus.[5] Not all, however, easily accepted this solution. Bishops in some of the dioceses in East Syria, especially those living near or within the Persian Empire, continued to be suspicious of the Alexandrian perspective and the attacks on Nestorius, who had resigned as Patriarch of Constantinople. Indeed, it appears that many of these bishops were not involved in Ephesus or in subsequent discussions.[6]

The church in the Persian Empire, later known as the Church of the East, eventually rejected the decision of Ephesus and its clarification of 433. This church, dating back to the second century, was centered in the region of upper Mesopotamia. The region was conquered by the Persian Empire during the third century. Persia never fully accepted Christianity. The ancient religion Zoroastrianism predominated. During the early fourth century, the bishops of the region were organized into an ecclesiastical structure under the leadership of a Catholicos, the bishop of the Persian royal capital at Seleucia-Ctesiphon. He later received the additional title of Patriarch. This ancient church had little formal connection with the church in the Roman-Byzantine Empire.[7]

The alienation became even more pronounced as time went on. Extremists in both traditions complicated this further. Indeed, the monk Eutychis expressed the extreme Alexandrian position by teaching that Christ's humanity was overtaken by his divinity. This was true doctrinal Monophysitism. Under the leadership of Patriarch Dioscorus of Alexandria this extreme position was accepted by another group of bishops who met at another council in Ephesus in 449. While this decision was subsequently repudiated at the Council of Chalcedon in 451, much damage to the relationships had already been done. The decision of Chalcedon opened up new opportunities for reconciliation.[8]

However, the decision of the Council of Constantinople in 553 to condemn posthumously the teachings of Diadore of Tarsus and Theodore of Mopsuestia only aggravated the tensions. Attempts to reconcile the divided churches, especially in the sixth century, were thwarted by the wars between the Roman-Byzantine Empire and the Persian Empire. A clear cleavage developed between the church in the Roman-Byzantine Empire and the church in the Persian Empire. This was solidified by the rapid rise of Islam in the early seventh century.

The Church of the East eventually came to be called the Nestorian Church by some or, in more recent times, the Assyrian Church. It continued its life independently from most of the subsequent developments that touched the churches in the Mediterranean world through the Middle Ages and into the modern period. Yet the Church of the East was engaged in remarkable missionary activity well into the fourteenth century. Missions were established in Ceylon, India, Burma, Thailand, Indochina, and China. Membership in this ancient church, however, was considerably reduced in recent centuries. In the sixteenth century, some members accepted the authority of the Roman Catholic Church. Some members were the objects of Protestant proselytism in the nineteenth century. A sizeable number of its faithful were the victims of persecution in the early twentieth century.[9]

DIVISIONS AFTER THE COUNCIL OF CHALCEDON OF 451

The second church division of great significance is centered on the statement of the Council of Chalcedon in 451. In order to heal the growing division over Christology and its expression, which was also affecting the life of the Roman-Byzantine Empire, a council of bishops met at Chalcedon, near Constantinople in 451. This council was a bold and swift reaction to the meeting of bishops held in Ephesus in 449. That gathering, dubbed the Robbers Synod by Pope Leo of Rome, had supported the monk Eutychis and his extreme Alexandrian Christology.[10] As we have said, Dioscoris and Eutychis pressed Cyril's theology to an extreme. They "maintained that in Christ there was not only a unity of personality but a single nature—Monophysitism." Kallistos Ware continues: "It seemed to their opponents—although the Monophysites themselves denied that this was a just interpretation of their views—that such a way of speaking endangered the fullness of Christ's manhood, which in Monophysitism became so fused with his divinity as to be swallowed up in it like a drop of water in the ocean."[11]

The bishops at Chalcedon were concerned with bearing witness to the fullness of the apostolic faith in opposition to extreme Alexandrian and Antiochian perspectives. The council was also concerned with reconciling the ever widening division between the churches associated with the Alexandrian theology and those associated with Antiochian theology. Therefore, the statement produced at the council must be understood within the context of the Christological debates reaching back to the Council of Ephesus and the differing emphasis in Christology.[12]

The famous Chalcedon statement says in part:

> So, following the saintly fathers, we all with one voice teach the confession of one and the same Son, our Lord Jesus Christ: the same perfect in divinity and perfect in humanity, the same truly God and truly man, of a rational soul and a body; consubstantial with the Father as regards his divinity, and the same consubstantial with us as regards his humanity; like us in all respects except for sin; begotten before the ages from the Father as regards his divinity, and in the last days the same for us and for our salvation from Mary, the virgin God-bearer as regards his humanity; one and the same Christ, Son, Lord, only-begotten, acknowledged in two natures which undergo no confusion, no change, no division, no separation; at no point was the difference between the natures taken away through the union, but rather the property of both natures is preserved and comes together into a single person and a single subsistent being; he is not parted or divided into two persons, but is one and the same only-begotten Son, God, Word, Lord Jesus Christ, just as the prophets taught from the beginning about him, and as the Lord Jesus Christ himself instructed us, and as the creed of the fathers handed it down to us.
>
> Since we have formulated these things with all possible accuracy and attention, the sacred and universal synod decreed that no one is permitted to produce, or even to write down or compose, any other creed or to think or teach otherwise. As for those who dare either to compose another creed or even to promulgate or teach or hand down another creed for those who wish to convert to a recognition of the truth from Hellenism or from Judaism, or from any kind of heresy at all: if they be bishops or clerics, the bishops are to be deposed from the episcopacy and the clerics from the clergy; if they be monks or layfolk, they are to be anathematized.[13]

The statement of Chalcedon wisely brought together the essential positive elements both from the moderate Alexandrian tradition and the moderate Antiochian tradition. It also reflected the language of the Agreement of 433 as well as an historic statement known as the Tome of Pope Leo. The Chalcedonian statement affirms that Christ is fully divine and fully human. While recognizing the mystery of the incarnation, the statement affirms that he is one person with two natures. Neither his divine nor his human nature are diminished or lost by the union in one person. "The council," says John Meyendorff, "appears in the history of the Church as the most perfect example of 'conciliarity' that enables the Church to discover and formulate a truly 'catholic' language, understandable to all, a permanent truth that no isolated local tradition can completely express."[14]

The churches related to the patriarchate of Rome and the patriarchate of Constantinople received the statement. The Council of Chalcedon was eventually recognized in these churches as the Fourth Ecumenical Council. In the decades following Chalcedon, however, portions of the church in Egypt and in West Syria as well as the churches in Armenia eventually rejected the statement of the council. For a time, the Church in Georgia joined them. Following the lead of these churches, the churches in Ethiopia and in Malankara, India subsequently also rejected the decision.[15]

At the theological level, those who rejected the statement presented a number of reasons that continued to reflect differences in emphasis in Christology. Upholding a very formal Alexandrian position, the opponents of the statement of Chalcedon felt that the use of the terminology of two natures went in the direction of the teaching of the followers of Nestorius. The council had in fact anathematized Nestorius. In some parts of the Christian East, these churches were already in conflict with the churches of the Persian Empire, which were accused of following Nestorian teachers. Moreover, the opponents of the statement claimed that the two nature terminology was a betrayal of Cyril's affirmation of "one nature of the incarnate Word." Of course, Cyril in the Agreement of 433 recognized the use of the two nature terminology, if understood properly.[16]

The rejection of the decision provided the basis for a new division. This church division not only reflected a difference in Christological interpretation, but also political and cultural differences among those within the Roman-Byzantine world, those living on its boundaries, and those living beyond it. During the period following Chalcedon, those who rejected the council's teaching made up a significant portion of the Christians living on the periphery of the empire. "Political and ecclesiastical rivalries, personal ambitions, imperial pressures aimed at imposing Chalcedon by force, abusive interpretations of Cyril in the Monophysite sense, as well as misinterpretations of the council by some Nestorianizing Antiochians who saw it as a disavowal of the great Cyril—all provoked the first major and lasting schism in Christendom."[17]

Major councils of bishops in 553 and 681 in Constantinople attempted to heal the growing division. They also struggled with ongoing questions related to describing the person of Christ. These councils came to be recognized as the fifth and sixth Ecumenical Councils by the churches of the Byzantine-Roman world.[18] However, by the seventh century differences in terminology and theological perspectives were greatly complicated by cultural, political, and linguistic factors. Moreover, the rise of Islam in the seventh century created a further wedge between those churches that accepted Chalcedon and the subsequent councils and those that did not.

While there was some contact and movements toward reconciliation during the Middle Ages, misunderstandings, language, and cultural differences prevented an enduring reconciliation.[19]

Today, the division of the fifth century is the basis for the two families of Orthodox Churches. The (Eastern) Orthodox Churches have accepted the Council of Chalcedon in 451 and have also recognized three additional Ecumenical Councils. The Oriental Orthodox Churches have not formally accepted the decision of Chalcedon.[20] Despite their formal division between themselves and the family of Orthodox Churches, theologians from both families established an unofficial bilateral theological dialogue in 1964. This theological dialogue became formal in 1972. Today, it is generally recognized by theologians and church leaders in both families that the Christological differences between the Oriental Orthodox and the Orthodox were primarily a matter of terminological differences and that in fact both families of churches profess the same faith in Christ but use different formulas.

DIVISION BETWEEN THE ORTHODOX CHURCH AND THE ROMAN CATHOLIC CHURCH

The division between the Orthodox Church and the Roman Catholic Church is the result of a gradual estrangement between the ninth and the fifteenth centuries. This division began initially as a break in relationship between the Church of Rome and the Church of Constantinople. The year 1054 is frequently identified as the date of the schism because representatives of Rome and Constantinople exchanged limited excommunications. Most church historians today reject this as the actual date of a permanent schism. Some point to the year 1204 when the crusaders sacked the city of Constantinople, and bishops related to Rome were installed for a brief period of time in Constantinople and other eastern cities. From that time on, the gradual alienation between the Latin West, centered on the Church of Rome, and the Byzantine East, centered upon the Church of Constantinople, became more real and much more complex. Within the regional churches of the Roman-Byzantine world, there had always been differences in theological emphasis and ecclesiastical organization. However, by the thirteenth century, the certain theological and organizational differences became much more aggravated. These tensions were seriously compounded by political and cultural differences as well.[21] There was a political and cultural estrangement between the Christian West and the Christian East that certainly contributed to the division of the churches.[22]

Between the ninth and thirteenth centuries, two major theological differences ultimately led to the unresolved schism between the Western Church centered on Rome and much of the Eastern Church centered on Constantinople.[23] The first issue was known as the *filioque*. This Latin word means "and the Son." The word was inserted by the Western Church into the Nicene-Constantinopolitan Creed of 381 after the affirmation that the "Holy Spirit, the Lord and Giver of Life, proceeds from the Father." This addition was first made to the creed in Spain during the sixth century. From there, the usage spread to churches in other parts of Western Europe. The addition may have been made initially to help counter the influence of the Arian heresy. In a strange twist of history, Emperor Charlemagne's theologians proclaimed that the *filioque* was part of the original creed and they accused the Easterners of omitting it. The addition was at first rejected formally by Rome. Pope Leo III had the original creed written in Greek and Latin inscribed on silver tablets in St. Peters Basilica. However, the creed, with the addition of the *filioque*, was eventually accepted by Rome in the eleventh century. After that, it became part of the creed used by Christians throughout church in Western Europe.[24]

Beginning in the ninth century, theologians in the Byzantine East identified the *filioque* as an unwarranted alteration of the original Nicene-Constantinopolitan Creed. The creed represented a succinct expression of essential aspects of the Christian faith. While the actual genesis of the addition may not have been known by them, the Easterners held that no one portion of the church could unilaterally tamper with the creed that had been composed by the early Ecumenical Councils of Nicaea and Constantinople and that had been so widely used in worship and teaching. Moreover, under the leadership of Patriarch Photius of Constantinople, Eastern theologians viewed the Western addition as an expression of Trinitarian theology that diminished the distinctive character of each divine person of the Holy Trinity.[25]

Under the leadership of Patriarch Photios, a union council was held in Constantinople in 879. With the concurrence of representatives of Pope John VIII, the bishops agreed to use the traditional version of the creed without the *filioque*. While the theological issues related to the *filioque* were not fully discussed or resolved, this council marked a formal end to disputes between Rome and Constantinople that had been simmering for decades.[26] "Rome and the Eastern churches still shared the idea that the Church is essentially an ordered communion of local churches. On Rome's side this meant that Constantinople was recognized as a real sister church—as fully church, one holy, catholic and apostolic, and not just a branch office of a universal organization. For its part, Constantinople freely recognized Roman priority. It was certainly the first among the churches of the pentarchy."[27]

The second major theological difference centered upon different understandings of the position and authority of the pope, the bishop of Rome, within the whole church. From the earliest centuries, there were differences in emphasis in the West and East with regard to the prestige and authority of the bishop of Rome and his relationship to other bishops.

By the fourth century, the church in the Roman-Byzantine world had structured itself along the lines of five patriarchates. These patriarchates brought together the dioceses of particular regions. A bishop or archbishop led each diocese. The archbishops of Rome, Constantinople, Alexandria, Antioch, and Jerusalem were known as patriarchs from the sixth century. The title pope, which means father, was in earliest times used by all bishops. At least from the fourth century, it came to be used in a more formal manner by the bishop of Rome and the bishop of Alexandria. As the president of a synod, each patriarch presided among the bishops of their patriarchal region. On a larger scale, this reflected the practice long found at the local and regional levels. There, metropolitans or archbishops would preside at synods of bishops of a geographical area.

From the earliest times, a certain primacy among the worldwide bishops was accorded to the pope of Rome, who was also the only patriarch in the vast Western portion of the church. The reason for this primacy reflects different perceptions. According to the Eastern perspective, this primacy and the hierarchial ordering of all the five patriarchates by the fourth century were based primarily upon decisions of the early councils of the church. These organizational decisions were made for the well-being of the church. The church of Rome, however, emphasized that the primacy of the bishop of Rome was not based primarily only upon conciliar decisions. Rather, according to Western theologians, it was based primarily upon a particular view of the apostle Peter and his successors.[28]The bishop of Rome was seen as the successor of Peter to whom Christ had given a particular leadership role among the Twelve Apostles.[29]

The two points of view were not mutually exclusive. Not all Easterners would necessarily deny that Peter had a role of leadership among the apostles. Indeed, some would claim that every bishop expressed a leadership role like Peter in his regional church. However, the Easterners staunchly held that the pope of Rome could not exercise authority beyond his own patriarchate. While a primacy of honor was generally accorded to the pope of Rome, the Easterners rejected Rome's claims to jurisdiction over the entire episcopacy of the whole church. The East tended to emphasize the authority of every bishop within his diocese. Likewise, the value of church councils, bringing together bishops of a region, continued to be seen as a means of affirming unity and of addressing difficulties facing the church. The reunion council of 879 in Constantinople also affirmed this principle. "Here again, the differing approaches of East and West were not mutually exclusive. Despite recurrent tensions relating to church order, the churches remained in communion for centuries save when dogmatic issues were at stake. But neither were these approaches neatly complementary. Issues relating to church order, above all to papal primacy, would in time prove church dividing."[30]

The differing theological understandings of the authority of the bishop of Rome in the West and East were undoubtedly compounded by political developments, especially in Western Europe. In the wake of the Germanic invasions and the growth of feudalism in the early Middle Ages, the Church in Western Europe developed a highly centralized structure. This feudal pyramid placed the pope at the top. All other Western archbishops and bishops were placed in subservient positions to him.

This model of church governance was compounded by political alliances between the papacy and the Franks in the late eighth and early ninth centuries. By the time of Pope Gregory VII (ca. 1021–85), the papacy was seeking to rid itself from political domination and other abuses that had developed during the feudal period. As part of the reforms, the papacy strongly emphasized its independence in relationship to secular rulers in Western Europe. The claims of the papacy came to be expressed with greater strength and emotion, but with little appreciation for the perspectives of the East.

This provides the background for the famous exchange of excommunications in 1054. In that year, Pope Leo IX sent three legates to Constantinople. The leader of the delegation was Cardinal Humbert, the bishop of Silva Candida. It appears that the primary mission of the delegation was to discuss growing tensions between Rome and Constantinople over theology and liturgical practices. Political issues related to the Norman control of parts of Italy may have also had a role to play. In Norman Italy, Eastern Christians were being forced to follow Western liturgical practices. And, in Constantinople, perhaps as a form of retaliation, Patriarch Michael insisted that Western churches follow the Byzantine liturgical practices. The type of bread being used in the Eucharist was among the major points of dispute. The East was using leavened bread. The West was using unleavened bread. Upholding a strong view of the authority of Rome and its practices, the legates appeared to be in no mood to discuss the issues. And Patriarch Michael seems to have had little regard for the legates. As a result, Cardinal Humbert arrogantly placed a letter of excommunication on the altar of St. Sophia's cathedral on July 16, 1054. The letter of excommunication was directed against Patriarch Michael and his immediate associates. It contained numerous accusations. Some dealt with liturgical matters. Others dealt with more serious theological or doctrinal issues. Among these was the Western affirmation that the East was using the creed without the *filioque*. The document also stated that Michael did not deserve his patriarchal status. After their dramatic gesture at St. Sophia's, the legates immediately left the city.

Patriarch Michael and his synod responded with moderation. They believed that the letter of excommunication did not come from the pope himself, but was composed by Humbert in his name. Perhaps the Byzantines also knew that Pope Leo had died in April of the same year, thus negating the mission of Humbert. In light of these facts, Patriarch Michael and the Synod excommunicated the author of the Western excommunication and those associated with it. There was no reference to the pope or to the Western church in general. Clearly, despite the intrigues of Cardinal Humbert, neither Rome nor Constantinople acted to declare a schism, although tensions were surely running high. After 1054, however, "friendly relations between east and west continued. The two parts of Christendom were not yet conscious of a great gulf of separation between them, and men on both sides still hoped that the misunderstandings could be cleared up without too much difficulty. The dispute remained something of which ordinary Christians in east and west were largely unaware. It was the Crusades which made the schism definitive: they introduced a new spirit of hatred and bitterness, and they brought the whole issue down to the popular level."[31]

The relationship between the church of Rome and the churches of Constantinople, Alexandria, Antioch, and Jerusalem was seriously strained during the period of the crusades and especially in the wake of the infamous Fourth Crusade. Western Crusaders sacked the great city of Constantinople, long the rival to the Venetians, in the year 1204. Western politicians and clergy dominated the life of the city until 1261. During this time, many of the religious treasures of Constantinople were transported to Venice. In many eastern cities, including Constantinople, the invaders installed Western bishops who professed loyalty to the pope. This process had begun in Jerusalem in 1099 and in Antioch in 1100. The installation of Western bishops who were loyal to Rome and to political powers in Western Europe became a tragic and visible expression of schism in Constantinople, Antioch, Jerusalem, and other cities. Clergy and the faithful in these cities did not easily accept bishops imposed upon them. The great centers of Eastern Christianity were not restored to Eastern bishops until after 1268. Even after that time, however, the church of Rome supported rival patriarchs who claimed the titles of Constantinople, Antioch, and Jerusalem. This was a clear sign that the papacy and its political supporters had little regard for the legitimacy of the ancient patriarchal churches of the East.[32]

The tragic sack of Constantinople by the crusaders, and the related disputes between them and the local population did much to stir up mistrust, animosity, and hatred. Up until this time, chiefly theologians and clergy had expressed mutual suspicion of theological perspectives. In the wake of the crusades, however, hostility between Easterners and Westerners was expressed with vengeance in many places. "After 1204 the sense of mutual interiority—of common participation in the mystery of the Church—which had persisted even after the schism of 1054 gives way to a sense of mutual exteriority. The Orthodox Church and Catholic Church are on their way to becoming mutually exclusive, each viewing itself as somehow 'outside' the one Church confessed in the Creed." Despite this, efforts at reconciliation continued.[33]

From the thirteenth century through the fifteenth century, there were numerous attempts on both sides to address the theological and ecclesiological differences. However, the attempts to resolve them were frequently stymied by a lack of historical perspective, cultural prejudices, and political intrigues. This was also a time when the Western church and the papacy in particular were being shaken by internal divisions and disputes. Moreover, during the period of estrangement, the more fundamental theological differences between Rome and Constantinople were compounded by others related to the sacraments, clerical marriages, and liturgical customs.

Major attempts to address differences and to restore full communion took place at councils in the city of Lyons in 1274 and the city of Florence in 1434. At the latter gathering, the Easterners were much better represented and key issues were discussed. However, in light of the political threat to the greatly weakened Byzantine Empire, the Easterners were at a disadvantage. Strongly reflective of medieval Roman Catholic theology, the decisions of these councils were never fully received and were eventually repudiated by the Orthodox. At the heart of their repudiation was the Orthodox rejection of the claim of absolute authority of the pope over and above all other bishops. This was consistently rejected. The Orthodox never recognized papal claims of universal jurisdiction and refused to submit to papal authority. As John Meyendorff says: "The Crusades did much to antagonize the two culturally distinct civilizations of the East and of the West. And when the Papacy, shaken by the Great Western Schism, and Byzantium, threatened by the Turks, finally agreed to hold a union council at Florence, it was too late to create the atmosphere of mutual respect and trust which alone would have permitted authentic theological dialogue."[34]

Less than 20 years after the Council of Florence, the City of Constantinople fell to the Ottoman Turks in 1453, thus ending the Roman-Byzantine Empire. The political assistance from the Christian West, for which the Byzantines had hoped, never arrived. While Orthodox Christians managed to maintain their church in the new political system, it was not without serious restrictions. Under the leadership of the Patriarch of Constantinople, the Christians in the Ottoman Empire were grouped into a separate *milet*, which gradually greatly restricted their freedoms. Within the church, there was also a gradual loss of educational and theological centers as well as the loss of a spirit of mission. Survival became the chief concern. Among the Orthodox of the time, only the Church of Russia, granted autonomous status in the year 1448, remained free from Ottoman political control. The Council of Florence was formally rejected in Constantinople in 1484. At the same time, it was decreed that individual Western Christians (Latins) would be anointed upon entry into one of the other Eastern patriarchates.[35] This was a visible expression of disunity between Rome and the Orthodox.

Within 50 years after the Fall of Constantinople, the Western Church was divided by the Protestant Reformation, which began in 1517. Undoubtedly, the theological debates of the Reformation and the Catholic response only helped to solidify the schism between the Roman Catholic Church and the Orthodox Church. The Reformation raised new theological questions that required a response from the Roman Catholic Church. While not directly involved in the Reformation debates, the Orthodox found themselves affected by the theological currents and by the growing divisions in Western Christianity.[36]

The Orthodox who lived in territories close to Catholic or Protestant countries eventually became the victims of various forms of proselytism. As time went on, many Protestants sought to spread their doctrines among the Orthodox of Eastern Europe. Likewise, many Roman Catholics sought to counter the spread of Protestantism by engaging in missionary work among Orthodox and by allying with some Orthodox. Within Roman Catholicism, "a new spirit of soteriological and ecclesiological exclusivism dominated thinking and only deepened the division."[37]

With political support from Poland, some Orthodox Christians living in the region of the Ukraine entered into communion with Rome with a council of bishops held in the city of Brest in 1595.[38] Both clergy and laity were permitted to maintain many of their Eastern liturgical customs and much of their administrative organization. However, they professed ultimate loyalty to the pope of Rome and, in principle, Rome's view of the papacy. These churches came to be known as "Greek Catholic" or "Uniate."[39] These unions would be eventually repeated in other parts of Eastern Europe and the Middle East in subsequent centuries under Roman Catholic influence.[40] Most Orthodox came to view these unions as tragic attempts to impose papal authority over a weakened Orthodox Church.[41]

By the year 1729, Rome formally forbid *communio in sacris* with the Orthodox, viewing them as schismatic.[42] Feeling threatened both by Roman Catholic missionaries and under Ottoman political influence, the patriarchate of Constantinople in 1755 responded and advocated the rebaptism of Roman Catholics who entered the Orthodox Church.[43] While this unprecedented recommendation did not reflect all of Orthodoxy and was overturned in 1888, the proposal indicated that the estrangement was profound and that the division had indeed become formalized.[44]

In the nineteenth century, Rome made some formal overtures to the Orthodox. The proposals, however, always called the Orthodox to return to the true faith and accept the ultimate authority of the pope. This mentality was expressed in an encyclical from Pope Pius IX in 1848 and Pope Leo XIII in 1894. The Orthodox repudiated these overtures and the papal claims implicit in them. For their part, the Orthodox called the Roman Catholic Church to renounce its innovations and return to the faith expressed by the Ecumenical Councils. When the Roman Catholic Church at the First Vatican Council in 1870 defined that the pope is infallible in matters of faith and morals when speaking formally, the gulf between Catholicism and Orthodoxy grew even wider.

As will be seen in subsequent chapters, the Orthodox Church and the Roman Catholic Church entered a new phase of relations during the 1960s.[45] Building upon informal contacts developed especially in the 1950s, the Roman Catholic Church and the Orthodox Church slowly began a process of renewed contact and theological dialogue. After more that five centuries, formal theological dialogues were established between Roman Catholics and Orthodox. The first began in the United States in 1965. A global theological dialogue was established in 1979.[46]

THE PROTESTANT REFORMATION

The Protestant Reformation is the term given to the broad movement for reform and renewal in Western Christianity in Western Europe beginning in the early sixteenth century. By the end of the sixteenth century, Western Europe was formally divided among those regional churches and countries that remained faithful to the Roman Catholic Church and those churches and countries that had adopted forms of Protestantism. From the beginning, there was a wide diversity in Protestant teachings preventing many of the Protestant churches from agreeing with themselves over significant matters.[47] The Protestant Reformation must be viewed within the wider context of religious and political developments of the fifteenth and sixteenth centuries especially. The many factors including the Renaissance leading to the division in Western Christianity during the sixteenth century were complex and interrelated.[48]

MARTIN LUTHER AND THE LUTHERAN TRADITION

The Reformation began in Germany on October 31, 1517 when Martin Luther (1483–1546), a Roman Catholic priest, monk of the Augustinian Order, and university professor at Wittenberg, posted Ninety-five Theses inviting debate over the legitimacy of the sale of indulgences.[49] The Roman Catholic Church taught that an indulgence was a pardon for a period of time one had to spend in Purgatory as a result of sin. Luther had encountered the teaching of the Dominican monk Johann Tetzel who was selling these indulgences in the region of Saxony.[50] The theses reflected Luther's growing concern over perspectives and practices in the Roman Catholic Church. Printed copies of his theses were soon circulated. From Luther's viewpoint, the Church appeared to place emphasis upon ones religious activities, or works, without appropriate regard for the primacy of faith in God's gift of salvation in Jesus Christ. Both from his study of Scripture and his own spiritual struggle, Luther was convinced that the essence of the Christian Gospel was that believers are justified by faith alone. One could not achieve salvation through good works. The debate over indulgences eventually had become a debate over the papacy and authority in the church.[51]

Luther declared that the teachings and practices of the church could not be contrary to Scripture. While not claiming to establish a new church, Luther called for radical reforms in the Roman Catholic Church. At the heart of Luther's teachings were three principles: *sola fide, sola gratia,* and *sola scriptura.* In opposition to appeals to tradition, Luther emphasized the primacy of Scripture. Against the emphasis upon religious activities, Luther emphasized the primacy of God's grace and faith in God's gift of salvation. In one degree or another, these three principles became central to the entire Reformation. They were a direct challenge to the authority of the Pope.

With the Papal Bull, *Exsurge Domine,* of June 15, 1520, Rome declared that 41 of Luther's theses were heretical and ordered his writings burned. With the sense of alienation growing, Luther responded by publicly burning the Papal Bull. He was formally excommunicated in 1521. In April of the same year at the Diet at Worms, Luther stood before Holy Roman Emperor Charles V and the German princes. He refused to recant his teachings unless proven wrong by the Scriptures or by reason. Frederick III, the elector of Saxony, and some other German princes supported Luther. This support came from mixed motives. About this time, Luther translated the New Testament into German. He also began to author many hymns that became part of worship services that eventually replaced Latin with German.[52]

A close collaborator of Luther and a New Testament professor at Wittenberg, Philip Melanchthon (1497–1560) eventually was asked to draft a common confession of faith that could serve as a document of reconciliation. Melanchton put together a series of affirmations that he believed could be received both by followers of Luther and by other Catholics. The resulting document, the *Augsburg Confession,* was presented to the emperor on June 25, 1530.[53] While some hoped that the text could prevent further divisions, religious and political factors precluded this.[54]

The *Augsburg Confession* of 1530 became a major statement of faith for those who accepted Luther's teachings. Roman Catholics viewed it as an attack upon traditional teachings and the authority of Rome. A number of German princes and cities' representatives signed the Augsburg Confession presented at the Diet of Augsburg. This marked a formal break with the Roman Catholic Church by many regional state churches of Germany. As a consequence, a civil war erupted in 1546. After years of conflict, the Peace of Augsburg in 1555 affirmed that each prince would determine the religious affiliation, either Roman Catholic or Evangelical (Lutheran), of the territory he ruled. By the middle of the sixteenth century, the state churches of Denmark, Sweden, Norway, and Finland also adopted the Lutheran tradition and broke with Roman Catholicism.[55]

THE REFORMED TRADITION: ULRICH ZWINGLI AND JOHN CALVIN

The Reformation in Switzerland began in the canton of Zurich under the leadership of the Ulrich Zwingli (1484–1531), a Roman Catholic priest ordained in 1506. An admirer of Erasmus, Zwingli was initially influenced by his concern for reform and interest in the biblical languages. Disturbed by abuses at the famous pilgrimage shrine at Einsiedeln, Zwingli's concern for church reform was strengthened. Like Luther, the development of his positions and his separation from the Roman Catholic Church were gradual. As a priest in the historic cathedral church in Zurich, he began to advocate for changes in church practices and teachings with the support of local politicians.[56] Early in 1519, Zwingli began a series of sermons on the New Testament that supported his positions. He held that church teachings and practices must be explicitly expressed in the Scriptures. He challenged the belief in purgatory, the invocation of saints, monasticism, and clerical celibacy. By the year 1524, Zwingli championed the abolition of the ceremony of the mass and its replacement by a simple and symbolic rite resembling a meal, as well as the removal of pictures and relics from Zurich's churches.[57]

A meeting with Luther known as the Colloquy of Marburg in 1529 did not yield a common view of the Eucharist and demonstrated the gap in teachings growing among the reformers.[58] Zwingli also found himself in debates with Anabaptists and sanctioned their persecution by the Zurich government. His influence initially spread to some other Swiss cantons. A convocation of clergy and laity in Berne accepted the "Theses of Berne," which had been sanctioned by Zwingli in 1528. The text was a defense of reformed thought based upon the supremacy of the Scriptures. A number of other Swiss cantons, however, refused to accept Zwingli's religious and political views. A war among the Swiss cantons erupted in the year 1531. During that war, Zwingli died in battle fighting as a solder. In the same year, the Second Peace of Kappel recognized the existence of Catholic and Protestant cantons and prohibited further spread of Protestant teachings in the Swiss Confederation.[59]

John Calvin (1509–64) was a French lawyer who traveled to Geneva in 1536, where the Reformation spirit had begun to take hold under the leadership of Guillaume Farel (1489–1565).[60] After much political and religious conflict, Geneva officially became Protestant in 1535.[61] Through his personal leadership and his writings, Calvin had a major influence upon the spirit of the Reformation that developed in a number of Swiss cantons within France, the Netherlands, and Scotland. His perspectives were central to the Puritans who left England and settled in New England in the seventeenth century.[62]

Based upon his interpretation of the Scriptures, Calvin drafted a new organization for the Geneva church in Ordinances of 1541. Together with

Farel, Calvin also imposed a strict moral code on the citizens of Geneva. Initially, Calvin's strict moral standards, based upon literal understanding of the Scriptures, were not well received. In early 1538, Calvin and the Protestant reformers were exiled from Geneva. Moving to Strasbourg, Calvin began writing commentaries on the Bible and finished his massive account of Protestant doctrine, known as *The Institutes of the Christian Church in 1536.*[63]

With new political leaders in Geneva, Calvin returned. Immediately, he set about turning Geneva into a theocracy based upon his interpretation of the Scriptures. Calvin introduced a number of reforms that imposed a strict and uncompromising moral code on the citizens of the city. Reflecting the perspectives of Zwingli, Calvin also greatly simplified Protestant worship and eliminated all liturgical practices that were not supported by Scripture. By the 1550s, Geneva was thoroughly Calvinist in thought and structure. Indeed, it became the most important Protestant center of Europe in the sixteenth century.[64]

At the heart of Calvin's teaching was the insistence on the primacy of the Scriptures, as he interpreted them. In principle, any teaching or practice not contained explicitly in the Scriptures was to be rejected. And a practice or teaching that was contained explicitly in the Scriptures was to be followed unwaveringly. Calvin took these principles to an extreme. He held that not only should all religious belief be founded on the literal reading of Scriptures but also that church organization, political organization, and society itself should be founded on the literal reading of Scripture. Of course, Scripture always needed interpretation. Calvin provided that interpretation, thereby establishing a new form of tradition for those who followed his teachings.[65]

Among the most distinctive theological positions that Calvin took was his affirmation of a doctrine of predestination. He believed that salvation was in no way the result of a choice by the human person. Rather, it was predetermined by God from the beginning of time. This meant that some were chosen and elected for salvation by God. Others were damned regardless of their faith, good intentions, or their good behavior. Although the elect obviously were expected to avoid sin, not all good people were among the elect. A strict moral life, while not determining salvation, could be seen as a sign of salvation.[66]

The reform views of Zwingli and Calvin were not confined to the Swiss Confederation. The reformed perspectives were firmly established in the Church of Scotland under the leadership of John Knox (ca. 1513–72).[67] In addition, French Calvinists, known as Huguenots, began to organize congregations by the mid-sixteenth century. Compounded by political conflicts between France and Spain as well as internal wars, the Huguenots were often subject to bitter persecution from the French government. Finally, the Edict of Nantes in 1598 affirmed religious toleration. This significant edict, however, was revoked in 1685, which led to the exile of many Huguenots to England, Holland, and America.[68]

THE REFORMATION IN ENGLAND

The Reformation in England developed in a manner that was distinct from Protestantism in the rest of Western Europe. It was centered initially upon King Henry VIII (1491–1547) who is remembered for his excesses. With the beginning of the Lutheran Reformation, Henry VIII became a staunch opponent of its teachings. Because of this, Pope Leo X honored him in 1521 with the title of Defender of the Faith. However, the rise of protest against the authority of Rome in church matters soon combined with Henry's desire to have a male heir to his throne. Thus, the Reformation in the Church of England occurred initially as a direct result of Henry's desire to divorce his first wife, Catherine of Aragon. The pope refused Henry's request in 1534, probably under the influence of Catherine's nephew who was Emperor Charles V.

Thomas Cromwell, the king's chief minister, masterminded the formal break of Henry and the Church of England from the Roman Catholic Church. In the spirit of the Reformation, Cromwell proposed that Henry break with Rome and declare himself as head of the Church in England. Henry agreed to the plan. Under the direction of Cromwell, Parliament passed the Act in Restraint of Appeals (to Rome in 1533). This was followed by the Act of Supremacy (1534), which affirmed the king's authority over the Church of England. By this time, Henry had been excommunicated by Rome. Among those who opposed Henry's actions were Sir Thomas Moore and the Archbishop of Canterbury, Sir John Fisher. They refused to break with Rome and were eventually tried for treason and beheaded in 1535. As the leader of clergy who followed Henry, Thomas Cranmer, the new Archbishop of Canterbury, formally annulled Henry's marriage to Catherine and permitted the king to marry Anne Boleyn.[69]

Henry appears to have little desire in altering the traditional faith and practice of the Church of England apart from securing its independence from the control of the pope. However, England could not easily avoid the impact of the Reformation once Henry had challenged the authority of Rome in the Church of England. Thomas Cromwell and Archbishop Thomas Cranmer soon authorized an official translation of the Bible into English. Concerned with developing worship services in English and with other liturgical reforms, Archbishop Thomas Cranmer was also largely responsible for the composition of the *Book of Common Prayer*, adopted under Henry's successor, Edward VI. Cranmer and others in the Church of England sought to find a middle way between Roman Catholics and the English Puritans, Calvinist sympathizers who felt that the reform in England had not gone far enough. For example, the Church of England continued to maintain a number of church practices, such as the threefold order of ministry, which was not accepted by the Puritans.[70]

Subsequent changes in heads of state led to deepened divisions between members of the Church of England (Anglicans), Roman Catholics, and Puritans. The religious settlement of 1559, under Elizabeth I, led to renewed persecution and guaranteed that both England and the Church of England would be free from any connection with Roman Catholicism. In seventeenth-century England, the Puritans achieved political influence under Oliver Cromwell, who had King Charles I beheaded and ruthlessly persecuted Roman Catholics.[71]

THE ANABAPTIST TRADITION

From the sixteenth century, not all those with Protestant sympathies could easily be accommodated within those churches that had adopted the Lutheran, Reformed, or Anglican perspectives. A number of Protestants felt that the reforms of Luther, Zwingli, and Calvin did not go far enough. Emphasizing a very literal approach to Scriptures, they wanted a more thorough reform of liturgical practices than those advocated by either Luther or Zwingli and their followers. For the most part, these radical reformers rejected the practice of infant baptism, maintained by most Protestants, in favor of adult baptism of persons who personally confessed the Christian faith. The various groups that rejected infant baptism came to be known generally as Anabaptists. Throughout the sixteenth and seventeenth centuries, this movement consisted of a wide variety of separatist groups. Luther, Zwingli, and Calvin vigorously opposed the Anabaptists. The sharp opposition of the Anabaptists to Lutheranism and Calvinism led to their persecution by a number of local governments. This also led the Anabaptists to a firm rejection of the accommodation between church and state that most Protestants and Roman Catholics accepted.[72]

Among the early spokesmen for the Anabaptist cause was the German Thomas Munzer (1490–1525). A former Roman Catholic priest, Munzer adopted the Protestant cause in 1520, claiming that he had a direct inspiration from the Holy Spirit. Following a disagreement with Luther, he traveled throughout Germany opposing both Catholicism and Luther's teachings. He took a leading role in the Peasants' War of 1524–26, which was suppressed by the Lutherans. After the defeat at the battle of Frankenhaausen in 1525, Munzer was captured and executed. His teachings led to the short-lived establishment in Munster in 1533 of an Anabaptists theocracy in which property was held communally. Lutherans too harshly suppressed this. By the middle of the sixteenth century, numerous Anabaptist congregations could be found throughout Germany, the Swiss Confederation, Moravia, and Holland. Among the more numerous groups were the Hutterites, Swiss Brethren, and the Mennonites.[73]

THE ROMAN CATHOLIC REFORMATION

The formal response of the Roman Catholic Church to the issues raised by Protestants is known as the Catholic Reformation or the Counter Reformation. Important efforts at renewal, reform, and response to the Protestant theologies began in earnest during the reign of Pope Paul III (1534–49). At the center of Paul's program was the intention to assert papal responsibility throughout the church. Recognizing the need for internal reform and to respond to issues raised by Protestants, Paul III decided to convene a council of bishops. While the council was delayed by 10 years due to internal resistance, Paul III sought to attack abuses in the church undeterred by powerful bishops and politicians.[74] The council finally opened in the northern Italian city of Trent in 1545. Bringing together Catholic bishops from throughout Europe, it met irregularly until they completed their work in 1563. Together with the bishops, the council also permitted some Protestant representatives to present their position, especially in the early sessions. Some Roman Catholics had hoped that the council would help to reconcile the principal Protestant churches. However, as the council progressed, the participants viewed it primarily as the opportunity to oppose Protestant perspectives.[75]

The Council of Trent's most important decrees dealt with those theological issues raised by the Protestants. The council affirmed the importance of Scripture and tradition as sources of faith as well as the sole right of the Church to interpret the scriptural texts. The council also affirmed the necessary relationship between faith and good works. The teaching of the seven sacraments was also reaffirmed together with the affirmation of the real presence of Christ in the Eucharistic bread and wine. Belief in purgatory, the invocation of the saints, the veneration of relics, and the practice of indulgences were also affirmed. Also of importance were the decisions of the council establishing seminaries and the procedures for the appointment of bishops.[76] The doctrinal statements and disciplinary practices of the Council of Trent greatly shaped Roman Catholicism until the First Vatican Council (1869–70) and the Second Vatican Council (1962–65).

Together with a revitalized papacy, the reforms and renewal dictated by the Council of Trent were carried out at the local level with the support of the Society of Jesus. Founded by Ignatius Loyola (1491–1556), the society, better known as the Jesuits, was a semimonastic order of clergy developed especially to the tasks of preaching, teaching, reconciling penitents through the sacrament of confession, and establishing missions. The activities of the Jesuits did much to prevent further gains in Western Europe by Protestants.[77]

By the middle of the sixteenth century, Western Europe was firmly divided between those states that had accepted Protestant teachings and those who had remained faithful to the Roman Catholic Church. Within some of these states, such as England, France, Spain, Scotland, and Germany, the religious minorities were often the victims of oppression. Indeed, the Protestant Reformation and the Catholic response set the stage for a bitter century of bloody wars that had religious differences at their center. As one popular study says: "But it was not enough for either side to remedy religious deficiencies and abuses. Each had to launch a fanatical and unrelenting attack on the enemy religion. In this atmosphere of hatred and violence, voices of moderation such as Erasmus' were ignored, and pleas for toleration went unheard, for there was a rare ferocity to the conflicts that now racked European civilization."[78] In the wake of the bitter war of religion, the differences between Protestants and Protestants as well as between Protestants and Roman Catholics were eventually transferred to America in the seventeenth and eighteenth centuries. The American colonies provided new territory where the religious differences found room both for protection and for further expansion throughout the seventeenth century.[79] As we shall see, additional divisions afflicted Protestantism in the post-Enlightenment period of the late eighteenth and early nineteenth centuries. In addition to this, slavery and the movement to abolish it in the United States led to new divisions within the churches.

CONCLUSIONS: SOME COMMON FEATURES OF THE PAST DIVISIONS

There are a significant number of common features in the four divisions examined in this chapter. These features remind us that the fundamental doctrinal or theological issues, which were highlighted at the time of division, were part of a wider context. None of the theological issues of divisions can be seen apart from their broader historical context.

First, the divisions took place over the course of time. For convenience sake, we sometimes use the dates 431, 451, 1054, and 1517 when we discuss church divisions. Often, some important historical events can be associated with these dates. However, on closer examination, we see that each of the historic divisions of the churches was part of a gradual process of estrangement. The particular historical event, which we often use to date a particular church division, is, in fact, one among many events that contributed to the division. In the study of church divisions, the identification of the convenient date of a schism should not obscure the reality of the actual historical development of gradual division among churches.

The divisions reflect serious disagreement in Christian teaching and theology. The great historic divisions of the churches have occurred because agreement or consensus could not be reached on major theological or doctrinal issues related to the Christian faith. In the case of each division, there was a crisis over the interpretation of Christian Scripture and tradition. At the same time, the breakdown in dialogue frequently led to an imbalance in theological perspective. Whether the issue was Christology or ecclesiology or the relationship between faith and works, the divisions frequently produced a lack of a holistic theological perspective and a lack of balance on both sides of the divide. This was reflected in a polemical theology of point and counterpoint, of action and reaction.

These historic divisions did not take place in a social and political vacuum. The theological issues were serious ones. Yet, within the historical context, the theological issues were compounded by the nationalistic, political, and cultural issues of the day. Often theological positions were taken to express these political or cultural differences. In addition to this, theological differences were often solidified by persecution and wars. This harsh reality is often overlooked in the more idealized story of divisions.

Perhaps the fundamental theological issues raised at each point of division could have been resolved if the atmosphere had not been contaminated, not only by polemics but also by politics, and polluted by the lack of mutual respect and good will. While not denying the importance of the theological issues raised in each division, there is a sense that the historical context was not conducive to genuine dialogue. Yes, in each of the historical periods there were attempts by many goodwilled people at dialogue for the sake of reconciliation and unity. However, the good intentions were frequently overshadowed by hostility, fear, and the political agendas of others.

The divisions between churches and traditions were expressed in a very visible manner through worship. As a consequence of divisions, the patterns of worship and liturgical life came to embody and express the separateness and even the distinctiveness of the divided churches. From the earliest days of Christianity, there were common liturgical practices such as the rites of baptism and the Eucharist, found throughout the church in all places. At the same time, there was a diversity of liturgical customs that reflected different cultures and histories. In the wake of major divisions, however, differences in worship were highlighted as expressions of the divided churches. For example, at one time, some asked whether the Eucharistic bread be leavened or unleavened. At other times, some asked whether infants should be baptized or not. For those unschooled in the subtleties of theological or doctrinal differences, the worship and worship space came to embody the distinctive character of a particular church or tradition. The divisions were expressed in the patterns and style of worship.

The divisions frequently led to subsequent divisions. The unresolved theological differences from earlier times frequently appeared in subsequent schisms. Indeed, the major church divisions of Europe and the Middle East were exported to North America, as well as to Africa, the Far East and South America from the sixteenth century.

In addition to this, a number of new Protestant traditions emerged from the seventeenth through the nineteenth centuries especially within the United States. While they shared common roots in the Reformation, they also expressed their own particularities in teaching and worship. Often they began as reform or renewal movements. Among the more prominent and influential were the Baptists, the Methodists, and the Disciples of Christ (Christian Church). They would have a major impact upon the development of Christianity in America, and upon the subsequent Christian missionary movement, especially of the nineteenth century.

Finally, these great divisions in Christianity took on a more or less permanent character by the middle of the sixteenth century, and this mentality continued for at least 400 years. The great divisions among the churches were seen as normative and acceptable. Some would even claim that they were necessary for the defense of the Christian faith. Prior to the late 1500s, one could find important efforts among the divided churches to examine their differences and to seek reconciliation. For example, between Orthodox and Catholics, there were the Council of Lyons (1274) and the Council of Florence (1438). While these councils did not accomplish their purpose and were ultimately rejected by the Orthodox, the meetings were attempts at reconciliation. Likewise, the Roman Catholic Council of Trent (1545–63) began with the intention of healing the Roman Catholic-Protestant division. While the council did not heal the estrangement, it did reflect in its early stages a desire to examine issues of theological and doctrinal differences.

By the seventeenth century, there was very little formal effort among the divided churches to examine and heal their divisions. Indeed, a formal isolation among the divided churches developed. Within the Orthodox Church, the Roman Catholic Church, and most Reformation churches, divisions came to be accepted as normative. This in tern led to expressions of ecclesiastical exclusivism, polemical theology, missionary conflicts, and proselytism. The divided churches and their theological concerns tended to evolve in isolation, but not without mutual antagonism.

NOTES

1. St. Basil the Great, *Epistle 203,* cited in Jean Danielou, "The Fathers and Christian Unity," *Eastern Churches Quarterly* 16 (1964), p. 16.

2. John Meyendorff, *Christ in Eastern Christian Thought* (Washington: Corpus Publications, 1969), pp. 3–16.

3. R. V. Sellers, *The Council of Chalcedon: A Historical and Doctrinal Survey* (London: SPCK, 1953), pp. 3–5.

4. Timothy Ware, *The Orthodox Church* (New York: Penguin Books, revised edition, 1964), p. 32.

5. Seller, *The Council of Chalcedon,* pp. 17–21. See also Karekin Sarkesian, *The Council of Chalcedon and the Armenian Church* (London: SPCK, 1965), pp. 75–110.

6. Sellers, pp. 21–29.

7. Aziz S. Atiya, *History of Eastern Christianity* (Notre Dame: University of Notre Dame Press, 1968), pp. 237–57.

8. Ibid., pp. 30–49.

9. Today the Church of the East has a greatly diminished presence in areas of Iran, Iraq, India, Turkey, and Syria. In recent decades, dioceses and parishes have been organized in the United States and Western Europe as a result of immigration.

10. Sellers, p. 78.

11. Ware, p. 33.

12. Sellers, pp. 132–81; Sarkesian, pp. 174–95.

13. "Statement of the Council of Chalcedon," in *Decrees of the Ecumenical Councils*, vol. 1, ed. Norman P. Tanner, (New York: Sheed and Ward, 1990), pp. 86–87.

14. Meyendorff, p. 12.

15. Sellers, pp. 254–55.

16. Ibid., pp. 256–75; Sarkesian, pp. 196–213.

17. John Meyendorff, *Byzantine Theology* (New York: Fordham University Press, 1974), p. 33.

18. Sellers, 302–50.

19. Each of the churches, which did not accept formally the statement of Chalcedon, has their own particular historical background and distinctive liturgical traditions. Each is quite distinctive and each has had its own particular historical development in the centuries following Chalcedon. Today, there are six ancient churches that make up the family known as the Oriental Orthodox Churches. According to their more popular designations, these churches are the Coptic Orthodox Church of Egypt, the Armenian Apostolic Church, the Syrian Orthodox Church, the Ethiopian Orthodox Church, the Malankara (India) Orthodox Syrian Church, and the Eretrean Orthodox Church. In addition to their presence in their historic homeland, these churches have also established dioceses and parishes in the Middle East, the Americas, and Western Europe, chiefly as a result of immigration. It is estimated that there are over 23 million Oriental Orthodox worldwide.

20. While they are in communion with one another, each is fully independent and possesses many distinctive traditions. Because they formally rejected Chalcedon's statement of two natures in Christ, these churches have often erroneously been called Monophysites, from the Greek word meaning "one nature." This is a description that these churches reject, noting that they reject. They reject the classical Monophysite position of Eutyches, who held that Christ's humanity was absorbed into his single divine nature. They prefer the formula of St. Cyril of Alexandria, who spoke of "the one nature of the incarnate Word of God." In this sense they may be considered to be linguistic Monophysites but not doctrinal Monophysites. The family of churches has also been referred to as the Lesser Eastern Churches, the Ancient Oriental Churches, the Non-Chalcedonian Churches, or the Pre-Chalcedonian Churches. The Oriental Orthodox Churches are active in the ecumenical movement. Each is a member of the World Council of Churches (WCC). They normally participate in the WCC and other ecumenical councils in close association with the Orthodox Churches.

21. George Every, *Misunderstandings Between East and West* (Richmond: John Knox Press, 1966), pp. 9–25.

22. Aidan Nichols, *Rome and the Eastern Churches* (Collegeville: The Liturgical Press, 1992), pp. 111–20.

23. Earlier breaks in communion in the fifth, sixth, and ninth centuries had been resolved through dialogue.

24. A Roman Catholic perspective can be found in Nichols, pp. 188–229.

25. A major reevaluation of the period is found in Francis Dvornik, *The Photian Schism* (Cambridge: University Press, 1948); see also Richard Haugh, *Photios and the Carolingians: The Trinitarian Controversy* (Belmont: Nordland Publishing Company, 1975).

26. Haugh, pp. 123–30.

27. John Borelli and John H. Erickson, *The Quest for Unity* (Crestwood, N.Y.: St. Vladimir's Seminary Press, 1996), p. 10.

28. Nichols, pp. 152–80.

29. Borelli and Erickson, p. 10.

30. Ibid., p. 6.

31. Timothy Ware, *The Orthodox Church,* p. 67.

32. Every, p. 59.

33. Borelli and Erickson, p. 12.

34. Meyendorff, *Byzantine Theology,* p. 101.

35. Ware, *The Orthodox Church,* pp. 66–67.

36. Timothy Ware, *Eustratios Argenti: A Study of the Greek Church Under Turkish Rule* (Oxford: Clarendon Press, 1964), pp. 1–42.

37. Borelli and Erickson, p. 15.

38. Ronald Roberson, *The Eastern Christian Churches: A Brief Survey* (Rome: Orientalia Christiana, 1999), p. 165.

39. Nichols, pp. 282–304.

40. Ibid., pp. 139–88.

41. See K.T. Ware, "Orthodox and Catholics in the Seventeenth Century: Schism or Intercommunion," in *Schism, Heresy, and Religious Protest,* ed. Derick Baker (Cambridge: University Press, 1972), p. 259.

42. Borelli and Erickson, p. 15.

43. Ware, *Eustratios Argenti,* pp. 65–79; Borelli and Erickson, p. 15.

44. Ware, *Eustratios Argenti,* p. 106.

45. The Orthodox had been actively involved in ecumenical dialogues with many Protestant Churches from the late nineteenth century and early twentieth century. The Roman Catholic Church, however, had refused to become involved formally in these early ecumenical dialogues.

46. Today, the Orthodox Church is composed of 14 autocephalous and two autonomous churches that are united in the same faith. These are the Churches of Constantinople, Alexandria, Antioch, Jerusalem, Russia, Serbia, Romania, Bulgaria, Georgia, Cyprus, Greece, Poland, Albania, and the Czech Lands-Slovakia. The Autonomous Churches are Finland and Estonia. In North and South America, Western Europe, and Australia, missions and migration in the nineteenth and early twentieth centuries have led to the establishment of vital Orthodox jurisdictions. These areas are often referred to as the so-called Orthodox Diaspora. However, this phrase is increasingly viewed with disfavour. The patriarchate of Constantinople affirms special responsibility for these developing churches based upon historic precedents. Some of the jurisdictions in these places, however, still maintain connections with other Mother Churches. It is estimated that there are over 300 million Orthodox Christians worldwide.

47. I am indebted to many observations from Lewis W. Spitz, *The Protestant Reformation* (New York: Harper and Row, 1985).

48. Owen Chadwick, *The Reformation* (Middlesex: Penguin Books, revised edition, 1972), pp. 1–31.
49. Jaroslav Pelikan, *The Christian Tradition 4, Reformation of Church and Dogma (1300–1700)* (Chicago: University of Chicago Press, 1984), pp. 127–81.
50. Chadwick, pp. 40–43.
51. Chadwick, pp. 47–54.
52. Ibid., pp. 54–56.
53. Pelikan, pp. 333–34.
54. Ibid., p. 66.
55. Ibid., p. 75.
56. See Jean Rilliet, *Zwingli: Third Man of the Reformation* (Philadelphia: Westminster Press, 1964).
57. Chadwick, pp. 76–78.
58. Ibid., pp. 78–80.
59. Ibid., p. 80.
60. Ibid., pp. 81–82.
61. Chadwick, pp. 82–83.
62. See John T. McNeill, *The History and Character of Calvinism* (Oxford: Oxford University Press, 1954).
63. Pelikan, pp. 183–87.
64. Chadwick, pp. 84–90.
65. Ibid., pp. 91–93.
66. Ibid., pp. 93–96.
67. Ibid., pp. 171–73.
68. Ibid., pp. 153–70.
69. Ibid., pp. 97–104.
70. Ibid., pp. 114–17.
71. Ibid., pp. 123–36, 238–40.
72. Ibid., pp. 188–90.
73. Ibid., pp. 190–92.
74. Ibid., pp. 264–70.
75. Ibid., pp. 273–76.
76. Ibid., pp. 277–81.
77. Ibid., pp. 255–64.
78. Mortimer Chambers et al., *The Western Experience to 1715* (New York: McGraw-Hill, Inc., 1991), p. 567.
79. Many English Puritans settled in Massachusetts Bay. Many Dutch Reformed settlers established New Amsterdam. A number of Roman Catholic immigrants found a haven in Maryland. Quakers went to Pennsylvania. Not tolerated in Massachusetts, Baptists settled in Rhode Island. Many Scandinavian Lutherans settled in Delaware. While many Anglicans could be found in the northern colonies, they dominated in the southern colonies especially. In most of the colonies, both before and during the American Revolution, an established church was maintained and the degree of toleration of other religious groups varied from place to place. In the United States, state churches were eventually disestablished during the early nineteenth century.

CHAPTER 4

First Steps Toward New Relationships

> The Federation will...unite in spirit the students of the world...in doing this it will be achieving a yet more significant result—the hastening of the answer to our Lord's prayer "that they all may be one."
>
> —John R. Mott[1]

INTRODUCTION

Throughout the second half of the nineteenth century, there were numerous developments both within the divided churches and among Christian leaders through which a concern for reconciliation and unity were expressed. Historic divisions among the churches continued to be the norm. Indeed, in some places new divisions arose. Yet, side by side with these divisions and their attendant misunderstandings, there were signs of dialogue, expressions of common witness in the society, calls for prayers for unity, and, in some cases, profound expressions of the desire for the reconciliation of the churches. This provided an impetus and a foundation for the ecumenical ventures of the twentieth century.

THE NINETEENTH CENTURY: CONTEXT AND TRENDS

There were a number of characteristic features of the second half of the nineteenth century that contributed to a renewed interest in greater cooperation among Christians and even to interest in the unity of the churches. This was a period in which the political powers of Western Europe and the

United States were extending greater influence and, in many cases, becoming more politically involved in Asia and Africa. With this imperial expansion, there was also increased interest in the churches for missionary work in these parts of the world. Earlier missionaries not only had preached the Christian faith but also had exported Christian divisions from Western Europe, especially to the Americas and Asia. The latter part of the nineteenth century saw intensified missionary activity not only in Asia but also in Africa, Asia Minor, and the Middle East.[2] These were encouraged by the various Protestant revivalist movements in the United States. In some cases, missionaries even engaged missionary activities among fellow Christians of other churches. Yet the challenge of the missions also began to raise some questions regarding both the practical and the theological significance of these competing missions.

The American Civil War and the issue of slavery dramatically affected all the churches in the United States and especially most Protestant churches. The slavery issue and questions of the rights of black citizens led to different interpretations of Scriptures. Some Christians and their churches helped to justify slavery through references to the bible. Also claiming biblical support, the Abolitionists strongly opposed the practice and gained the support of many northern church families.[3] These differences led to a number of divisions within Protestant churches in the United States. Baptists, Presbyterians, and Methodists experienced divisions. "The church," says Edwin Scott Gaustad, "could be a station in the underground railroad, helping to spirit the run away slave to freedom. Or the church could be the gathering place from which to send out patrols to recapture slaves or to break up their religious gatherings."[4]

The nineteenth century was also a time of significant developments in travel and communications. The steamship, the telegraph, and the railway dramatically altered life, especially in Western Europe and North America. These factors greatly aided the establishment of new national and international societies and organizations, many of which were devoted to religious and philanthropic causes. In a certain sense, the world was becoming smaller, and distant concerns were taking on new significance for Americans and Europeans.

In addition to this, major political changes and industrial developments marked the nineteenth century. The century began not long after the French Revolution and it concluded on the eve of the Balkan Wars. Dramatic political changes occurred through most of Western Europe at the same time that the old Ottoman Empire was undergoing a slow demise, dramatically affecting all the Balkans. At the same time, the fruits of industrialization led to increasing dissatisfaction among workers in America and Western Europe. These tensions often provided a basis for political changes as well as new social policy. Gradually, many of the Christian organizations and churches in Western Europe and America responded to the plight of the workers and the urban poor. Among the more significant responses were the Encyclicals from Pope Leo XIII, issued in 1888 and 1891, and the Social Gospel movement, originating in the 1870s, which found expression in many American Protestant churches.

Finally, the nineteenth century was a period of massive immigration from Europe to the United States. Waves of immigrants from Ireland arrived prior to the Civil War. Their presence often led to an increase of anti-Catholicism and nativism among some Protestants.[5] Following the Civil War, there was a massive immigration to the United States from southern Europe, the Balkans, the old Austro-Hungarian Empire, and Asia Minor. Most of these immigrants came as members of either the Roman Catholic Church or the Orthodox Church. Their coming to America frequently introduced new tensions between the various divided churches as a result of different beliefs and practices. For many Protestants in America, the growing presence of Roman Catholics and Orthodox Christians was not always welcome.[6] Eventually, however, their presence dramatically altered the religious landscape of the United States and contributed to new relationships between the churches.

COOPERATIVE SOCIETIES

During the early 1800s, a number of associations developed, especially in the United States and in Britain, that brought together persons from a number of Protestant churches for specific tasks. These organizations were interdenominational in terms of their composition. Many were concerned with missionary and evangelistic challenges. Among the more prominent organizations in the United States were the American Board of Commissioners for Foreign Missions (1810), the American Home Missionary Society (1826), and the American Bible Society (1816).[7]

While having strong religious motivations, other organizations were concerned more directly with reforms in American and British society. In the United States, there were, for example, the American Society for the Promotion of Temperance (1826), the American Peace Society (1828), and the American Antislavery Society (1833). Although they often reflected the Protestant revivalist theology of the early nineteenth century, none of these organizations was directly linked to particular Protestant churches. They did, however, provide opportunities for a measure of Christian cooperation that cut across the traditional church boundaries.

Of particular interest are the Bible societies. The Bible Society movement began in 1804 with the establishment of the British and Foreign Bible Society. Its principal purpose was to distribute Bibles without any theological commentary. Because of this approach, Bible societies soon were founded in over 14 countries. The societies were not considered to be related to any particular church tradition. One could find Anglicans, Protestants, Roman

Catholics, and Orthodox involved in particular societies in various places. Again, this was an important and tentative sign of cooperation.

By the year 1826, however, the new ecumenical thrust of the societies was greatly diminished. Under pressure from Protestants, especially in Scotland, the British Bible Society abandoned the publication of the Bible that contained the deuterocanonical books. Roman Catholics and Orthodox accepted certain deuterocanonical books as part of the Old Testament tradition. From the time of the Reformation, most Protestant churches, however, rejected these deuterocanonical books. Not all the local Bible societies accepted the decision of the British Bible Society. However, the controversy in England became more widely known in time and tended to alienate both those Roman Catholics and Orthodox who had been involved in the Bible Society activities. The controversy demonstrated that even the publication and distributions of Bibles could reflect serious unresolved, historical differences among the churches.[8]

THE EVANGELICAL ALLIANCE

As a result of numerous regional initiatives, the Evangelical Alliance was formally established in 1846 at a conference in London. The gathering brought together about 500 persons from Europe and the United States. The participants came from 52 different Protestant churches. The participants declared that they were "deeply convinced of the desirableness of forming a Confederation on the basis of great evangelical principles held in common by them which may afford opportunity to members of the Church of Christ of cultivating brotherly love, enjoying Christian intercourse, and promoting such other objects as they may hereafter agree to prosecute together."[9]

From the start, the Alliance was not meant to be composed of official representatives of churches but of individual Protestant Christians who could accept the basis of the association. While not considered to be a creed or a confession of faith, the basis identified nine affirmations that reflected general Protestant teachings.[10]

The Alliance initially produced some significant results for its day. A number of international conferences were subsequently held in London in 1851, in New York in 1873, and in London in 1896. These gatherings bore witness to a certain degree of unity among the Protestant participants that transcended their church affiliations. These conferences also gave a powerful impetus to the establishment of chapters of the Alliance in various countries. One in the United States was established in 1867. At both the global and national levels, the Alliance encouraged the establishment of a special week of prayer beginning on the first Sunday of the year. This practice also had the practical consequence of highlighting the unity among Christians in spite of their church divisions. Finally, the Alliance became a powerful advocate of Protestant missionary activity. Many of the participants in the Alliance also were active in various missionary boards of particular Protestant churches.[11]

There were some severe internal limitations to the Alliance that prevented its growth and adaptation. While the Alliance generally lacked leadership, coordinated organization, and a clear mission throughout much of its life, there were two fundamental factors that stymied its growth past the late nineteenth century. First, as we have said, the organization appealed to individual Christians. Even before its first conference in 1846, Alliance leaders decided in 1845 that it should not be a federation or a union of churches. The decision to leave membership open to individual Christians was most welcomed by those who were tired of the doctrinal disputes among the churches. At the same time, this meant that the Alliance never could really attend to the critical issues dividing even the Protestant churches of its day. While emphasizing the unity of the members of the invisible church, the Alliance simply could not address the need for the visible unity of the churches and the resolution of doctrinal differences. "It aimed," says Ruth Rouse, "at making the invisible church visible...but the truth that the invisible church is one lacks missionary power so long as the members of the invisible church remain in visibly separate and competing folds."[12]

The second major weakness of the Alliance was that it pursued objectives that were ultimately at odds with each other. From the beginning, the Alliance spoke of uniting Christians in the bonds of brotherly love. At the same time, however, it was a strong opponent of both the Anglo-Catholic movement within Anglicanism and Roman Catholicism, which, in those days, was referred to in a derogatory manner as popery or Romanism. In many places, such as the United States, the Alliance drew strength from the fact that it was viewed as a bastion of nativism and anti-Catholicism. While some farsighted participants in the work of the Alliance saw the need for reconciliation and unity of all the Christian churches, the Alliance had acquired a reputation that could not easily be disavowed.[13]

CHRISTIAN YOUTH MOVEMENTS

Two great Christian youth movements were founded in England in the mid-nineteenth century that would also contribute to the developing process of Christian reconciliation. The Young Men's Christian Association (YMCA) was founded in 1844 in London. Ten years later the Young Women's Christian Association (YWCA) was established. Neither of these organizations was explicitly concerned with the formal reconciliation and unity of the Christian churches, especially in the early years of their existence. Yet they became international Christian organizations bringing together young people from many different churches and countries. Like the Evangelical Alliance, both organizations reflected a Christian perspective that was both evangelistic and missionary in spirit. At the same time, neither organization was explicitly identified with a particular church. The Basis of the YMCA, adopted in 1855, declared that its purpose was "to unite young men who, regarding Jesus Christ as their God and Saviour, according to the Holy Scriptures, desire to be His disciples in their faith and in their life, and to associate their efforts for the extension of His Kingdom amongst young men."[14] Throughout the late nineteenth and early twentieth centuries, the YMCA and YWCA served as a valuable training ground for many young men and women who eventually became active in the early ecumenical movement of the 1920s and 1930s.

THE WORLD STUDENT CHRISTIAN FEDERATION

During the last quarter of the nineteenth century, loosely organized Christian student associations could be found in the United States and Western Europe. Out of these, students chiefly from the United States and Western Europe founded the World Student Christian Federation (WSCF) at Vadstena Castle, Sweden, in 1895.[15] While there was a close association in its early years with the YMCA and YWCA, the federation sought to be more inclusive and brought together representatives from various Christian youth movements.[16] Among its founders were John Mott (1865–1955) from the United States and Karl Fries from Sweden. Mott had been one of the principal organizers of the YMCA in the United States.

Through the early part of the twentieth century, Mott was actively involved in early ecumenical discussions, especially regarding missions, and he became the driving force behind the International Missionary Council established in 1921. Mott was concerned from the beginning with establishing truly ecumenical associations and organizations that could incorporate not only Protestants but also Orthodox and Roman Catholic members. Shortly after its formation, Mott expressed his vision for the federation saying: "The Federation will... unite in spirit the students of the world... in doing this it will be achieving a yet more significant result—the hastening of the answer to our Lord's prayer 'that they all may be one.' We read and hear much about Christian union. Surely there has been recently no more hopeful development towards the real spiritual union of Christendom than the World Student Christian Federation, which unites in common purpose and work the coming leaders of Church and State in all lands."[17]

Mott's words indicate that he viewed the central purpose of the federation to be the restoration of Christian unity in accordance with the prayer of Christ. This unity was indispensable for missionary activity. Mott recognized that the divisions of the churches had to be recognized and that actions needed to be taken to address these divisions. He recognized that the disunity of the churches was a tragic impediment to world mission.

Therefore, he viewed the federation as a unique forum for advancing the cause of Christian unity. Undoubtedly, it was this clear vision that set the WSCF apart from other organizations such as the Evangelical Alliance and the YMCA. Like these organizations, the WSCF was not directly and formally linked to any particular church. This fact undoubtedly made some church leaders suspicious of the federation. Yet, unlike the Alliance, the WSCF was not identified solely with evangelical Protestantism and it was also not an explicit proponent of any particular theological tradition. In fact, Mott was especially active in involving Orthodox students in the federation. Likewise, as his travels indicate, he recognized that the federation had to incorporate Christian youth leaders from the Middle East, Eastern Europe, the Far East, and the Pacific.[18] The WSCF was truly an association that not only inspired Christian students to appreciate the importance of mission but also to appreciate the value of personal encounters and dialogue that transcended traditional church boundaries. A remarkable number of Christian leaders, who helped to organize the Faith and Order movement and the Life and Work movement following World War I, were inspired by their involvement in the WSCF.

GREATER UNITY WITHIN CHURCH FAMILIES

Throughout most of the nineteenth century, not all of the divided churches were ready to commit themselves to formal theological dialogue, which would address the issues of unity and reconciliation. Indeed, even official cooperation between churches of different doctrinal traditions in areas of social concern and charity were not easily sanctioned. In many of these churches, however, there were important signs that the status quo began to be questioned. Some leaders began to call for mutual respect, cooperation, and theological dialogue. Indeed, their call frequently challenged the churches to look at the alienation and divisions that afflicted their own tradition. Some church families had internal divisions that reflected different theological emphasis. Other divisions, especially in the United States, arose as a result the organization of churches along ethnic and racial lines. The antislavery movement, the Civil War, and racism in the United States led to new divisions among Protestant churches during the mid-1800s. Throughout the later part of the nineteenth century, therefore, there was a growing desire within the various church families to heal where necessary their own internal divisions and to strengthen their bonds of fellowship throughout the world.

THE ANGLICAN COMMUNION

As early as 1865, the Anglican Church in Canada proposed a conference of the members of the Anglican Communion to address common problems. This proposal led directly to the first Lambeth Conference in 1867. At the invitation of the Archbishop of Canterbury, the conference gathered together 76 Anglican bishops from throughout the world. Owing to the particular structure of the Anglican Communion, the conference from the beginning was not viewed as a synod but as a consultative body. In the course of time, it was determined that a conference would be scheduled to meet about every 10 years.[19]

By the year 1888, it was becoming clear that the Lambeth Conference would be an appropriate forum for the Anglican bishops to address the broader question of the relationship between Anglicanism and other churches. Already in 1878, the conference had discussed relationships with the Moravians and the Old Catholics. At the conference in 1888, ecumenical issues had gained a higher visibility, and committees were established to discuss Anglican relations with the Orthodox, the Scandinavian Lutherans, the Reformed, the Free Churches in England, and the Old Catholics.

The bishops also had before them a report from the 1886 Convention of the Protestant Episcopal Church in America that sought to identify the basic elements that were essential for the restoration of unity. With some minor alteration, this report was adopted by the Lambeth Conference and came to be known as the Chicago-Lambeth Quadrilateral. The statement declares:

> We do hereby affirm that Christian unity so earnestly desired...can be restored only by the return of all Christian Communions to the principles of unity exemplified by the undivided Catholic Church during the first ages of its existence; which principles we believe to be the substantial deposit of Christian faith and order committed by Christ and His Apostles to the Church unto the end of the world, and therefore incapable of compromise or surrender by those who have been ordained to be its stewards and trustees for the common and equal benefit of all men.[20]

Building upon the American statement, the Lambeth Conference identified four features of church life that came to be the basis of Anglican discussions with other churches from the year 1888 onward. These were: first, the Old and New Testaments; second, the Apostles' Creed and the Nicene Creed; third, baptism and the Lord's Supper; and fourth, the historic episcopate. In a broader sense, the Chicago-Lambeth Quadrilateral helped to raise the question of what essential elements would be necessary to restore visible unity to the divided churches. This was an important and farsighted proposal.[21]

THE OLD CATHOLIC CHURCHES

The various Old Catholic Churches joined in an association known as the Union of Utrecht in 1889.[22] Already in the early 1700s a division had taken place in the Netherlands between those Catholics who remained in communion with the Church of Rome and those who did not. This division was intensified there and also grew in areas of Germany, Switzerland, and Austria-Hungry following the proclamation of the doctrine of Papal Infallibility by the First Vatican Council in 1870. From this time onward, the Old Catholic Churches intensified contacts with both the Anglican Communion and the Orthodox Churches. Emphasizing the importance of the faith and liturgical practices of the early Church, the Old Catholics generally became staunch proponents of the unity of the churches. Theological dialogue from the late nineteenth century with the Anglicans led subsequently to the establishment of full communion in 1931.[23] While the dialogue with the Orthodox dating from 1874 did not yield the same result, the formal theological discussions between the two traditions established a valuable foundation for subsequent dialogue on the unity of the churches.[24]

Among the staunchest advocates of the reconciliation of the churches among the Old Catholics at this time was Ignatius von Döllinger (1799–1890). Widely respected as a church historian, Döllinger was among the first to articulate theological principles that challenged existing divisions and that looked toward a time of reconciliation. In addition to this, he envisioned an association of Christians from the various churches that would become the nucleus of the reunited churches.[25] His work contributed to the Old Catholic interest in establishing formal dialogues with Orthodox, Anglicans, and Lutherans.[26] A meeting held in Lucerne Switzerland in 1892 led to the establishment of a new journal, Internationalen Theologische Zeitschrift, which was especially devoted to ecumenical issues. This was most probably the first journal of its kind.[27]

THE PROTESTANT CHURCHES

Throughout the nineteenth century, a number of major Protestant church families began to establish organizations that brought together representatives from throughout the world to strengthen their own unity and witness.

The first meeting of the "Alliance of Reformed Churches throughout the World holding the Presbyterian System" was held in 1875. The meeting brought together delegates representing 21 separate Reformed and Presbyterian churches in America and Western Europe. This meeting led to the establishment in 1877 of the Conference of World Presbyterian Alliance in Edinburgh. This conference subsequently was known as the Alliance of Reformed Churches. The Alliance played an important role in bringing together representatives from a variety of Reformed churches, which often had different theological emphasis and social policies.[28]

During the 1870s and 1880s, there were calls among some Congregationalist leaders in America, Canada, and Britain for the establishment of a world conference. This led to the first International Congregational Council being held in 1891 in London. Subsequent meetings were held in 1899, 1908, and 1920. At a meeting in 1949 in Wellesley, Massachusetts, a formal organization was established.

In the year 1970, the Alliance of Reformed Churches merged with the International Congregational Council to establish the World Alliance of Reformed Churches, representing more than 150 church bodies in more than 80 countries. It maintains its offices in Geneva.

The General Conference of the Methodist Episcopal Church in 1876 passed a resolution that directed its bishops to correspond with other Methodist churches in America and to raise the question of a possible meeting with representatives from each body. Throughout the middle of the nineteenth century, a number of schisms had afflicted Methodism as a result of differences in church polity, discipline, and social issues, most especially slavery and racism. Positive responses from a number of American Methodist bodies to the inquiries led to overtures being made in 1879 to British Methodists. Because of these contacts, the first Ecumenical Methodist Conference was held in London in 1881. The meeting gathered together representatives from 30 Methodist groups in 20 countries. The conference marked a turning point in the relationship among the various Methodist groups. The dialogue within Methodism in the late nineteenth century led directly to the healing of a number of divisions in American and British Methodism throughout the early 1900s. In 1951 the World Methodist Council was established, with more than 50 regional church bodies. It subsequently established an office in Geneva.[29]

Among some Baptists there were calls for a worldwide association as early as the late eighteenth century. However, it was not until 1905 that the first Baptist World Conference was established in London, with representatives from Baptist bodies in 23 countries. The organization, subsequently known as the Baptist World Alliance, gathered together over one hundred regional Baptist organizations.

Preliminary efforts to bring about more contacts among Lutheran churches could be found in Germany and Scandinavia in the later part of the nineteenth century. A number of regional Lutheran churches throughout the world became part of the Lutheran World Convention in 1923. Subsequent assemblies were held in 1929 and 1935. The convention was transformed into the Lutheran World Federation (LWF) in 1949. It was composed of about 100 member churches in more than 20 countries. It also established offices in Geneva.[30]

The early associations of regional Protestant church families beginning in the late nineteenth century became even more formalized throughout the twentieth century. They were significant for a number of reasons. Initially, they helped to bring about a greater sense of unity and common mission within the particular church family through personal contacts, common studies, and meetings. These associations also created a greater sense of a confessional identity and served to emphasize the particularity of each church tradition. This was particularly true during the early period of their organizational existence. Yet the discussions about the visible unity and mission within the context of a particular church family could not ultimately ignore the relationship with other church traditions within Protestantism as well as with the Orthodox Church, the Anglican Communion, and the Roman Catholic Church. From the 1960s onward, therefore, these Protestant associations, which came to be known as Christian World Communions, have been active in contributing to the ecumenical witness of each particular church family. They have also been instrumental in establishing and maintaining a number of international bilateral theological dialogues.

PROTESTANT MISSIONARY SOCIETIES

The Christian missions of the nineteenth century express both the tragic character of Christian divisions as well as a growing interest in cooperation. This century was one that witnessed the dramatic growth of Christianity in Asia, the Pacific, and in parts of Africa. These missions, however, clearly reflected the divisions among Christians. Orthodox, Roman Catholics, and Protestants were engaged in their own specific missionary activities with little positive regard for the other. This proved to be the case generally even among the various Protestant missionary teams until the second half of the century. The tendency toward cooperation among some Protestants and some Protestant churches in Western Europe and America occurred at the same time that Protestant missionaries were also concerned with overcoming rivalries and establishing procedures for cooperative ventures.

The Protestant missions of the late eighteenth and early nineteenth centuries were not undertaken chiefly by the churches themselves. "In many cases," says Stephen Neill, "the Protestant Churches as such were unable or unwilling themselves to take up the cause of missions. This was left to the voluntary societies, dependant upon the initiative of consecrated individuals, and relying for financial support on the voluntary gifts of interested Christians."[31] In order to emphasize the importance of missions and to gain financial support from patrons, a number of missionary societies were established. Founded in 1795, the London Missionary Society began as an organization that was not related to a specific church. This tradition was continued by the British and Foreign Mission Society founded in 1804. This was followed in 1810 by the American Board of Commissioners for Foreign Missions, the Basil Mission of Switzerland in 1815, and the

Berlin Society in Germany in 1824. Similar Protestant missionary societies were established in a number of other countries.[32] While committed to the Protestant tradition broadly understood, these societies generally were not directly linked to a particular Protestant church. The development of these societies generated a great deal of interest in missions and led directly to the establishment of additional missions.

By the second half of the nineteenth century, there was also a growing desire for greater cooperation among the Protestant missionaries serving in the mission fields. As early as 1810, William Carey (1761–1834), a prominent British Baptist missionary, proposed that a missionary conference should be held at the Cape of Good Hope.[33] It was not until 1855, however, that a missionary conference was held in Calcutta and attended by 55 missionaries. Similar conferences were held in Bangalore in 1879, Osaka in 1883, Shanghai in 1887, Mexico in 1888, and South Africa in 1900. These local conferences provided the foundation for the historic Edinburgh Missionary Conference of 1910. As we shall see in the next chapter, this conference is frequently viewed as a major event, which contributed to the ecumenical movement of the twentieth century.[34]

The various Protestant missionary conferences of the second part of the nineteenth century established the principle of comity in Protestant missions.[35] The missions of the first part of the century generally lacked comprehensive planning, mutual respect, and a spirit of cooperation. The conferences helped to identify territories for missions and to establish agreements among separate Protestant missionary bodies not to work in another's region. Not all accepted the proposals. And, of course, their agreements did not apply to relations with Orthodox or Roman Catholic missions. Where there was agreement, however, there was a lessening of rivalries and misunderstandings among the Protestant missionaries. The cooperative spirit sometimes led to more profound questions being raised about the tragedy of division and the imperative of unity.

THE ORTHODOX CHURCH

Contacts between representatives of the Orthodox Church and those of the Anglican, Old Catholic, and some Protestant churches also began to increase from the early decades of the nineteenth century. Some of these contacts were the direct result of the activities of the Bible societies and Protestant missionaries. Others resulted from the growing numbers of Orthodox who had settled in Western Europe and especially in the United States.

These contacts coincided with some important developments within the Orthodox world. The nineteenth century began with the Orthodox Church being organized along the lines of five regional patriarchates. These were Constantinople, Alexandria, Antioch, Jerusalem, and Moscow. Because of political revolutions in the Balkans, the Ottoman Empire had essentially crumbled by the end of the nineteenth century. The development of new nation states in the Balkans also led to the gradual establishment of new Autocephalous Orthodox Churches in Greece, Serbia, and Romania.[36]

The Russian Bible Society was established in 1804 in St. Petersburg and was associated with British and Foreign Bible Society. In the following years a number of local branches were established throughout the Russian Empire under the patronage of leading Orthodox clerics and political figures. While the society initially concentrated its efforts on distributing the Slavonic version of the Bible, work on translating the text into Russian began in 1816. The task was completed in 1825. While the society sought to be nondenominational in its activity, many Russian Orthodox became suspicious of its ideology, which had little regard for the historic Orthodox Church and its teachings. Consequently, this new translation was not formally received by the Church. The Bible Society was formally disbanded in 1826 by an edict of the government. A translation sanctioned by the Church was formally approved some 50 years later.[37]

The experience of the Bible Society in Greece and in Ottoman controlled Asia Minor was ultimately not very different. Indeed, it proved to be more problematic for two reasons. First, Protestant missionaries in the Ottoman Empire were successful in establishing centers in Constantinople and a number of major cities in Asia Minor during the early nineteenth century. As a rule, the Patriarchate of Constantinople did not look favorably upon the work of these missionaries. In the year 1836, the very conservative Patriarch Gregory VI bitterly attacked the teachings of the Protestant missionaries and sought, with the assistance of the Ottoman government, to close the Protestant schools.[38]

Following the successful Greek Revolution of 1821 against the Ottomans, a number of Protestant missionaries from the United States set up mission centers and schools. Among these were missionaries from the Congregational, Baptist, and Protestant Episcopal churches. While these missionaries were not usually directly connected to the Bible Society, their common perspectives could not be easily overlooked. Initially, many leaders of the Orthodox Church in their newly liberated country welcomed the assistance of the Protestant missionaries. However, within a decade, many Orthodox in Greece also began to question the motives of the missionaries and their Protestant perspectives on traditional Orthodox beliefs and liturgical practices. The Holy Synod of the Church of Greece raised formal objection in 1834. Of special concern were tracts and pamphlets from the missionaries that challenged Orthodox doctrines and practices. The synod also declared that the Scriptures could not be taught objectively as the missionaries claimed. By the year 1843, most Protestant missionaries had left the Kingdom of Greece because of the growing opposition from the Orthodox.[39]

The work of the Bible Society in Greece and the Ottoman Empire was also complicated by a debate regarding the translation of the Bible into Modern Greek. While many Greeks opposed the move for a modern translation, others sought to work with the society. The debate became more aggravated over the question of whether to use the Septuagint or the Hebrew version as the basis for the translation of the Old Testament. This debate was further compounded by suspicions over the motives of the Protestant missionaries. As early as 1819, the patriarchate had concluded negotiations with the Bible Society to assist in the translation and distribution of the Bible into Modern Greek.[40] However, this agreement did not bear fruit. By the year 1824, the patriarchate was opposed to the new translation produced by the society.[41]

ORTHODOX AND ANGLICANS

From the time of the Reformation in the sixteenth century, there were a series of contacts between Orthodox and Anglicans. In the early years of the nineteenth century, these early contacts began to lead to a greater degree of theological discussion on issues dividing the churches. In the year 1839, Rev. George Tomlinson undertook a mission on behalf of the Archbishop of Canterbury. In meeting with the patriarch of Constantinople, Tomlinson explained some of the teachings of the Anglican Church. He also assured the patriarch that the Anglican Church was not concerned with undertaking missionary work in Asia Minor but was concerned with establishing better relationships between the two churches.[42]

This encounter appears to have set the stage for numerous exchanges between Anglicans and Orthodox throughout the remainder of the century. Among the better known are the attempts of the Anglican William Palmer (1782–1867) to demonstrate that both churches did in fact share the same faith. He sought to explain this to representatives of the Orthodox Church in Russia during visits there in 1840 and 1842. The Russians refused to consider him as holding the same Orthodox faith and refused to admit him to Holy Communion. However, they did enter into a significant dialogue with him. While Palmer came to be viewed by his English contemporaries as something of an eccentric, his book *The Harmony of the Anglican Doctrine with their Eastern Catholic and Apostolic Church*[43] provoked a lively discussion on doctrinal and unity questions within the Church of England.[44]

The perspectives of Metropolitan Philaret (1782–1867) of Moscow undoubtedly made the visits of William Palmer to Russia more pleasant. Among the Orthodox in Russia, this distinguished bishop was not only one of the great theologians of the period, but also one of the first to encourage better relationships among the divided churches. He took an active interest in Palmer's visits as well as other contacts between Anglicans, Old Catholics, and Orthodox. The metropolitan published an important work in 1832 entitled *Conversations between a Seeker and a Believer Concerning the truth of the Eastern Greco-Russian Church.*[45] While emphasizing the fact that the Orthodox had maintained the authentic Christian faith, Philaret refused to condemn other Christian bodies. He was among the first to articulate ecclesiological issues that would later occupy the attention of others involved in the ecumenical movement in the nineteenth and twentieth centuries. During a visit with representatives of the Protestant Episcopal Church in the United States in 1864, Philaret identified a number of topics that deserved study. These included the Anglican Thirty-nine Articles, the *filioque,* apostolic succession, Holy Tradition, and the Sacraments, especially the Eucharist.[46]

Two organizations were established in England that contributed to this growing relationship between the churches. Founded in 1857, the Association for the Promotion of the Unity of Christendom brought together Anglicans, Orthodox, and Roman Catholics with the express intention not simply for study, but most especially to offer united prayer that unity may be restored to the churches.[47] The association also published a book with essays from Anglicans and Orthodox regarding the issues to be addressed by those seeking reconciliation.[48] The association is said to have had over six thousand members from the Anglican, Orthodox, and Roman Catholic churches. However, in 1864 the Roman Catholics were forced to withdraw under pressure from Rome.[49]

Less than 10 years later in 1864, the Eastern Churches Association was founded by the Anglican scholar John Mason Neale. While the former association placed an important emphasis upon the theme of prayer for unity, the latter emphasized the importance of theological and historical study as a means of reconciliation. Related to these contacts, an important round of theological dialogue between Anglicans and Orthodox in England took place at Ely in 1870, during the visit of the Orthodox bishop of the Greek island of Syros, Alexander Lycurgus. In a very systematic manner, representatives of the two churches discussed points of agreement and disagreement. Chief subjects among the topics discussed were the *filioque* and the Sacraments. This dialogue was remarkable for its time and it set the stage for similar ones throughout the last quarter of the nineteenth century.[50]

All of these new and dramatic developments contributed to the decision of the Anglican bishops to take note of the relationship between their church and the Orthodox Church during the course of the Third Lambeth Conference in 1888. Their resolution states: "The conference, rejoicing in the friendly communications which have passed between the Archbishop of Canterbury and other Anglican Bishops, and the Patriarch of Constantinople and other Eastern Patriarchs and Bishops, desire to express its hope that the barriers to full communion may be, in course of time, removed by further intercourse and extended enlightenment." Reflecting on some on those barriers that the Anglicans perceived, the bishops continued by saying that "it would be difficult for us to enter into more intimate relations with that Church so long as it retains the use of icons, the invocation of the saints, and the cult of the Blessed Virgin."[51]

ORTHODOX AND OLD CATHOLICS

Orthodox relations with the Old Catholic Church were significant, especially during the last quarter of the century. In the wake of the First Vatican Council of the Roman Catholic Church in 1870, a number of Catholics, especially in parts Germany and present-day Switzerland, refused to accept the decision on papal infallibility and related teachings. They separated from the Roman Catholic Church and eventually began to be called Old Catholics or Catholic Christians. Because of their concern with the teachings of early Christianity and their concern with genuine Christian unity, they began to establish contacts with the Orthodox. Likewise, many Orthodox theologians looked favorably upon the Old Catholics, chiefly because of their rejection of the infallibility and universal jurisdiction of the pope.

The hope of reconciliation between the Old Catholics and the Orthodox was formally expressed in the first congress held in Munich in 1871. Orthodox guests were present at that meeting as well as those in the next three years. Under Old Catholic auspice, a Reunion Conference brought together several of their theologians with Orthodox and Anglicans in 1874. The main point of discussion was the historic Nicene Creed and the *filioque* addition. A second conference was held in Bonn in 1875. Among the Orthodox participants were official delegates sent by a number of regional churches including the Ecumenical Patriarchate of Constantinople and the churches of Russia and Greece. Again, the delegates discussed the doctrine of the Holy Spirit. While general agreement was reached between the Orthodox and the Old Catholics, the Anglican delegates were divided over the continued use of the *filioque* in the creed and its significance. Political difficulties in Europe prevented formal contacts between the Orthodox and the Old Catholic theologians for over a decade. These contacts were renewed in 1889 and continued into the twentieth century.[52]

ORTHODOX AND ROMAN CATHOLICS

Formal relations between the Orthodox and the Roman Catholic Church during the nineteenth century underwent little change, despite some informal contacts among both clergy and laity. The principal doctrinal differences related to the authority of the pope and to the understanding of the Holy Spirit, the *filioque* question, remained from the Middle

Ages as the major reasons for division. Yet these historic differences had been compounded by the activity of Roman Catholic missionaries and the development of Eastern Catholic Churches from the seventeenth and eighteenth centuries especially. Known at that time as Uniates, the clergy and laity in these regional churches were once Orthodox but subsequently were integrated into the Roman Catholic Church. Initially found especially in the Ukraine and in the Middle East, these churches continued to follow Orthodox liturgical practice but affirmed loyalty to the pope. The Orthodox viewed these Eastern Catholics as an expression of the Roman Catholic proselytism.

The activity of Roman Catholic missions in the territory of Orthodox Churches and the development of Eastern Catholic Churches led to deepening of tensions. Undoubtedly, this situation served as the backdrop to Orthodox reaction to papal encyclicals of the nineteenth century. With the encyclical, *Praeclara Gratulationis Publicae,* in 1894 Pope Leo XIII described the traditions of the Christian East with admiration. But the pope continued to call the Orthodox to return to the Roman Catholic Church.[53]

The Orthodox Patriarchate of Constantinople responded forcefully to the papal encyclical in 1896. The patriarch said:

> The Orthodox Church of Christ is always ready to accept any proposal of union, if only the Bishop of Rome would shake off once and for all the whole series of the many and divers anti-evangelical novelties that have been "privily brought in" to his Church, and have provoked the sad division of the Churches of the East and West, and would return to the basis of the seven Holy Ecumenical Council, which having assembled in the Holy Spirit, of representatives of all the Holy Churches of God... have a universal and perpetual supremacy in the Church of Christ.[54]

DEVELOPMENTS IN THE ROMAN CATHOLIC CHURCH

As we have seen, the nineteenth century was a time of some important but tentative contacts between Orthodox, Anglicans, Old Catholics, and some Protestant churches. Despite these historic steps, the Roman Catholic Church formally avoided theological dialogue with representatives of other churches on the issue of reconciliation. While a number of papal encyclicals during the late nineteenth century addressed issues of Christian unity, their recommendation was rather straightforward. The popes called for the return of Orthodox, Anglicans, Old Catholics, and Protestants to the Roman Catholic Church.[55] Indeed, a number of unilateral decisions taken by the Roman Catholic Church in the late nineteenth century created new sources of difficulties for relationships between the churches.

The first instance was the understanding of the Immaculate Conception of Mary, which was proclaimed a Catholic doctrine by Pope Pius IX in 1854.

The Pope stated that "the most blessed Virgin Mary on the first instance of her conception was, by the singular grace and privilege of Almighty God and in view of the merits of Christ Jesus the savior of the human race, preserved immune from all stains of original guilt."[56] Such a statement, which had its roots in Catholic teachings for centuries, could only appear to be an additional obstacle to relations, especially with many Orthodox and Protestants who found such perspectives to lack a biblical justification.

During the pontificate of the same pope, a letter was sent from the Holy Office on September 16, 1864, entitled *Ad omners episcopos Angliae.* This document forbids Roman Catholic participation in Association for the Promotion of Christian Unity, which was established in 1857. As has been noted, this was one of the first ecumenical organizations to bring together Roman Catholics, Orthodox, Anglicans, and some Protestants.[57]

Under the leadership of Pope Pius IX, the First Vatican Council formally proclaimed the doctrine of the Infallibility of the Pope. Considered to be the nineteenth Ecumenical Council of the Catholic Church, the Vatican Council opened on December 8, 1869, and closed one month after the Italians seized Rome from the pope on October 20, 1870. The council declared that when "the Roman Pontiff speaks *ex cathedra,* (that is, when—fulfilling the office as pastor and teacher of all Christians—on his supreme Apostolical authority, he defines a doctrine of faith or morals to be held by the universal Church), through the divine assistance promised him in blessed Peter, is endowed with that infallibility, with which the divine Redeemer has willed that his Church—in defining doctrines concerning faith and morals—should be equipped."[58]

A final blow to new relationships with other Christian churches came when Pope Leo XIII, in his encyclical *Apostolicae curae* of September 18, 1896, declared that Anglican ordinations were null and void. Despite differences among Roman Catholic theologians at the time, the pope stated that Anglican orders were defective in the rite of ordination since the sixteenth century and that there was also a lack of proper intention in performing the rites.[59] The pope expected that this statement would put an end to the discussion on this matter.

Despite the decision on the validity of the Anglican Orders, the pontificate of Pope Leo did mark a certain turning point in the relationship between the Roman Catholic Church and other churches. There is certainly not a formal change in Roman Catholic policy toward the Orthodox Church and the Protestant churches. Both are viewed as being separated from the unity of the Roman Catholic Church. The concern for unity, therefore, is a concern from the pope's perspective for the return of dissidents to the unity of the Roman Catholic Church. It is also true, however, that Pope Leo expressed more sensitivity to the distinctive characteristics and historical developments of the other Christian churches. Indeed, Leo had a special concern for the Orthodox Church, which was looked upon quite differently from the Protestants. Similarly, Leo laid a foundation for future theological dialogue with Protestants in his apostolic letter *Amantissimae voluntatis* of April 14, 1895, and his encyclical *Caritatis studium* of July 25, 1898.[60] As the Roman Catholic theologian George Tavard says, "Leo XIII was the first Pope to take up ecumenism. He must be given credit for laying the basis of modern Catholic ecumenism. It will be possible for Benedict XV, Pius XI, and Pius XII to elaborate a highly developed ecumenical position on this foundation. The main point was already made by Leo XIII."[61] However, it was not until Pope John XXIII and Pope Paul VI and the Second Vatican Council (1963–65) that the Roman Catholic Church truly entered into formal dialogue with both the Orthodox Church and various Protestant churches.

CONCLUSIONS

The concern for Christian reconciliation and for the visible unity of the churches has significant expressions in the second half of the nineteenth century. Serious expressions of isolation, bigotry, and misunderstanding continue to be present in the relationship among the divided churches. Yet this was also a time when the issues of church disunity and unity were beginning to receive fresh attention both in Europe and in North America. A number of voluntary Christian organizations and the Bible societies brought Christians together in activities of service and witness that transcended the boarders of the divided churches. The YMCA, YWCA, and the World Student Christian Association provided young people with a vision of the reconciliation of Christians and with opportunities to foster it. Movements toward greater unity in Protestant church families developed. The relationship between mission and unity was raised. The Association for the Promotion of Unity of Christendom emphasized the importance of prayer for unity. The theological dialogues among Anglicans, Orthodox, and Old Catholics began to address historic points of difference. Many of the elements of the ecumenical movement that would become more prominent during the twentieth century have their roots in the nineteenth.

NOTES

1. Cited in Ruth Rouse, "Voluntary Movements and the Changing Ecumenical Climate," in *A History of the Ecumenical Movement, 1517–1948,* ed. Ruth Rouse and Stephen Charles Neill (Philadelphia: The Westminster Press, 1967), p. 341.
2. Stephen Neill, *A History of Christian Missions* (New York: Penguin Books, 1964), pp. 322–96.
3. Edwin Scott Gaustad, *A Religious History of America* (New York: Harper and Row, revised edition, 1966), pp. 164–75.

4. Ibid., p. 170.
5. Ibid., pp. 153–56.
6. Ibid., pp. 178–97.
7. See William H. Brackney, *Christian Voluntarism in Britain and North America,* (Westport: Greenwood, 1995).
8. Ruth Rouse, "Voluntary Movements and the Changing Ecumenical Climate," in *A History of the Ecumenical Movement, 1517–1948,* ed. Rouse and Neill, pp. 311–12.
9. Ibid., p. 320.
10. See J. W. Massie, *The Evangelical Alliance* (London, 1847).
11. Rouse, pp. 321–22.
12. Ibid., p. 322.
13. Ibid., p. 323.
14. Ibid., p. 327.
15. Ibid., p. 341.
16. See Ruth Rouse, *The World Student Christian Federation* (London: SCM Press, 1948).
17. Rouse, "Voluntary Movements and the Changing Ecumenical Climate," p. 341.
18. Stephen C. Neill, *Brothers of the Faith* (New York: Abingdon Press, 1960), pp. 16–28.
19. Henry Renaud Turner Brandreth, "Approaches of the Churches Towards Each Other in the Nineteenth Century," in *A History of the Ecumenical Movement, 1517–1948,* ed. Ruth Rouse and Stephen Charles Neill (Philadelphia: The Westminster Press, 1967), p. 364.
20. Protestant Episcopal Church, *Journal of the General Convention* (New York, 1886), p. 80.
21. Brandreth, p. 265.
22. Ibid., p. 267.
23. Ibid.
24. See U. von Arx, ed., "Koinonia auf Altkirchlicher Basis," *Internationalen Kirchlichen Zeitschrift* 79:4 (1989); H. Meyer and L. Vischer, *Growth in Agreement* (WCC, 1984), pp. 389–419.
25. See Ignatius von Döllinger, *Lectures on the Reunion of the Churches* (Naperville, Ill.: Alph Press, 1973).
26. Brandreth, p. 293.
27. This journal continues to be published under the name *Internationalen Kirchlichen Zeitschrift.*
28. Brandreth, p. 266.
29. Ruth Rouse, "Other Aspects of the Ecumenical Movement," in *A History of the Ecumenical Movement, 1517–1948,* ed. Rouse and Neill (Philadelphia: The Westminster Press, 1967), pp. 613–14.
30. Ibid., pp. 614–16.
31. Stephen Neill, *A History of Christian Missions,* p. 252.
32. Ibid., pp. 540–41.
33. Ibid., pp. 252–53.
34. Ibid., pp. 540–44.
35. Ibid., pp. 541–42.

36. John Meyendorff, *The Orthodox Church* (New York: Pantheon Books, 1962), pp. 82–101.

37. Georges Florovsky, *Ways of Russian Theology* (Belmont, Mass.: Nordland Publishing Company, 1979), pp. 181–201.

38. N.M. Vaporis, *Translating the Scriptures into Modern Greek* (Brookline: Holy Cross Orthodox Press, 1994), p. 70.

39. Ibid., pp. 72–84.

40. Ibid., p. 41.

41. Ibid., p. 55.

42. Methodios Fouyas, *Anglicanism, Orthodoxy, and Roman Catholicism* (Brookline: Holy Cross Orthodox Press, 1984), p. 38.

43. See William Palmer, *The Harmony of the Anglican Doctrine with their Eastern Catholic and Apostolic Church* (London, 1946).

44. Owen Chadwick, *The Mind of the Oxford Movement* (Stanford: Stanford University Press, 1960), p. 30.

45. Georges Florovsky, *Ecumenism II* (Valduz: Buchervertriebsanstalt, 1989), p. 112.

46. Ibid., 113–14.

47. Ibid., p. 127.

48. Ibid., p. 157. The book was titled *The True Basis for Reunion: Essays on the Reunion of Christendom,* by F.G. Lee (London, 1867).

49. Rouse, "Voluntary Movements and the Changing Ecumenical Climate," p. 347.

50. Florovsky, *Ecumenism II,* pp. 130–32.

51. R. Davidson, *The Five Lambeth Conferences, 1867–1920* (London, 1929), p. 168; Fouyas, p. 40.

52. Florovsky, *Ecumenism II,* pp. 140–41.

53. George Tavard, *Two Centuries of Ecumenism* (New York: Mentor-Omega Book, 1962), p. 71.

54. Cited in Fouyas, p. 201.

55. Ibid., pp. 71–74.

56. Cited in Jaroslav Pelikan, *The Christian Tradition 5* (Chicago: The University of Chicago Press, 1989), pp. 208–9; Fouyas, pp. 163–67.

57. Tavard, *Two Centuries of Ecumenism,* p. 68.

58. Cited in Henry Bettenson and Chris Maunder, eds., *Documents of the Christian Church* (Oxford: Oxford University Press, revised edition, 1999), p. 288. See also Pelikan, p. 250.

59. Ibid., pp. 289–90.

60. Tavard, p. 73.

61. Ibid., p. 74.

CHAPTER 5

Early Church Unity Movements

> We humbly acknowledge that our divisions are contrary to the will of Christ, and we pray God in His mercy to shorten the days of our separation and to guide us by His Spirit into fullness of unity.
>
> —The Edinburgh Faith and Order Conference, 1937[1]

INTRODUCTION

There were many important indications during the latter nineteenth century that Christians both in Europe and America were becoming increasingly dissatisfied with the divisions among them and their churches. Some leaders sought to bring Christians together in Christian associations not directly related to the churches. Others proposed more formal contacts and dialogues between the divided churches. Through all this was the indication that many old divisions were giving way to new opportunities for important contacts among clergy and laity of different churches. New associations were developing that transcended church boundaries. These deepened personal relationships, increased mutual respect, and opened up new perspectives on divisive issues. This, in turn, led to recognition among many that the de facto divisions among the churches could not be ignored. There was, therefore, a growing interest in finding ways in which the official representatives from divided churches could formally come together to address doctrinal issues, pray together, and to cooperate in social witness.

PRELIMINARY CONCERNS OVER DOCTRINAL DIFFERENCES

The World Missionary Conference in Edinburgh in 1910 is often identified as a seminal gathering, sparking greater interest in the difficulties inherent in the disunity of the churches and the need to find opportunities for cooperation. Bringing together over one thousand participants, the Edinburgh Conference was a gathering composed only of Protestant representatives who met primarily to discuss Christian missions and cooperation in the mission field. Roman Catholics and Orthodox were not invited to this event. Yet the tragedy of Christian disunity could not be ignored. The participants recognized that the advance of Christian mission was severely impaired by conflicting theologies, the real divisions between the churches, and the lack of a common witness. The conference led to the establishment of the International Missionary Council in 1921, which united a number of Protestant missionary societies.[2]

Even before the Edinburgh Conference, the Orthodox Church of Constantinople, known as the Ecumenical Patriarchate, began a new series of discussions on issues related to church divisions as early as the year 1902. On June 12 of that year, Patriarch Joachim III addressed an encyclical to the Autocephalous Orthodox Churches that took note of the need of the Orthodox to examine issues of common concern. Among these were issues related to dialogue with other Christian churches. In the encyclical, the patriarch affirmed that the Orthodox are concerned with unity. However, he also took note of the serious doctrinal differences that divide the churches. In one portion of the letter addressed to other Orthodox, he says:

> Of course, the union of them and all who believe in Christ with us in the Orthodox faith is the pious and heartfelt desire of our Church and of all genuine Christians who stand firm in the evangelical doctrine of unity, and it is the subject of constant prayer and supplication; but at the same time we are not unaware that this pious desire comes up against the unbroken persistence of these Churches in doctrines on which, having taken their stand as on a base hardened by the passage of time, they seem quite disinclined to join a road to union, such as is pointed out by evangelical truth; nor do they evince any readiness to do so, except on terms and basis on which the desired dogmatic unity and fellowship is unacceptable to us.[3]

Despite the profound concern over doctrinal differences, the patriarch calls upon the other Orthodox Churches to consider a common approach to other Christian churches that are concerned with the issue of unity. Indeed, the record indicates that a number of Autocephalous Orthodox Churches responded favorably to the encyclical of Patriarch Joachim. Their positive response appears to have led directly to Orthodox involvement in the early ecumenical meetings. The responses also led to the historic Patriarchal Encyclical of 1920, which called for the establishment of a

Fellowship of Churches and offered proposal through which the divided churches could engage in doctrinal discussions and common witness.[4]

Among the participants in the Edinburgh Conference was Bishop Charles Brent (1862–1929) of the Episcopal Church in the United States.[5] Brent was among those who were touched with the vision of a united church through the Edinburgh meeting. Before leaving Scotland, Brent appears to have become convinced of the need for another conference that would address the theological issues of Church disunity. Upon his return to the United States, Brent continued to raise up his concern. At the General Convention of the Episcopal Church in October 1910, the bishop reviewed the activity of Edinburgh and appealed for support in proposing a Conference on Faith and Order. Some days later, on October 19, 1910, the General Convention approved a resolution that created a commission "to bring about a conference for the consideration of questions touching Faith and Order, and that all Christian Communions throughout the world which confess Our Lord Jesus Christ as God and Saviour be asked to unite with us in arranging for and conducting such a Conference."[6]

The decision by the Episcopal Church in the United States was but one of many actions taken formally by a number of churches. These actions sought to seek means to address together doctrinal issues affecting unity. Dr. Peter Ainslie addressed the Annual Convention of the Disciples of Christ a day earlier on October 18, 1910, on issues of Christian unity. His remarks led to the establishment of their Commission on Christian Unity and an agreement to work with the Commission of the Episcopal Church. Likewise, the National Council of Congregational Churches agreed to a similar commission on the same day. When the Episcopal Church Commission met less than a year later in April 1911, 18 Protestant Churches in the United States had established similar commissions. In addition to those noted, they included the Methodists and Presbyterians.[7]

Bolstered by the support found in the United States, representatives of the Episcopal Church took the responsibility to publicize the proposal as well as to contact European church leaders. During the year 1911, the proposal for a Conference on Faith and Order had been submitted to the leaders of churches throughout the world. This included not only Anglican and Protestant churches but also the Orthodox and the Roman Catholic. The proposal called upon churches "which confess Our Lord Jesus Christ as God and Saviour" to join in arranging a conference "based upon a clear statement and full consideration of those things in which we differ, as well as those things in which we are one."[8] While the Orthodox tended to be predisposed to participating in a conference, the Roman Catholic Church in 1914 formally but politely indicated that it would not be able to participate.[9]

An important meeting of representatives of various churches took place in New York on May 8, 1913. Participants included Anglican, Protestant, and Orthodox delegates. Reports indicated that the interest in convening a Conference on Faith and Order was growing not only in the United States but also in Europe. With this in mind, the participants established some broad principles for the conference. It was affirmed that the conference would seek participation from all Christian churches, that issues of difference and agreement would be discussed, that no plan of unity would be immediately proposed, that a conference agenda would be established in advance, and that the participants in the conference would need to be truly representative of the churches.[10]

With the coming of World War I, much of the dramatic movement toward convening a conference was brought to a halt. When the war did come to an end, however, the Episcopal Church Commission rapidly dispatched a delegation to Europe to meet especially with Orthodox and Catholic leaders. The delegation had with them a proposal from an American Preparatory Meeting of 1916 that outlined the subjects to be addressed at the conference. These included:

1. The Church, its nature, and function.
2. The Catholic creeds as the safeguards of the faith of the Church.
3. Grace and the Sacraments in general.
4. The Ministry, its nature, and function.
5. Practical questions connected with missionary and other administrative functions of the Church.

Orthodox Church leaders in Constantinople, Athens, Alexandria, Cairo, Damascus, and Jerusalem warmly received the delegation. However, attempts to meet with Pope Benedict XV in Rome were fruitless. The delegation subsequently received a letter from the Vatican on May 16, 1919, indicating that the Roman Catholic Church was not able to participate in the proposed conference. The letter also said that the pope hoped that the participants would "see the light and become reunited to the visible head of the Church, by whom they will be received with open arms."[11] The fact that the Roman Catholic Church was not willing at that time to participate disappointed many members of the Episcopal Church Commission. Yet this was offset to some degree by the positive reaction of most Orthodox leaders as well as a number of Protestant Church leaders in France, Norway, and Sweden. Protestant Church leaders in Germany, however, consistently refused to become involved in the conference at that time.

Delegates from 75 churches in over 40 countries met in Geneva, Switzerland, during August 12–20, 1920. The participants appointed a Continuation Committee that met and formulated a series of questions related to church unity to be discussed by the churches before the conference. This committee met again in Stockholm in 1925 and proposed that the long anticipated conference be held in Lausanne, Switzerland, in 1927.

FAITH AND ORDER AT LAUSANNE IN 1927

The first Conference on Faith and Order was held in Lausanne, Switzerland, during August 3–21, 1927. The gathering brought together about four hundred participants representing 127 Orthodox, Anglican, Old Catholic, and Protestant churches.[12] Many of the participants were truly ecumenical pioneers who had been active in a number of interchurch groups and associations, such as the Student Christian Movement. Yet, at the same time, this gathering was among the first of the twentieth century to bring together people from vastly different Christian traditions, churches, and countries. As with most international meetings of the time, the conferences operated in English, French, and German with the greatest portion of the discussions in English. Among the prominent leaders of the conference were Episcopal Bishop Charles Brent of the United States, Swedish Lutheran Bishop Nathan Söderblom, and Orthodox Metropolitan Germanos Strenopoulos from Constantinople.

The discussions were cordial but not always easy. American and European participants predominated. Asians and Africans were few. The participants had their own cultural peculiarities and manners of expression. Orthodox and some Protestants did not always speak the same theological language. The themes proposed for discussion touched upon the very issues of doctrinal differences between the churches. Questions of creeds and confessions and ministry and sacraments had divided the churches in ages past. Many of these differences involved bitter debates in previous centuries. There was much learning to be done in a new atmosphere of mutual respect. Much of the discussions, therefore, were simply devoted to comparing the different theological perspectives and emphases from the churches. Nonetheless, most of the delegates clearly recognized that the unique vocation of the Faith and Order tradition was to examine differences as well as similarities within a context of mutual respect and common prayer. In their statement, the delegates said: "God's Spirit has been in our midst...He has enlarged our horizons, quickened our understanding, and enlivened our hope. We have dared and God has justified our daring. We can never be the same again."[13]

FAITH AND ORDER AT EDINBURGH IN 1937

The Second World Conference on Faith and Order was held in Edinburgh, Scotland, during August 3–18, 1937. About 400 participants were present representing 122 churches. Archbishop William Temple (1881–1944) of York of the Church of England was elected the president.[14] Based upon responses to the Lausanne, the assembly examined five major themes. These were: first, The Grace of Our Lord Jesus Christ; second, The Church of Christ and the Word of God; third, The Church of Christ: Ministry and Sacraments; fourth, The Church's Unity in Life and Worship; and fifth, The Communion of Saints.[15]

The discussions at Edinburgh were somewhat smaller than the earlier ones at Lausanne. About one hundred of the delegates had been present at the earlier meeting. These delegates had come to know each other and a sense of mutual respect and trust had been built up, despite the difficult topics that were under discussion. Most of the delegates at Edinburgh were well aware of the theological discussions at Lausanne as well as the responses that had been submitted in subsequent years from the churches and interested persons. Moreover, the Edinburgh meeting began with 10 days devoted primarily to group discussions of the topics. This methodology created an atmosphere where the delegates felt comfortable in engaging in genuine dialogue.[16]

One theme, which was not on the preliminary agenda, was the proposal to support the establishment of a World Council of Churches. About one month prior to the Faith and Order Conference, Life and Work held its conference in Oxford. There, the delegates approved a motion that the two movements come together and form the World Council of Churches. After a long and difficult discussion, the delegates to the Edinburgh Conference passed a motion supporting the establishment of the World Council of Churches.[17]

The approval of the reports of the discussion at Edinburgh was complemented with the approval of an affirmation that captured many of the concerns of the conference. This report captures many of the fundamental principles of reconciliation and the quest for the visible unity of the churches. A portion of it says:

> We are one in faith in our Lord Jesus Christ, the incarnate Word of God. We are one in allegiance to Him as Head of the Church, and as King of king and Lord of lords. We are one in acknowledging that this allegiance takes precedence of any other allegiance that may make claims on us.
>
> This unity does not consist in the agreement of our minds or the consent of our wills. It is founded in Jesus Christ Himself, who lived, died, and rose again to bring us to the Father, and Who through the Holy Spirit dwells in the Church. We are one because we are the objects of the love and grace of God, and called by Him to witness in all the world to His glorious gospel.
>
> Our unity is of heart and spirit. We are divided in the outward forms of our life in Christ, because we understand differently His will for His Church. We believe, however, that a deeper understanding will lead us towards a united apprehension of the truth as it is in Jesus.
>
> We humbly acknowledge that our divisions are contrary to the will of Christ, and we pray God in His mercy to shorten the days of our separation and to guide us by His Spirit into fullness of unity.
>
> We are thankful that during recent years we have been drawn together; prejudices have been overcome, misunderstandings removed, and real, if limited, progress has been made towards our goal of a common mind.

We have lifted up our hearts together in prayer; we have sung the same hymns; together we have read the same Scriptures. We recognize in one another, across the barriers of our separation, a common Christian outlook and a common standard of values. We are assured of a unity deeper than our divisions.

We believe that every sincere attempt to cooperate in the concerns of the Kingdom of God draws the severed communions together in increased mutual understanding and goodwill. We call upon our fellow Christians in all communions to practice such cooperation...and constantly to pray for that unity, which we believe to be our Lord's will for His Church.[18]

THE EARLY LIFE AND WORK MOVEMENT

During the late nineteenth and early twentieth century, a number of church leaders began to emphasize the need for Christians and their churches to apply Christian principles to the relations among nations and to the strengthening of the rule of international law. With the participation of religious and political leaders, two international Peace Conferences at The Hague, in 1899 and in 1907, crystallized many of these concerns. In the year 1914 a number of religious leaders helped to establish the Church Peace Union with a grant from the American industrialist Andrew Carnegie.[19]

Both the short-lived Church Peace Union and its funds provided the basis for the establishment of the World Alliance for Promoting International Friendship Through the Churches in Constance, Switzerland, on August 2, 1914. Plans called for about one hundred fifty persons representing Protestant churches in Europe and America to attend.[20] Due to the fear of a possible war in Europe, however, only about 75 participants attended the abbreviated meeting. Little more could be done at Constance because on the previous day, Germany had declared war on Russia and participants were advised to make plans to leave Switzerland before rail lines were closed. During the early years of the war, meetings of Alliance representatives were held in London and in Berne. There, in 1915, the name of the organization was changed to The World Alliance for Promoting Friendship through the Churches. The change of name was deemed necessary because the participants in the alliance did not formally represent their churches.

With the close of the war, there were new efforts among religious leaders to address issues related to humanitarian services and to the resolution of disputes among nations. The World Alliance held a conference in The Hague during September 30–October 3, 1919. There were about 60 participants. Most were part of the alliance's International Committee or members of similar national committees. "To a large extent the delegations were made up of men who, during the war, had been carrying on Christian work of mutual understanding between the different countries."[21] The delegates welcomed the establishment of the League of Nations and urged it to be protective of the rights of religious minorities in its work. The delegates affirmed also that the alliance in the future would concern itself with support for the rule of international law. Clearly, from the start, the concerns of the alliance were not oriented directly toward issues of Church unity.

Within the context of the alliance meeting of 1919, however, Lutheran Archbishop Nathan Söderblom (1866–1931) of Uppsala had the opportunity to speak about his view of creating a Council of Churches. According to him, this council could be a means through which the churches, divided in doctrine, could work together to address social problems. While the delegates meeting gave general approval to Söderblom's plan, they also stated that the proposal was beyond the competence of the World Alliance. "The plan for an international Christian conference was thus taken out of the hands of the World Alliance and the new endeavors appear as an independent undertaking; they developed into the Life and Work Movement."[22] The fact that the delegates chose formally not to associate with Söderblom's plan was a clear sign that they viewed the alliance as an organization separate from the churches. Some delegates, however, were greatly supportive of the proposal and immediately established an independent committee to work with Söderblom.

Following a preliminary meeting in Paris in 1919, a conference was held in Geneva during August 9–12, 1920 with 90 participants from 15 countries.[23] The participants included only Protestants. This fact appears to have reflected the view of some organizers that the future council should only include representatives from Protestant churches. Under the leadership of Söderblom, the participants set about to plan the conference and the extent of participation. Söderblom clearly envisioned a conference that would include representatives from all the churches. He believed that such a conference, addressing pressing moral issues, would be of great value in itself and lay the groundwork for a ecumenical Council of Churches. Therefore, he forcefully argued that both the Orthodox Churches and the Roman Catholic Church be invited to send representatives to the conference. He stated that an ecumenical conference of Protestant churches alone would not truly be ecumenical. Since not all agreed with his position, especially some Swiss Protestants, a lengthy debated took place over the issue of participation. Supported by the majority, Söderblom's perspectives prevailed. The debate led to the decision that all Christian churches should be invited to the international conference. "This decision," says Nils Karlström, "made on 11 August 1920, marks one of the greatest victories of the ecumenical movement."[24] At long last, invitations were sent to the churches in April 1924.[25]

LIFE AND WORK AT STOCKHOLM IN 1925

The Universal Christian Conference on Life and Work met in Stockholm, Sweden, during August 19–29, 1925. More than 600 delegates from Protestant and Orthodox churches in 37 countries participated in the historic gathering.[26] Despite receiving an invitation, the Roman Catholic Church did not send any delegates.

The phrase Life and Work reflected a concern primarily for issues of Christian living and the activities of the churches in the society. Since many of the same people were involved in the planning for a Faith and Order meeting, the organizers of Life and Work tended not to be concerned with the historic issues of church divisions. There concern was to find avenues through which the divided churches could cooperate within the society. The planning committee had established six topics to be examined at the Stockholm meeting, and preliminary essays on each were prepared in advance. These were:

> The general obligation of the Church in the light of God's plan for the world—the basic and fundamental questions.
>
> The Church and economic and industrial problems.
>
> The Church and social and moral problems.
>
> The Church and international relations.
>
> The Church and education.
>
> Ways and means for promoting cooperation between Churches and for their closer association on federal lines.[27]

Each of the topics was substantial and contained far more subtle issues than the participants could easily handle. But this was not the only challenge. The planners had intentionally sought to avoid all discussions of issues dealing with Faith and Order since another body was considering them. As we have said, Life and Work was designed to highlight those issues that the churches could address despite their doctrinal differences. Yet it became clear during the course of the deliberations that differences in theology and in church teachings could not be easily ignored. A major theological debate arose over the issue of the Kingdom of God on earth. Some participants, rooted in the Social Gospel perspective spoke of the role of persons in contributing to the establishment of God's Kingdom on earth. Others objected and declared that humans should not be so arrogant in claiming that they can inaugurate the Kingdom. "The tension between these different conceptions of the Kingdom of God came to dominate much of the discussion and, because not squarely faced, led to continual misunderstanding. This misunderstanding was not eased when the theological issue was confused with national or confessional categories—such as American activism versus German otherworldliness, or Calvinism against Lutheranism. Here the antithesis was revealed—partly theological, partly geographical and cultural—which in changing manifestations was to preoccupy the movement for many years to come."[28]

The cry of the Stockholm Conference had been: "Doctrine Divides but Service Unites. Yet it was clear at Stockholm that the various theological and doctrinal differences among the churches could not be easily ignored. The fact that there were some serious theological differences expressed during the conference deliberations accounts for the fact that no formal reports were approved by the delegates. The Message of the Universal Christian Conference on Life and Work was the only official document to be approved by the assembly. The message makes a strong affirmation of the need of churches to apply the message of the gospel to all aspects of life including the industrial, social, political, and international. Yet the message also affirms that Christian faith is at the heart of the Church's concern for the well-being of the society. A portion says:

> The sins, sorrows, the struggles, and losses of the Great War and since have compelled the Christian Churches to recognize humbly and with shame, that "the world is [too] strong for a divided Church." Leaving for the time our differences in Faith and Order, our aim has been to secure united practical action in Christian Life and Work. The Conference itself is a conspicuous fact. However, it is only a beginning.
>
> The Conference has deepened and purified our devotion to the Captain of our Salvation. Responding to the call "Follow Me," we have in the presence of the Cross accepted the urgent duty of applying His Gospel in all realms of human life—industrial, social, political and international.
>
> Only as we become inwardly one shall we attain real unity of mind and spirit. The nearer we draw to the Crucified, the nearer we come to one another, and in however varied colours the light of the world may be reflected in our faith. Under the cross of Jesus Christ, we reach out hands to one another. The Good Shepherd had to die in order that He might gather together the scattered children of God. In the Crucified and Risen Lord alone lies the world's hope.[29]

LIFE AND WORK AT OXFORD IN 1937

The Second Conference on Life and Work was held in Oxford, England, during July 12–26, 1937. With over four hundred participants, there were about three hundred official delegates from 120 churches in 40 countries. While the Roman Catholic Church did not send official delegates, a small number of Roman Catholic observers were present. "The absence of Rome," says Nils Ehrenström, "was accepted as a fact, deeply regrettable, yet perfectly comprehensible in view of Rome's dogmatic position."[30] Also absent from the conference were representatives of Germany's Lutheran Churches. While many took part in the preparations for Oxford, the Nazi government prohibited representatives from the Lutheran Churches in

Germany from attending. This was a sign of the potent political and ecclesiastical difficulties that were rapidly developing in Germany.[31]

A number of important developments had occurred since Stockholm. First and most important, there were the harsh economic and political realities that especially had affected Europe and North America between 1929 and 1933. The impact of communism in Russia and the rise of National Socialism in Germany contributed to a souring of the optimistic spirit that was expressed at Stockholm. Much of the optimism of the Social Gospel movement had vanished. The whole ecumenical movement, and especially those active in Life and Work, had to reassess their view of society and the position of the churches within it.

This provided an important impetus for major theological reflection by notable theologians such as Karl Barth, Dietrich Bonhoffer, and Reinhold Niebuhr among Protestants, and Sergius Bulgakov, and George Florovsky among the Orthodox. Moreover, the Life and Work Movement was greatly inspired by the theological and administrative leadership of Archbishop William Temple and J. H. Oldham of England. Under their direction, seven major theological studies were published in anticipation of the Oxford Conference.

These studies provided the participants in the Oxford Conference with profound theological insight into a number of the social and moral questions of the day. As Paul Albrecht says: "This preparatory study for the Oxford Conference was a remarkable intellectual achievement for the Life and Work movement. It involved contributions from several hundred foremost theological and lay thinkers of that period, and representatives of all major denominational and confessional communities."[32] The preparations for Oxford recognized the importance of theological reflection as well as the centrality of the gospel of Christ and the Church for any ecumenical discussion of social and moral issues. As J. H. Oldham said at the time: "No question more urgently demands the grave and earnest consideration of Christian people than the relationship between the Church, the State and the community, since on these practical issues is focused the great and critical debate between the Christian faith and the secular tendencies of our time. In this struggle, the very existence of the Christian Church is at stake."[33]

Because of the depth of theological preparation and the profound concern for the world situation, Oxford has been called "an ecumenical study conference on a world scale. It was designed to be a culminating point in a continuing process of clarifying and crystallizing Christian thought and strategy in regard to burning issues of human society."[34] Under the leadership of Archbishop Temple and Dr. John Mott, the conference began with a number of addresses that addressed both the concerns of the Christian gospel and the state of the world in 1937. The delegates then broke into small groups that examined a number of related topics. The delegates then prepared a report dealing with five themes to be submitted to the churches. Among the major themes discussed was the relationship of Church and state.

Upon reviewing the reports, it would be wrong to say that Life and Work at Oxford was concerned only with practical issues. If there was a concern for many of the practical issues facing Christians and their churches, this concern was not unrelated to thoughtful theological reflection based upon the Church's Scripture and rich tradition. The reports clearly demonstrate this.

In addition to their theological reflections, the delegates at Oxford also approved a motion favoring the establishment of a World Council of Churches, which would bring together both the Life and Work Movement and the Faith and Order Movement. Indeed, the very methodology of Oxford, as well as the theological reflections, led many to believe that Faith and Order and Life and Work were not mutually exclusive. Rather, they were best seen as complementary in the quest for Christian unity.[35]

A portion of the message of the conference says:

> The first duty of the Church, and its greatest service to the world, is that it be in very deed the Church—confessing the true faith, committed to the fulfillment of the will of Christ, its only Lord, and united in him in a fellowship of love and service.
>
> In God is the secret of true unity among men and in Christ is revealed the secret of God. The first task of the Church, now as always, is to make known the gospel, and to assert the claim of Jesus Christ as the incarnate Word of God to the lordship of all human life.
>
> There is a call from God today:
>
> To every local congregation, to realize at any cost in its own self that unity, transcending all differences and barriers of class, social status, race and nation, which we believe the Holy Spirit can and will create in those who are ready to be led by Him.
>
> To different churches in any district, to come together for local ecumenical witness in worship and work.
>
> To all Christians, to a more passionate and costly concern for the outcast, the underprivileged, the persecuted, and the despised in the community and beyond the community. The recrudescence of pitiless cruelty, hatreds, and race discriminations (including anti-Semitism) in the modern world is one of the major signs of its social disintegration. To these must be brought not the weak rebuke of words but the powerful rebuke of deeds. Thus, the unity of the Church is advanced. The Church has been called into existence by God not for itself but for the world. Only by going out of itself in the work of Christ can it find unity in itself.[36]

OPPORTUNITIES FOR COMMON PRAYER FOR CHRISTIAN UNITY

The fact that Christians from divided churches were gathering together in associations such as the Student Christian Movement, or in formal Conferences on Faith and Order and Life and Work, naturally raised questions about prayer and common worship. The great divisions of the churches manifested themselves most concretely in separate worship services. Divided Christians were accustomed to separate services of worship. With the increase of activities devoted to the unity of the churches, however, new opportunities were also developing for Christians of different traditions and cultures to gather together for prayer and worship.

The first formal proposal for a union for prayer for Christian unity appears to have been made in 1840 by Fr. Ignatius Spencer, a Roman Catholic priest in England. During a visit to Oxford, Spencer presented his proposal to a number of leaders of the Church of England. Spencer's simple proposal advocated that Christians of divided churches join together at times to offer prayers for the unity. At that time, there were many in the Oxford movement who were becoming concerned with issues of Christian unity. As a result of the proposal, John Henry Newman devised a Plan of Prayer for Union that was meant to encourage the idea among Anglicans. At that time, however, the proposal received little support from Anglican bishops. However, elements of the plan undoubtedly influenced subsequent developments both within the Anglican Church and beyond it.[37]

A number of Anglican and Roman Catholic leaders in England joined together to establish the Association for the Promotion of the Unity of Christendom in 1857. Rev. Fredrick George Lee, an Anglican priest, and Ambrose Philip de Lisle, a Roman Catholic layman, took the initiative for this historic association.[38] Over the course of the next few years, Orthodox participants also became involved in the association. There is some reason to believe that this was the first organization to be established to pray for the unity of the churches. For a number of years, the association also published the *Union Review,* a periodical devoted to issues of reconciliation and unity. This journal was most probably the first to be devoted to such issues. Most importantly, the association had as its primary objective the offering of daily prayers for unity by its members. The members were asked to offer daily a simple prayer before the Lord's Prayer, which said: "O Lord Jesus Christ, who said unto Thine apostles, peace I leave with you: my peace I give to you; regard not my sins, but the faith of Thy Church and grant her that peace and unity which is agreeable to Thy will, who livest and reignest for ever and ever. Amen."[39]

About six thousand Anglicans, Catholics, and Orthodox had become members of the association by 1864. The genuine ecumenical character of the association, however, would not last. Although the Roman Catholic Church had formally approved the association in 1857, support was withdrawn in 1864 at the recommendation of the Roman Catholic bishops in England. This compelled Roman Catholic members to withdraw from membership. In the year 1895, Pope Leo XIII suggested that the Rosary be used by Catholics to pray for the return of the dissidents to the Roman

Catholic Church. Two years later, he asked that a novena of prayers be offered before the Feast of Pentecost for the reunion of Christians under the authority of the pope.[40]

The association's influence, however, continued to be found especially among Anglicans who were concerned with the issues of Church unity. The early Lambeth Conferences of Anglican bishops consistently emphasized their concern for Christian unity and for the importance of prayer for unity.[41]

Some of the earliest conferences devoted to the study of Christian divisions also emphasized the importance of prayer for reconciliation. Between 1892 and 1895, representatives from a number of Anglican, Protestant, and Old Catholic churches met six times in Grundelwald, Switzerland. Prayer for the reunion of the churches became a prominent element of these Grundelwald conferences. In an appeal issued after the conferences in 1884 and 1885, the participants proposed that the churches establish a Reunion Sunday that would coincide with the Feast of Pentecost (Whitunday) every year. In response to the Grundelwald proposal, the archbishop of Canterbury in 1884 and 1885 asked clergy in England to use a Prayer for Unity as part of the worship services on that day. In the year 1885, the Roman Catholic Church in England also directed that prayers be offered on Pentecost for reunion of the churches.[42] Despite the fact that Roman Catholics were forced to withdraw from the association for the Promotion of the Unity of Christendom in 1864, this decision was an early and very remarkable expression of ecumenical cooperation.

THE WEEK OF PRAYER FOR CHRISTIAN UNITY

The most significant and enduring proposal for prayer for unity comes out of this period. Now known as the Week of Prayer for Christian Unity, the proposal has one root in a proposal of 1908, in a very different form, under the title Church Unity Octave.[43] Two Anglican priests, Fr. Spencer Jones and Fr. Paul Watson, proposed a period of prayer between January 18 and January 25 that would be concerned with the reunion of Christians. According to the Roman Catholic Calendar, January 18 was the Feast of St. Peter's Chair and January 25 was the feast of the conversion of St. Paul. Initially, the underlying assumption of the Church Unity Octave was that Anglicans, Old Catholics, Protestants, and Orthodox would be united with the Roman Catholic Church. Following the reception of Fr. Paul Watson into the Roman Catholic Church, Pope Pius X gave his blessing to the Octave.[44] The Church Unity Octave gained support among Roman Catholics who, at that time, generally saw reunion in terms of the return of Orthodox, Anglicans, Old Catholics, and Protestants to Rome. Anglicans, Protestants, and Orthodox, however, could not accept this doctrinal presupposition.

The perspective on church unity, which was basic to the Church Unity Octave, was dramatically altered through the untiring work of another Roman Catholic priest, Abbé Paul Couturier (1881–1953) of Lyon, France.[45] Initially, he introduced a three-day period of prayer for unity in the region of Lyon in 1933. With the success of this practice in mind, Abbé Paul turned his attention to creating an octave of prayer that would be more congenial to Anglicans, Old Catholics, Orthodox, and Protestants. With the encouragement of the archbishop of Lyons and as a result of contacts with Orthodox theologians, he refashioned the basis of the octave. He began to refer to it as a Universal Week of Prayer for Unity. No longer would it be based upon the idea of the return of other Christians to the Roman Catholic Church. Rather, Abbé Paul stressed prayer for unity on the basis that "Our Lord would grant to His Church on earth that peace and unity which were in His mind and purpose when, on the eve of His Passion, He prayed that all might be one."[46] Abbé Paul realized that common prayer for unity was essential to the restoration of the unity of the churches.

The new basis for the Universal Week of Prayer proved to be a great success. On this basis, Anglicans, Old Catholics, Orthodox, and Protestants could join with Roman Catholics in a prayer for unity that was not bound to a particular view of unity but open to the movements of God. The dates of January 18 through 25 remained the time of the Week of Prayer, but there was a better basis for broader participation.

Abbé Paul's approach to church unity also was expressed in theological conferences that he organized at the Monastery of La Trappe des Dombes near Lyons as well as through his yearly Calls to Prayer, which were issued until his death in 1953. His emphasis upon the importance of prayer for Christian unity also contributed to the establishment of the Community of Taizé, founded in 1940. Speaking of the importance of the prayer for unity, Abbé Paul said: "If we were to examine every single difficulty which must be overcome so that progress towards Christian Unity may be made, we should always come to the same conclusion: The problem of Christian Unity is for everyone a problem of the orientation of the inner life, for unless it is orientated, even in secret, towards Christian Unity, how can Christians face this burning question? Unless it succeeds in gripping, even torturing the Christian conscience, what hope is there for resolution?"[47]

The Faith and Order Movement and the Life and Work Movement also formally provided opportunities for prayer for unity as part of their planning and their conferences. The Faith and Order planning meeting of 1920 in Geneva resolved to appeal for a Week of Prayer for the Unity of the Church, which led up to the Feast of Pentecost. As a result of this initiative, Faith and Order took the responsibility to issue Suggestions for an Octave of Prayer for Christian Unity each year until 1941. At that time, the Faith and Order organizers decided to adopt the dates of the January Week of Prayer tradition.[48]

The Faith and Order Conferences, in Lausanne in 1927 and Edinburgh in 1937, and the Life and Work Conference, in Stockholm in 1925 and Oxford in 1937, provided important opportunities for the delegates to come together for common prayer. These conferences began and concluded with formal services of worship that brought together Anglicans, Protestants, and Orthodox. The fact that the participants could not join in the common celebration of the Eucharist was a powerful sign of the real divisions among the churches. Nonetheless, the services of prayer were also a sign of the new relationship that was developing among the churches and their members.

TAIZÉ

Brother Roger Schuz (1915–), then a 25-year-old pastor in the Swiss Reformed Church, established a very important ecumenical community of prayer and hospitality in 1940 in Taizé, Burgundy, France.[49] During a long battle with tuberculosis, Brother Roger envisioned the creation of a new monastic community that would be rooted in regular prayer, characterized by simplicity and committed to the unity of the churches. Finding an abandoned farmhouse not far from the old and historic monastic center of Cluny, Brother Roger began his community as the Second World War was beginning. The village of Taizé was close to the demarcation line that divided France in half, and the house became a place of hospitality for refugees fleeing the war. Among them were many Jews who were fleeing Nazi persecution. Brother Roger responded to the immediate need to offer aid to all people, as his grandmother had done during the First World War. The house had to be abandoned briefly between 1941 and 1943 because of threats. However, the small community of brothers was reestablished there in 1944. In the next few years, Taizé welcomed orphans and former prisoners of war.

Brother Roger viewed the community as a place that would be a parable of communion among divided Christians. This unique monastic community became a center where Protestants, Catholics, and Orthodox monks could come together in prayer, reflection, and service. Since that time, Taizé has become a place of pilgrimage and common prayer for countless thousands of Christians from various traditions. The worship services of Taizé, which have been open to Christians of all churches, have become a very important expression of the importance of prayer in the quest for Christian unity.

Speaking about the relationship of prayer and reconciliation, Brother Roger says:

After a long separation, we are convinced that God is visiting us at this time and pouring out on us his gifts. He is asking us more than ever to keep ourselves in his presence, to give him thanks for his "today" and to refuse henceforth to look back on the history of our divisions.

Keeping ourselves in God's presence means letting God penetrate us without our knowing it; it means to agree to his changing our own viewpoints little by little, and giving us the same viewpoint as Christ from which to look at our separated brother, and even at the brother who belongs to the same confession as ourselves.[50]

CONCLUSIONS

The first four decades of the twentieth century witnessed some profound developments in the quest for Christian reconciliation and the restoration of the unity of the churches. These developments marked a bold assault on historic Christian divisions and the isolation of the churches. First, there was a recognition that the doctrinal issues, which divided the churches for centuries, had to be seriously examined with a new spirit and with a new commitment to resolve the wounds of the past. The doctrinal differences were real and could not be ignored. These divisions manifest themselves in sharp differences in worship, church organization, ministry, and worship. The doctrinal differences were obvious both to believers and nonbelievers. Clearly, the emphasis of the Faith and Order Movement reflected these concerns. These concerns were manifest at the Conferences of 1927 and 1937.

Second, there was recognition that the churches had an obligation to come together, even in spite of their divisions, to provide a Christian witness in the society. The tragedy of the First World War and its aftermath haunted many Church leaders, clergy, and laity. Likewise, the vicious expressions of Communism in Russia and the rise of National Socialism in Germany challenged the churches and their leaders to affirm together the dignity and value of human life. Many saw a connection between Christian divisions and the brokenness within the society. The emphasis of the Life and Work Movement was upon the duty of the churches to work together to address the critical challenges facing the nations and the society. The Stockholm Conference of 1925 spoke of applying the gospel to all aspects of life. The Oxford Conference of 1937 boldly spoke of the needs of the underprivileged and persecuted as well as the evils of racial discrimination and anti-Semitism.

Finally, there was the recognition that the churches and their members had the obligation to pray for reconciliation and unity. The reconciliation of Christians and the unity of the churches would result not simply from theological reflection and common witness but also from common prayer. Prayer for unity was an essential thread that had to link every aspect of the ecumenical movement. Indeed, the fact that Protestants, Anglicans, Old Catholics, and Orthodox believers could pray together during the course of the early Faith and Order and Life and Work Conferences was truly significant. In both of these movements, there was constant reference to the importance of prayer for unity and for the creation of opportunities when the representatives of the divided churches could pray together. The establishment of Week of Prayer for Christian Unity and its subsequent recognition by the Anglican, Old Catholic, Protestant, Orthodox, and Roman Catholic churches cannot be underestimated. It was a bold expression of the importance of Christians from divided churches coming together to pray for reconciliation and unity.

These three characteristics of the early movement reflected a number of important common features that deeply related them to each other. Most importantly, at the heart of each was an affirmation of the centrality of Jesus Christ and his gospel. The participants in these movements were unyielding in their devotion to Christ and they were not afraid to boldly proclaim the importance of his coming both for the Church and for the world. Christ was at the heart, not only of the prayers for unity, but also of the work of Faith and Order and Life and Work. Indeed, the documents of the early conferences frequently affirmed a profound unity in Christ and his Church, which existed, they claimed, in spite of historic divisions.

Closely related to this is the emphasis one finds on the importance of the Church. In each of the movements, there is the explicit concern for restoring the unity of the churches. This was expressed in the prayers for unity. It was expressed in the work of Faith and Order. It was expressed in the work of Life and Work. This, of course, did not diminish the importance of personal encounters and contacts that transcended ecclesiastical divisions. Yet, in sharp contrast to some of the organizations of the nineteenth century, there was a firm recognition of the relationship of believers to the historic churches. The mission and witness as well as the divisions of the churches were not to be ignored. Indeed, the participants in the early conferences were for the most part official representatives of their churches. When they gathered for prayer for unity, they often met within church buildings of a particular tradition. When they met for discussion, they linked the important activities of Faith and Order and Life and Work to the churches.

One cannot overlook the fact that these early endeavors were guided by persons of deep Christian conviction who came together as representatives of their churches. Together, they shared a common commitment to Jesus Christ and to the process of unity in all its dimensions. Many of these pioneers were active in various aspects of the early ecumenical movement. For example, John Mott, a Methodist layman, was active in the YMCA, the Student Christian Movement, and Life and Work. J. H. Oldham, a Baptist layman, was involved in the International Missionary

Council and Life and Work. The Orthodox Metropolitan Germanos Strenopoulos, the Swedish Lutheran Archbishop Nathan Söderblom, the Anglican missionary Bishop Charles Brent, and Anglican Archbishop William Temple were active both in Life and Work and Faith and Order Movements. These persons also contributed to the early discussions leading to the establishment of the World Council of Churches. Willem Visser 't Hooft, a member of the Dutch Reformed Church, who had been active in the YMCA and the Student Christian Federation, became the council's first General Secretary in 1948. These names reflect the depth and breath of the early ecumenical movement.

NOTES

1. Lucas Vischer, ed., "Final Report, Second World Conference on Faith and Order," *A Documentary History of the Faith and Order Movement* (St. Louis: The Bethany Press, 1963), p. 73.

2. Kenneth Scott Latourette, "Ecumenical Bearings of the Missionary Movement and the International Missionary Council," in *A History of the Ecumenical Movement, 1517–1948,* Ruth Rouse and Stephen Charles Neill (Philadelphia: The Westminster Press, 1967), pp. 355–62.

3. "Patriarchal and Synodical Encyclical of 1920," in *Orthodox Visions of Ecumenism,* ed. Gennadios Limouris (Geneva: WCC Publications, 1994), p. 3.

4. Thomas FitzGerald, *The Ecumenical Patriarchate and Christian Unity* (Brookline, Mass.: Holy Cross Orthodox Press, 1997), pp. 6–7.

5. See A. Zabriskie, *Bishop Brent, Crusader for Christian Unity* (Philadelphia: The Westminster Press, 1948).

6. Cited in Tissington Tatlow, "The World Conference on Faith and Order," in *A History of the Ecumenical Movement, 1517–1948,* Rouse and Neill, p. 407.

7. Ibid., p. 408.

8. "Report of the Committee, April 20, 1911," *Faith and Order Pamphlet,* no. 1, 1911 (Geneva: World Council of Churches, 1963), p. 1.

9. *Faith and Order Pamphlet,* no. 30 (Geneva: World Council of Churches, 1963), p. 12.

10. *Faith and Order Pamphlet,* no. 24 (Geneva: World Council of Churches, 1963), p. 46.

11. Cited in Tissington Tatlow, "The World Conference on Faith and Order," p. 416.

12. Ibid., pp. 420–21.

13. "Final Report, First World Conference on Faith and Order," in *A Documentary History of the Faith and Order Movement*, ed. Vischer, p. 28.

14. Tissington Tatlow, "The World Conference on Faith and Order," p. 431.

15. Ibid., p. 432.

16. Ibid., p. 433.

17. Ibid., p. 434.

18. Leonard Hodgson, ed., *The Second World Conference on Faith and Order* (London: SCM, 1938) p. 275. See Tissington Tatlow, "The World Conference on Faith and Order," p. 434.

19. Nils Karlström, "Movements for International Friendship and Life and Work, 1910–1925," in *A History of the Ecumenical Movement, 1517–1948,* Rouse and Neill, p. 513.
20. Ibid., p. 513.
21. Ibid., p. 530.
22. Ibid., p. 534.
23. Ibid., p. 535.
24. Ibid., p. 538.
25. Ibid., p. 542.
26. Nils Ehrenström, "Movements for International Friendship and Life and Work, 1925–1948," in *A History of the Ecumenical Movement, 1517–1948,* Rouse and Neill, p. 545.
27. Karlström, "Movements for International Friendship and Life and Work, 1910–1925," in *A History of the Ecumenical Movement, 1517–1948,* Rouse and Neill, p. 541.
28. Ehrenström, p. 547.
29. G.K.A. Bell, ed., *The Stockholm Conference, 1925: Official Report* (London: Oxford University Press, 1926), p. 710. See also Ehrenström, "Movements for International Friendship and Life and Work, 1925–1948," in *A History of the Ecumenical Movement, 1517–1948,* Rouse and Neill, p. 548.
30. Ehrenström, p. 588.
31. Ibid.
32. Paul Albrecht, "Life and Work," in *Dictionary of the Ecumenical Movement,* ed. Nicholas Lossky et al. (Geneva: WCC Publications, 1991), p. 612.
33. Cited in W.A. Visser 't Hooft, *The Genesis and Formation of the World Council of Churches* (Geneva: World Council of Churches, 1987), p. 22.
34. Ehrenström, p. 589.
35. Visser 't Hooft, *The Genesis and Formation of the World Council of Churches,* pp. 43–51.
36. J.H. Oldham, ed., *The Oxford Conference: Official Report* (Chicago: Willet, Clark, 1937), pp. 55–63.
37. Ruth Rouse, "Voluntary Movements and the Changing Ecumenical Climate," in *A History of the Ecumenical Movement, 1517–1948,* Rouse and Neill, p. 347.
38. Gaius Jackson Slosser, *Christian Unity,* pp. 213–16; H.R.T. Brandreth, *Dr. Lee of Lambeth* (London: SPCK, 1951), pp. 76–117.
39. Rouse, "Voluntary Movements and the Changing Ecumenical Climate," p. 347.
40. Ibid.
41. *The Five Lambeth Conferences* (London, 1920), pp. 53, 86, 205.
42. Rouse, "Voluntary Movements and the Changing Ecumenical Climate," p. 340.
43. Charles Angel and Charles LaFontaine, *Prophet of Reunion: The Life of Fr. Paul of Graymore* (New York: The Seabury Press, 1975), pp. 84–85.
44. Ibid., p. 177.
45. See G. Curtis, *Paul Couturier and Unity in Christ* (London: SCM Press, 1964); M. Villain, *The Life and Work of Abbe Paul Couturier* (Hayward Heath: Holy Cross Convent, 1959).

46. Cited in Rouse, "Voluntary Movements and the Changing Ecumenical Climate," p. 348.

47. Curtis, *Paul Couturier and Unity in Christ*, p. 351.

48. A common text for the Week of Prayer was prepared yearly between 1957 and 1965 by the Faith and Order Commission and the Roman Catholic center *Unite Cretienne* in Lyons. Since 1966, The Pontifical Council for Christian Unity has joined with Faith and Order in preparing the common text. This means that the text is jointly prepared by representatives of Orthodox, Catholic, Anglican, and Protestant churches.

49. J. L. Balado, *The Story of Taizé* (London: Mowbray, 1988); K. Spink, *A Universal Heart* (London: SPCK, 1986).

50. Roger Schutz, *Unity: Man's Tomorrow* (London: Faith Press, 1962), pp. 87–88.

CHAPTER 6

The Founding and Development of the World Council of Churches

> The World Council of Churches began its journey in faith with the determination to stay together. We experienced this same determination at Harare, even when we were aware of the difficulties that we faced. As churches long committed to staying together, we now commit ourselves to being together in a continuing growth towards visible unity—not only in assemblies and ecumenical gatherings but each in every place.
>
> —WCC Harare Assembly, 1998[1]

INTRODUCTION

Throughout the first few decades of the twentieth century there were a number of associations and organizations that were bringing together Christians of various traditions for particular activities or concerns. Among these were local Church Councils, the YMCA, the YWCA, the World Student Christian Movement, the World Missionary Council, the World Council of Christian Education, and the World Alliance for Friendship through the Churches. Concern for prayer for reconciliation and unity was expressed through gatherings associated with the World Day of Prayer and the Week of Prayer for Christian Unity. In addition to these, there were the conferences and meetings associated with the Faith and Order Movement and the Life and Work Movement. These two movements were for the most part closely related and linked in a more formal manner with the churches.

All of these organizations and activities contained some strands of the early ecumenical movement. There was truly a remarkable "variety of ecumenical experiences"[2] both at the local, regional, and international levels. Yet there was a growing sense that many of these activities and concerns needed greater coordination. The duplication of efforts could be avoided so that limited resources could be better utilized.

At the same time, there was a growing recognition that the churches had to be brought more fully into the heart of the concerns for reconciliation and unity. It was certainly necessary that individual Christians from different churches and cultures meet one another, cooperate, and pray together. However, this was not sufficient if the real tragedy of the disunity of the churches was to be addressed. The churches themselves, in a more formal manner, had to become committed to the quest for reconciliation and unity both in word and in deed. These concerns were at the heart of the move to establish the World Council of Churches.

THE PATRIARCHAL ENCYCLICAL OF 1920

Following the tragedy of the First World War, there were some significant signs that the major churches and church leaders were beginning to address in a new manner the difficulties of Christian disunity as well as the need to change attitudes and to seek reconciliation. The bilateral theological dialogues and opportunities for prayer that developed during the late nineteenth century led to the involvement of Anglican, Orthodox, Old Catholic, and Protestant churches in the Faith and Order and Life and Work movements of the early twentieth century.

As early as 1919, the Orthodox Church of Constantinople, known as the Ecumenical Patriarchate, formally began a study of the possibility of proposing the establishment of a League of Churches that would bring them together for discussion and common witness. The clear intention of this discussion was to fashion a proposal for a body that would contribute to the unity of the churches. Even before the First World War, the patriarchate in 1902 had been in contact with other Orthodox Churches regarding the issue of dialogue among the various Christian churches. This had produced a number of favorable responses. The discussions of 1919, therefore, were part of an ongoing concern over issues of Christian reconciliation and unity that were being discussed in Constantinople for nearly 20 years.[3]

One of the most forceful proponents of greater contacts was Metropolitan Germanos Strenopoulos (1872–1951) of Seleukia, the dean of the famous Orthodox Theological School of Halki. Having studied in Leipzig, Strasburg, and Lausanne, Metropolitan Germanos had come to know well the theological perspectives of the Christian West. Moreover, in the year 1911 at the Conference of the World Student Christian Federation, Germanos had come to know a number of notable Christian leaders from Europe and America. Among these were John Mott and Nathan Söderblom, who would also become leaders in the early ecumenical movement.[4]

The discussions within the patriarchate led to the publication in January 1920 of an unparalleled encyclical addressed "Unto all the Churches of Christ Everywhere."[5] The letter is the first formal statement of the twentieth century to be addressed from a church to other churches of different Christian traditions that raises the issue of reconciliation and unity.[6] The encyclical sent greetings to all the churches and invited them to consider seriously the formation of a Fellowship (koinonia) of Churches. In addition, the encyclical boldly declared:

> Our own church holds that rapprochement between the various Christian Churches and fellowship between them is not excluded by the doctrinal differences which exist between them. In our opinion such a rapprochement is highly desirable and necessary. It would be useful in many ways for the real interest of each particular church and of the whole Christian body, and also for the preparation and advancement of that blessed union which will be completed in the future in accordance with the will of God. We therefore consider that the present time is most favorable for bringing this important question and studying it together.[7]

The patriarchal encyclical says that there are two presuppositions to the establishment of a Fellowship of Churches. First, the patriarchate says that it considers "as necessary and indispensable the removal and abolition of all the mutual mistrust and bitterness between the different churches, which arise from the tendency of some of them to entice and proselytize adherents of other confessions. For nobody ignores what is unfortunately happening today in many places, disturbing the internal peace of the churches, especially in the East." And second, the patriarchate says that "above all love should be rekindled and strengthened among the churches, so that they should no more consider one another as strangers and foreigners, but as relatives, and as being a part of the household of Christ and 'fellow heirs, members of the same body and partakers of the promise of God in Christ' (Eph. 3. 6)."[8]

In addition to proposing the establishment of a Fellowship of Churches, the document made a number of practical recommendations for dialogue and cooperation that were remarkable for the time. The encyclical advocated both theological reflection on doctrinal differences and cooperation in the areas of religious relief and charity. The entire text of the encyclical was anticipatory of both the Faith and Order Movement and the Life and Work Movement as well as the World Council of Churches.

The proposal of the patriarchate for the creation of a Fellowship of Churches was bold and farsighted. In addition to this, the recommendations of the patriarchate were remarkable. They set out some very practical ways that the churches could come out of their isolation, overcome misunderstandings, and work together for reconciliation and common witness. In one form or another, the Life and Work Movement immediately took up these proposals by the Faith and Order Movement. Eventually, these recommendations served as a valuable indication of many of the tasks that would become part of the mission of the World Council of Churches when it was founded in 1948.

COMPLEMENTARY PROPOSALS: THREE VISIONARIES

The proposal of Constantinople was unique because it came in a formal manner from a church. Indeed, the proposal originated from the senior patriarchate of Orthodox Christianity. During the same time, there were a number of Anglican and Protestant church leaders who also made similar proposals to establish some form of global council that would bring together representatives of the churches for the sake of reconciliation and unity.

Archbishop Nathan Söderblom (1866–1931) of the Lutheran Church of Sweden, in September 1919, had also raised the possibility of organizing a global, ecumenical Council of Churches.[9] This proposal was a reflection of his strong desire to bring the Christian churches closer together in the period following the First World War. Söderblom was not content simply to bring together Protestant churches. He envisioned an organization that would bring together official representatives of all the churches: Orthodox, Roman Catholic, Anglican, and Protestant. As we have already noted, Söderblom's proposal led initially to the establishment of the Life and Work Conferences.[10]

In subsequent years, J.H. Oldham (1874–1969) also made a strong contribution to the plan. This distinguished Baptist layman from England had been very active in the work of the International Missionary Council and in the Life and Work Movement.[11] As a result of his early ecumenical work, Oldham also came to recognize the importance of establishing a global body, which would be rooted in the churches and would also bring together the various elements of the developing ecumenical movement. Oldham envisioned a body that would be an instrument of the churches. As W.A. Visser 't Hooft says, Oldham "believed that there had been a constitutional ambiguity in Life and Work because its members included not only leading churchmen, appointed by their churches, but also persons who had not been so appointed and who had no voice in the churches' controlling organs."[12] Oldham also envisioned a global ecumenical organization that would involve key laypersons. While he saw the future body as connected to the churches, he also recognized that its mission required the involvement and support of the laity. Finally, Oldham recognized that the future body had to give much room to serious theological reflection. He had emphasized the importance of theological reflection in the preparation for the Oxford Life and Work Conference in 1937.[13] This concern was carried over to his view of a global body that would bring together representatives of the churches.

The views of Archbishop William Temple (1881–1944) of England also had a profound impact on the movement to establish an organization to serve the churches in their ecumenical activities.[14] As a result of his own involvement in a number of early ecumenical organizations, Temple had also come to see the importance of council related directly to the churches. He was also aware of the encyclical of Constantinople as well as the advocacy of his colleagues Nathan Söderblom and J. H. Oldham. During a meeting with American church leaders at Princeton in 1935, Temple clearly articulated his vision. He called for "an interdenominational, international council representing all the churches with committees to carry on various projects now forming the objectives of distinct world movements."[15]

THE CONFERENCES OF FAITH AND ORDER AND LIFE AND WORK

The Conferences of Faith and Order and Life and Work were scheduled to meet during the summer of 1937. Prior to these conferences, key representatives of the two movements met in London during July 8–10, 1937. Among these were Orthodox Metropolitan Germanos, J. H. Oldham, William Temple, and W. A. Visser 't Hooft (1900–1985). Based upon prior proposals and discussions, the 35 members decided to bring the two movements together and to set up a fully representative assembly of the churches. They said:

> The new organization which is proposed shall have no power to legislate for the churches or to commit them to action without their consent; but if it is to be effective, it must deserve and win the respect of the churches in such measure that the people of greatest influence in the life of the churches may be willing to give time and thought to its work. Further, the witness which the Church in the modern world is called to give is such that in certain spheres the predominant voice in the utterance of it must be that of lay people holding posts of responsibility and influence in the secular world. For both these reasons, a first-class intelligence staff is indispensable in order that material for discussion and action may be adequately prepared.[16]

Based upon the recommendation of Samuel McCrea Cavert from the United States, the participants decided to propose that the new organization be named the World Council of Churches.[17]

The Life and Work Conference at Oxford and the Faith and Order Conference at Edinburgh in 1937 accepted the proposal for the establishment of the World Council of Churches. Each body appointed seven members to a committee that would discuss the basis and structure of the new council.

Not all of the ecumenical bodies agreed to be part of the plans for the World Council. The leaders of the World Alliance for International Friendship through the churches formally decided in 1938 to maintain their independence and not become associated with the proposed council.[18] They desired "the maintenance of the World Alliance as a movement based upon individual loyalty, with no official relationship to any religious organization."[19] Likewise, the International Missionary Council decided in 1938 to continue at that time as a separate organization, which would cooperate with the proposed World Council.[20] In both cases, there was a fear that the particular mission of each organization would somehow be minimized within the World Council. At the same time, there appeared to be reluctance in both organizations to become associated directly with a council that would be the creation of the churches.

The Organizational Committee of Fourteen met in Utrecht in May 1938. There, a Provisional Committee responsible for establishing the WCC in process of formation was established. Archbishop William Temple was named the chairman, and W. A. Visser 't Hooft was selected as the general secretary. The immediate tasks of the Provisional Committee was to establish a firm foundation for the council by resolving questions concerning its basis, membership structure, and authority. Each of these issues presented particular challenges. Perhaps most important was the question of the basis for the council. After much discussion, it was felt that the council had to have a basis for the membership of the churches. Favoring an emphasis from the Faith and Order tradition, the committee stated that: "The World Council of Churches is a fellowship of Churches, which accept Our Lord Jesus Christ as God and Saviour."[21]

Speaking about the council and its basis, Archbishop Temple said: "It stands on faith in our Lord Jesus Christ as God and Saviour. As its brevity shows, the basis is an affirmation of the Christian faith of the participating churches, and not a creedal test to judge churches or persons. It is an affirmation of the incarnation and Atonement." He then noted that the "Council desires to be a fellowship of those churches, which accept these truths. But it does not concern itself with the manner in which the churches interpret them. It will therefore be the responsibility of each particular church to decide whether it can collaborate on this basis."[22]

Having struggled with a number of key constitutional questions, the committee sent out formal invitations to 196 churches during October and November 1938. A number of prominent church leaders and theologians of the time representing Anglican, Orthodox Reformed, Lutheran, Methodist, and Baptist churches around the world signed the letter. Among them were: Archbishop William Temple, Archbishop Germanos Strenopoulos, Marc Boegner, Bishop George Bell, William Adams Brown, John Mott, Georges Florovsky, and M. E. Aubrey.[23] A portion of the letter of invitation says, "the very nature of the Church demands that it shall make manifest to the world the unity in Christ of all who believe in him. The full unity of the Church is something for which we must work and pray. But there exists a unity of allegiance to our Lord for the manifestation of which we are responsible. We may not pretend that the existing unity among Christians is greater than in fact it is; but we should act upon it in so far as it is already a reality."[24]

The committee was also concerned about the position of the Roman Catholic Church. Already, the Roman Catholic Church had declined earlier invitations to conferences of both Faith and Order and Life and Work. Indeed, some Protestants were opposed to the involvement of the Roman Catholic Church in these early ecumenical efforts. Yet there were many Anglicans, Protestants, and Orthodox who believed that the door should not be closed to possible Roman Catholic involvement in the council. With this in mind, Archbishop Temple wrote a personal letter to the Vatican Secretary of State regarding the plans for the council. While the Roman Catholic Church indicated that it would not participate, there were also signs that it was open to confidential consultation and to the exchange of viewpoints.[25]

As early as 1939, the Provisional Committee proposed that the first general assembly of the council be held in August 1941. Yet the much-feared World War intervened. Between 1940 and 1946, the Provisional Committee could not function fully. A number of its leaders, however, had the opportunity to meet in the United States, England, and Switzerland. Under the leadership of the council's new general secretary W. A. Visser 't Hooft in Geneva, activities of the proposed council already began. These included interchurch aid, chaplaincy services, the pastoral care of prisoners of war, the assistance to Jews and other refugees, and the exchange of information among the churches. When the war concluded, the Provisional Committee finally met in 1946 in Geneva and in 1947 in Buck Hills, Pennsylvania. Many of these leaders had experienced first hand the tragedy of the war, and this only increased their commitment to the establishment of the council. By the year 1948, 90 churches throughout the world had accepted the invitation to join the council.[26]

THE AMSTERDAM ASSEMBLY OF 1948

The First Assembly of the World Council of Churches was held in Amsterdam on August 22 through September 4. Following the tragedy of the Second World War, the theme of the assembly was Man's Disorder and God's Designs.[27] In modern church history, this was an unprecedented event. The assembly brought together representatives from 147 churches in 44 countries. These included delegates from Orthodox, Anglican, and most traditions of Protestantism. The assembly was truly a meeting of church representatives and it marked an important stage in directly involving the churches in the fledging ecumenical movement. In bringing together representatives of both the Faith and Order tradition and the Life and Work tradition, the assembly pointed to the importance of integration of ecumenical activities in the quest for Christian reconciliation and unity. From then on, the World Council was seen as the organization through which both the agenda of Faith and Order and the agenda of Life and Work would be supported and brought together.

The participants engaged in a number of theological discussions related to the general theme of the assembly and its subthemes. Significant addresses were made by such distinguished theologians as Karl Barth, C.H. Dodd, and Georges Florovsky. These speakers reflected both upon the theme of the assembly as well as the significance of the World Council.

Much of the work of the assembly, however, was devoted to formalizing the basis, constitution, and structure of the World Council. The Amsterdam Assembly established 12 departments under the guidance of the general secretariat at the Geneva, Switzerland, headquarters. These were: Faith and Order, Study, Evangelism, Laity, Youth, Women, Inter-church Aid and Refugees, International Affairs, the Ecumenical Institute, Publications, Library, and Finance. There was a clear recognition that the World Council was something of a work in progress and that the first assembly alone could not be expected to resolve immediately all the questions related to the significance of the council, its relationship to the churches, and its relationship to preexisting ecumenical traditions and organizations.[28]

A portion of the historic statement from the Amsterdam Assembly says:

> We bless God our Father and our Lord Jesus Christ, who gathers together in one the children of God that are scattered abroad. He has brought us here to Amsterdam. We are one in acknowledging Him as God and Saviour. We are divided from one another not only in matters of faith, order and tradition, but also by pride of nation, class and race. But Christ has made us his own, and He is not divided. In seeking Him we find one another. Here at Amsterdam we have committed ourselves afresh to Him, and have covenanted with one another in constituting the World Council of Churches. We intend to stay together. We call upon Christian congregations everywhere to endorse and fulfill this covenant in their relations one with another. In thankfulness to God we commit the future to Him.[29]

Two years after Amsterdam, the Central Committee of the council had a significant meeting in Toronto in 1950. Its fundamental purpose was to clarify the meaning of church membership in the World Council. On behalf of the council, the Central Committee approved an historic statement on "The Church, the Churches and the World Council of Churches." The text came to be known as the Toronto Statement.

According to the Toronto Statement, the council "is not and must never become a super-church." The council "does not negotiate union between churches" and it "cannot and should not be based on any one particular conception of the church." Membership in the council does not "imply that a church treats its own conception of the church as merely relative" or accepts a "specific doctrine concerning the nature of church unity." Yet the common witness of the member churches "must be based on the common recognition that Christ is the divine head of the body," which, "on the basis of the New Testament," is the one Church of Christ. Membership of the Church of Christ "is more inclusive" than the membership in one's own church, but membership of the World Council "does not imply that each church must regard the other member churches as churches in the true and full sense of the word." Membership in the council implies in practice that the churches "should recognize their solidarity with each other, render assistance to each other in case of need, and refrain from such actions as are incompatible with brotherly relationships."[30]

The Toronto Statement sought to strike a balance between the centrality of the member churches and the significance of their participation in the council. At the same time, it recognized that the member churches had different ecclesiologies and views of the others. The underlying tensions of the Toronto Statement have been with the council since its beginning. It stands in opposition, however, to those who would view the council as an expression of an already united Church. From the beginning, the Orthodox Churches, for example, have refused to accept the denominational model, which says that the one Church is comprised of many denominations, each with their own organization and beliefs and each present at the council.

Two years later, the Faith and Order Commission meeting in Lund, Sweden, in 1952 issued a significant statement that emphasized the importance of the churches in cooperating where possible, even in the face of other divisive issues. In a sense, the Lund Statement complements the Toronto Statement. A portion of the Lund Statement says:

> The measure of unity which has been given to the churches to experience together must now find clear manifestation. A faith in the one Church of Christ which is not implemented by acts of obedience is dead. There are truths about the nature of God and His Church which will remain forever closed to us unless we act together in obedience to the unity which is already ours. We would, therefore, earnestly request our Churches to consider whether they are doing all they ought to do to manifest the oneness of the People of God. Should not our Churches ask themselves whether they are showing sufficient eagerness to enter into conversations with other Churches, and whether they should not act together in all matters except those in which deep differences of conviction compel them to act separately? Should they not acknowledge the fact that they often allow themselves to be separated from each other by secular forces and influences instead of witnessing together to the sole Lordship of Christ who gathers his people out of all nations, races and tongues?[31]

The Lund Principle became an immediate challenge to the churches that were involved in the ecumenical movement. It was not sufficient for the churches to meet and simply compare their viewpoints. Lund indicated that simple encounter was not sufficient to regain unity. The churches had to enter into a true dialogue that sought to transcend old differences. Moreover, the churches had to actively relate to and cooperate with one another whenever possible.

THE EVANSTON ASSEMBLY OF 1954

The Second Assembly of the council met in Evanston, near Chicago, Illinois, and served to more closely link the council with developing ecumenical work in the United States. The gathering met from August 15 to August 31, 1954, and had 502 delegates from 161 member churches. The theme of the assembly was "Christ—The Hope of the World."[32]

Against the background of the cold war and the concern of racism, the assembly struggled with the theme of Christian hope. Among many of the European Protestants, the emphasis was upon the theme of the future Kingdom of God. Many American Protestants, however, rooted in the Social Gospel tradition, stressed the importance of the present actions of Christians in society. This provided the context for discussions on Christian disunity, the mission of the Church, the responsible society, world community, racial and ethnic tensions, the laity, and the Christian vocation. The harsh distinctions, rooted in Western Christianity and expressed in these discussions, however, were generally alien to Orthodox participants and their theological perspectives. Indeed, the nature of the theological discussions placed the Orthodox delegates in a very difficult position, for they were not sympathetic to the various Protestant perspectives. Because of this, the Orthodox delegates produced two separate statements that spoke of their understanding of the main theme "Christ, the Hope of the World" and of the Assembly Report dealing with "The Division of the Christian Churches."[33] Both of these statements indicated that the Orthodox could not accept the view of the church as comprised of a number of denominations with their own perspectives and teachings.

THE NEW DELHI ASSEMBLY OF 1961

The assembly in New Delhi, India, held from November 19 to December 5, 1961, expressed boldly the fact that neither the churches not the council should be identified with either European or American churches and their perspectives. The gathering brought together 577 delegates from 197 member churches. At the assembly, the council received into the membership the sizeable Orthodox Churches of Russia, Romania, Bulgaria, and Poland. These were added to the other Autocephalous Orthodox Churches, which had been a part of the council from the beginning. At the same assembly, 20 additional Protestant churches also joined. Many of these were from Asia and Africa.[34]

The theme of New Delhi was "Jesus Christ—The Light of the World." This theme was the basis for discussions of three subthemes, which were: Witness, Service, and Unity. With this in mind, the participants examined the theological challenge of non-Christian religions, political and social change especially in the Third World, and the meaning of church unity.

The assembly approved the integration of the International Missionary Council (IMC) into the council and it became the Division of World Missions and Evangelism. The IMC had cooperated with the WCC since its establishment in 1948.[35]

The assembly also approved an important change in the basis of the council that clearly emphasized the Trinitarian character of membership. In meetings before New Delhi, many churches expressed the opinion that the basis provided by Amsterdam was not sufficient since it did not have an explicit expression of the faith in the Trinity and a specific reference to the Scriptures. The result was the reformulation that still stands: It says, "The World Council of Churches is a fellowship of churches which confess the Lord Jesus Christ as God and Saviour according to the scriptures, and therefore seek to fulfill together their common calling to the glory of the one God, Father, Son and Holy Spirit."[36]

The revised basis was significant. It was not an attempt to make a new confession of faith. Rather, it was an attempt to state more clearly the essential faith affirmations of those churches that were part of the council. The clear reference to the Trinity was a means of expressing the essential faith conviction of the member churches.

The New Delhi Assembly also approved an important statement on the meaning of church unity. The statement reflects ongoing discussions, especially in the area of Faith and Order, about the characteristics of ecclesial unity toward which the member churches were striving. The statement is important because it marks an important attempt to identify those issues that are essential to reconciliation and, therefore, those issues that require further study by the churches. A portion of the statement says:

> We believe that the unity which is both God's will and his gift to his Church is being made visible as all in each place who are baptized into Jesus Christ and confess him as Lord and Saviour are brought by the Holy Spirit into one fully committed fellowship, holding the one apostolic faith, preaching the one Gospel, breaking the one bread, joining in common prayer, and having a corporate life reaching out in witness and fellowship in all places and all ages in such wise that ministry and members are accepted by all, and that all can act and speak together as occasion requires for the tasks to which God calls his people.[37]

THE UPPSALA ASSEMBLY OF 1968

The Fourth Assembly was held in Uppsala, Sweden, from July 4 through July 20, 1968, with the theme "Behold, I Make All Things New."

There were 704 delegates from 235 member churches. The participants discussed the theme in relation to a number of diverse topics: the Holy Spirit and the Catholicity of the Church, renewal in mission, world economic and social development, justice and peace in international affairs, worship, and new styles of living.[38]

Following the Second Vatican Council (1963–65) and the remarkable ecumenical developments in the Roman Catholic Church, there were those who believed that the Uppsala Assembly could forge a new relationship with Rome. For the first time, the Roman Catholic Church sent 15 official observers to the assembly. In an address to the assembly, the Roman Catholic theologian Roberto Tucci referred to the possibility of the Roman Catholic Church joining the WCC in the future. This opened the door for further discussions in coming years about degrees of cooperation. The Vatican and the WCC established a Joint Working Group in 1965. At the same time, official Roman Catholic delegates began to participate in the work of the Faith and Order Commission and in other selected activities of the council. Yet the other developments in the council from Uppsala onward appear to have prevented a deeper relationship.

Many observers have noted that the Uppsala Assembly of 1968 was distinct from previous ones. The discussions and statements reflected the world issues of the war in South East Asia, racism, poverty, and the youth revolution. The Uppsala Assembly also came to be identified with radical changes in the internal life of the WCC and in its institutional concerns. Racism, economics, and social justice issues were major items discussed at the assembly. The opening sermon at the assembly was to be delivered by Dr. Martin Luther King, Jr. The great minister and civil rights leader, however, had been assassinated only four month earlier. The writer James Baldwin spoke forcefully to the delegates about the history of the churches' involvement in racism. In light of these concerns, the assembly participants became deeply concerned with issues of social justice, and this led to practical developments in the subsequent ongoing work of the council.

In the years following the assembly, the WCC inaugurated a number of new programs in the area of social witness and action. Among these were the Programme to Combat Racism, the Commission on the Churches' Participation in Development, the Christian Medical Commission, and the Dialogue with Peoples of Living Faiths and Ideologies. Many of these programs received support primarily from agencies and organizations that were not necessarily associated directly with the member churches. From that point on, the majority of WCC funding and staff were devoted to issues of social witness and service. Not all these developments received enthusiastic support from the member churches. As Marlin Van Elderen says: "There were tensions as well as excitement in the ecumenical fellowship over the new developments in the WCC after Uppsala. Programmes sometimes overlapped and were not easy to coordinate. Awareness of and support for what the Council was doing varied greatly among member churches. And financial difficulties imposed stringent limits on creative innovation."[39]

THE NAIROBI ASSEMBLY OF 1975

The first assembly to be held in Africa took place in Nairobi from July 24 through August 10, 1983. The gathering had 847 delegates from 301 member churches. The theme of the assembly was "Jesus Christ Frees and Unites." With this theme in mind, the delegates considered six subthemes. These were confessing Christ today, seeking community, education for liberation and community, structures of injustice and struggles for liberation, and human development.[40]

Two major concerns dominated the assembly. The first had to do with the significance of other religions and the issue of interfaith dialogue. During heated debate, many delegates responded negatively to aspects of a document on interfaith dialogue. Many expressed the fear that the call for dialogue with other religions, while important, would diminish the concern for Christian mission and lead to a relativizing of the significance of Christ and the Christian message. The second issue that also created some controversy was the ongoing discussion on the Programme to Combat Racism. In the end, the assembly chose not to weaken the program and its special fund. It did, however, seek to relate these issues with deeper theological reflection on the meaning of a just society. Moreover, issues such as faith and science, militarism and disarmament, ecology, and the role of women in church and society began to receive greater attention.

Within this broad context, the assembly did approve a major statement on "What Unity Requires" prepared by the Faith and Order Commission. The statement says in part: "The one Church is to be envisioned as a conciliar fellowship of local churches which are themselves truly united. In this conciliar fellowship, each local church possesses, in communion with the others, the fullness of catholicity, witnesses to the same apostolic faith, and therefore recognizes the others as belonging to the same Church of Christ and guided by the same Spirit." The statement says the members of the Church "are bound together because they have received the same baptism and share in the same Eucharist; they recognize each other's members and ministries. They are one in their common commitment to confess the gospel of Christ by proclamation and service to the world. To this end, each church aims at maintaining sustained and sustaining relationships with his sister churches, expressed in conciliar gatherings whenever required for the fulfillment of their common calling."[41]

THE VANCOUVER ASSEMBLY OF 1983

With the theme "Jesus Christ—The Light of the World," 847 delegates from 301 member churches met in Vancouver, Canada, for the Sixth Assembly from July 24 through August 10, 1983. The delegates discussed eight issues. These were witnessing in a divided world, taking steps toward unity, moving toward participation, healing and sharing in community, confronting threats to peace and survival, struggling for justice and human dignity, learning in community, and communicating credibly.[42]

The assembly received the text "Baptism, Eucharist, and Ministry" completed by the Faith and Order Commission in Lima in 1982 after decades of study. The churches were called upon to respond to this historic text by 1986.[43]

The assembly also recommended that the council engage the member churches in a conciliar process of commitment to justice, peace, and the integrity of creation. This process was meant to encourage the churches to struggle together against such issues as racism, sexism, economic exploitation, the violation of human rights, and the misuse of science and technology.

THE CANBERRA ASSEMBLY OF 1991

"Come, Holy Spirit—Renew the Whole Creation" was the theme of the Seventh Assembly held in Canberra, Australia, from February 7 through February 20, 1991. There were 842 delegates from 317 member churches. The delegates discussed four subthemes: Giver of Life—Sustain your creation, Spirit of Truth—set us free, Spirit of Unity—reconcile your people, and Holy Spirit—transform and sanctify us.[44]

The assembly took place within the larger context of the Gulf War, which had only recently begun. Discussion on a statement on war revealed deep differences of opinion over the justifiability of war, as well as differences between local and global concerns. In addition to this, discussions about worship and the ordained ministry revealed deep differences of opinions about their significance and their place in WCC activities. A statement prepared by the Orthodox delegates insisted that the WCC's principle task is to assist in the restoration of the unity of the churches and proposed that Faith and Order be given greater prominence in the council's agenda. This reflected the grave concern of some that the council had deviated from its fundamental vocation to serve the goal of unity.

As a result of the activities of the Faith and Order Commission, the assembly did produce an important statement on "The Unity of the Church as Koinonia: Gift and Calling." This statement builds upon the New Delhi and Nairobi Statements, and further refined the vision of the visible unity of the churches. A portion of this statement says:

The Unity of the Church to which we are called is a koinonia given and expressed in the common confession of apostolic faith, a common sacramental life entered by the one baptism and celebrated together in eucharistic fellowship; a common life in which members and ministries are mutually recognized and reconciled; a common mission witnessing to all people to the gospel of God's grace and serving the whole creation. The goal of full communion is realized when all the churches are able to recognize in one another the one, holy, catholic and apostolic church in its fullness.[45]

THE HARARE ASSEMBLY OF 1998

The Eighth Assembly in Harare, Zimbabwe, marked the 50th anniversary of the World Council of Churches. Meeting from December 3 through December 14, 1998, the assembly gathered 966 delegates from 336 member churches. Because of the anniversary and the immediate challenges facing the World Council, the participants were called to examine larger questions related to the council, the churches, and the wider ecumenical movement.

The assembly took place at a time when the World Council was facing serious financial difficulties, leading to the elimination of staff members and to the reorganization of programmatic concerns in the period between 1996 and 1999. This was a painful development that led to deeper questions about the true meaning and purpose of the council. In addition, there was a growing concern about the coherence and integrity of the various activities of the council. Moreover, these programmatic activities did not always have the support of member churches. This fact led to alienation between the World Council and many of the member churches.

Representatives from Orthodox Churches, as well as others, had raised serious questions about the ethos and direction of the World Council in the period between Canberra and the Eighth Assembly. Initially, the leadership of the council tended to diminish the significance of these concerns. However, in the period before the assembly, the Orthodox Church of Georgia and the Orthodox Church of Bulgaria withdrew from membership. On the eve of the assembly, many feared that the Orthodox delegates would not fully participate and that other Orthodox Churches, notably the Church of Russia, would formally withdraw from the council.

With these facts dominating the deliberations, the assembly participants examined the issues facing the churches and nations of Africa, prepared a new statement on "Human Rights," and marked the conclusion of the "Ecumenical Decade: Churches in Solidarity with Women."

Central to the work of the assembly was the review of the text known as "Towards a Common Understanding and Vision of the World Council of Churches (CUV)." The criticism of the council, its financial crisis, and its internal restructuring in 1991 and 1997 contributed to the development of this important self-study process, which began in earnest in 1989. A number of consultations were held and the member churches were invited to examine the council and its tasks before the assembly. As Aram Keshishian said, there was one basic question that had to be answered: "How can the WCC as an instrument of the ecumenical movement best serve the churches in their continuous search for visible unity and in their common witness in a rapidly changing world?"[46] A clear answer was not given at the assembly. The CUV report presented and discussed at Harare reflected this process. It was meant to be a guide toward the future. While the assembly had a festive character, many realized that the WCC was in the midst of a crisis of its own identity and purpose. Some of these concerns were reflected in the fact that the Harare Assembly requested that a Special Commission be created to study the various issues related to Orthodox participation in the WCC and that this commission make proposals regarding the necessary changes in structure, style, and ethos of the council.

Already at the assembly, the delegates approved some significant changes in the council's constitution that were significant. For one thing, the new constitution makes explicit the fact that "The World Council of Churches is constituted by the churches to serve the one ecumenical movement." It also says that the "primary purpose of the fellowship of churches in the World Council of Churches is to call one another to visible unity in one faith and in one eucharistic fellowship, expressed in worship and common life in Christ through witness and service to the world, and to advance towards that unity in order that the world may believe."[47] These modifications reflected the concern of many of the churches that the fundamental relationship between them and the council had to be renewed and strengthened if the WCC was to continue.

A portion of the Assembly Message says:

> The World Council of Churches began its journey in faith with the determination to stay together. We experienced this same determination at Harare, even when we were aware of the difficulties that we faced. As churches long committed to staying together, we now commit ourselves to being together in a continuing growth towards visible unity—not only in assemblies and ecumenical gatherings but each in every place. It is this being together that all ecumenical work at every level must serve. The mission to which God calls the church in the service of God's reign cannot be separated from the call to be one. In Harare we saw once again the immensity of the mission in which God invites us to share. In this mission we who are reconciled to God through the sacrifice of Christ on the cross are challenged to work for reconciliation and peace with justice among those torn apart by violence and war.[48]

OTHER ASPECTS OF THE WCC

The significant activities of the World Council of Churches cannot be fully reflected in the list of assembly themes and activities alone. The assemblies have been significant events that brought together church delegates and others for worship, bible studies, theological reflection, and affirmations of concerns. The delegates have come from a wide variety of church traditions, theological perspectives, and cultural backgrounds. Because of the assemblies, many have come to a deeper understanding of the traditions and histories of churches in various parts of the world. They have experienced both the tragedy of the disunity of the churches as well as the hopeful expressions of reconciliation. Many who have attended the assemblies have brought this appreciation back to their churches and parishes. The assemblies have contributed to a rediscovery of the catholicity of the Church and a reaffirmation of the desire for the visible unity of the churches, and for their common witness and mission in the world.

Together with the assemblies, the WCC has also provided many more opportunities for the churches to come together and to address critical issues on the ecumenical agenda at the regional and global levels. The period from one assembly to another is one in which there are numerous conferences and meetings of church delegates and theologians. These conferences address more traditional topics of church unity and disunity as well as more recent challenges facing the churches.[49] It is a time when the WCC sponsors visitations to churches. Delegations have the opportunity to experience first hand the challenges facing churches and the ecumenical movement in various parts of the world. It is also a period when the council assists needy churches and church related institutions and responds to the humanitarian needs through the sharing of resources.

In addition to this, the Ecumenical Institute, known as Bossey, brings together students from around the world for programs of ecumenical formation and it also provides opportunities for theologians to address together common concerns. The Library at the Ecumenical Center in Geneva contains an unparalleled collection of 100,000 books and journals devoted to the ecumenical movement. It is the largest collection of its type in the world. In addition to this, WCC Publications has published hundreds of books and monographs devoted to various aspects of the ecumenical movement.[50]

CONCERN OVER PURPOSE AND DIRECTION

Throughout its 50-year history, the World Council of Churches has not been without criticism. From the beginning, some of this criticism has come from those fundamentalist Christians who have opposed all expressions of the ecumenical movement. They have claimed that the WCC opposes the teaching of the Scriptures and has been a tool of Marxist political ideology. Some have criticized it for the inclusion of Orthodox Churches and for cultivating relationships with the Roman Catholic Church.[51]

Other forms of legitimate criticism have come from those who are deeply committed to the goal of the visible unity of the churches and have been active in various activities of the council. These persons, and indeed member churches, have generally called the WCC to remain an instrument of the churches and to be faithful to its primary purpose, which is to contribute to the restoration of the visible unity of the churches so that the world may believe in the gospel of Christ. With this in mind, a number of insightful concerns about the life and direction of the World Council have been voiced in recent years. The following observations are especially important.

The World Council must remain, first of all, a Christian Council of Churches, which exists to serve the churches in their quest for reconciliation, unity, and witness. This was the clear vision of the founders. Since the Uppsala Assembly, however, there was a growing sense among some that the council, as an institution, was developing a life of its own and that the member churches did not support many of its endeavors. From the beginning, the council was not meant to be a substitute or replacement for the churches. It was meant to be their instrument. As Hanfield Kruger says, "the WCC can not fulfill its many different tasks unless its thought and actions are adequately supported by its member churches. Otherwise, the balance would shift from the life of the member churches to the Geneva headquarters, which would conger up the specter of 'secretariocracy.'"[52] On the eve of the 50th anniversary, some feared that this was taking place.

The World Council must remain committed to the goal of the visible unity of the churches. As we have noted, this goal has been forcefully stated again in the recent revision of the WCC constitution. In recent years, however, there has been a growing concern that the leadership of the council has settled for an approach that stresses only cooperation and that has diminished the theological efforts to address historic church dividing issues.[53] Because of this perception, some have even proposed in recent years that the Faith and Order Commission separate itself from the WCC because of diminishing support from the council's leadership.

This means that the council must support and encourage solid theological reflection that is rooted in the divine revelation, centered upon Christ, and expressed in the Scripture and Tradition of the member churches.[54] All the activities and programs of the council must be firmly supported by Christian faith perspectives. "Clearly, theology—reflection on the faith in ongoing dialogue with Tradition," says Marlin Van Elderen, "will continue to be on the ecumenical agenda. If the WCC is true to the best of its heritage, it will avoid both abstract intellectualism which does not touch and is not touched by the conditions of people everywhere, and the parochialism of supposing that our talk about God and the church need not inform or be informed by thoughtful reflection on the rest of the world."[55] The "irresponsible negation of the theological task,"[56] which comes from some quarters in the leadership of the WCC, must be forcefully countered.

The World Council must develop new structures and an ethos that is open to the full and equal participation of the Orthodox Churches in all aspects of its life.[57] Many Orthodox Churches were among the founders of the WCC, and all Autocephalous Orthodox Churches have been members of the WCC. Yet there is a fundamentally different manner in which Orthodox Churches and Protestant churches have been structured over history. Now, there are about 20 Orthodox member churches[58] and about 300 Protestant, Anglican, and Old Catholic member churches. This structural imbalance has reflected itself in staffing, in program concerns, and in the ethos.[59]

The World Council must continue to look for opportunities to involve more directly the Roman Catholic Church in its life and activities. Likewise, opportunities to involve Evangelical and Pentecostal churches, which are open to ecumenism, should also be investigated. If the council is genuinely concerned with the restoration of visible unity, the possibility of membership of these churches in the council and its work should be pursued. This may also require structural changes in the council's administrative life.[60]

The council must identify the essential tasks it can best accomplish on behalf of the churches at a global level, which is sensitive to the local. Much has happened in the past 50 years in the ecumenical movement generally. There has been a remarkable growth in local and regional councils of churches as well as other ecumenical bodies. There have been dramatic contacts and cooperative efforts between the churches at regional and local levels. There has also been an increase in bilateral theological dialogues between the churches. Undoubtedly, the WCC has contributed to these historic developments. Now, the council must recognize the unique and global tasks through which it can serve as an instrument of the churches in this period of ecumenical life. Such a recognition must clearly see not only the council's true strengths but also its limitations. This will require a certain institutional humility. Yet the words of one of the founders are more than helpful here.[61]

> We are a council of churches, not the Council of the one undivided Church. Our name indicates our weakness and our shame before God, for there can be and there is finally only one Church of Christ on earth. Our plurality is a deep anomaly. But our name indicates that we are aware of the situation, that we do not accept it passively, that we would move forward towards the manifestation of the One Holy Church. Our Council represents therefore an emergency solution—a stage on the road—a body living between the time of complete isolation of the churches from each other and the time—on earth or in heaven—when it will be visibly true that there is one shepherd and one flock.[62]

CONCLUSIONS

Throughout its five decades of existence, the World Council of Churches epitomized for many both the accomplishments and the promise of the ecumenical movement. The council provided a unique opportunity at the global level to bring together representatives of the member churches from throughout the world. It offered valuable opportunities for theological dialogue, for common witness, and for the sharing of resources. While the Roman Catholic Church did not become a member of the council, it has cooperated in a number of its activities, most especially in theological dialogue since 1965.

As the council observed its 50th anniversary in 1998, however, it was an organization in the midst of serious difficulties. These difficulties resulted from many factors related to leadership and finances as well as to programs and organization. Most important, the difficulties related to differing perceptions of the council's fundamental purpose. A number of member churches began to raise serious questions about its ethos and direction. At the heart of these concerns was the conviction that the WCC must remain faithful to its essential identity and mission. It must be a Council of Churches that is primarily concerned with the restoration of the visible unity of the churches so that together they may give a common witness in the world.

NOTES

1. "Being Together Under the Cross in Africa: The Assembly Message," in *Together On the Way: Official Report of the Eighth Assembly of the World Council of Churches,* ed. Diane Kessler (Geneva: WCC Publications, 1999), p. 3.
2. Ruth Rouse uses this phrase in her "Other Aspects of the Ecumenical Movement: 1910–1948," in *A History of the Ecumenical Movement 1517–1948,* Ruth Rouse and Stephen Charles Neill (Philadelphia: The Westminster Press, 1967), p. 599.
3. "Patriarchal and Synodical Encyclical of 1902," in *Orthodox Visions of Ecumenism,* ed. Gennadios Limouris (Geneva: WCC Publications, 1994), pp. 1–8.
4. See V. Istravidis, "The Inter-Orthodox and Inter-Christian Work of Germanos Strenopoulos Prior to His Elevation to the Metropolis of Thyateira," *The Greek Orthodox Theological Review* 4 (1958), pp. 66–76.
5. "Encyclical of the Ecumenical Patriarchate, 1920: Unto the Churches of Christ Everywhere," in *Orthodox Visions of Ecumenism,* ed. Limouris, p. 9.
6. Thomas FitzGerald, "The Patriarchal Encyclicals on Christian Unity," *The Greek Orthodox Theological Review* 22:3 (1977), pp. 303–04.
7. Limouris, ed., *Orthodox Visions of Ecumenism,* "Encyclical of the Ecumenical Patriarchate, 1920," p. 9.
8. Ibid., pp. 9–10.
9. See C.J. Curtis, *Söderblom: Ecumenical Pioneer* (Minneapolis: Augsburg Publishing Company, 1967).
10. W.A. Visser 't Hooft, *The Genesis and Formation of the World Council of Churches* (Geneva: WCC Publications, 1982), pp. 12–13.

11. See Keith Clements, *Faith on the Frontier: A Life of J.H. Oldham* (Geneva: WCC Publications).

12. Visser 't Hooft, *The Genesis and Formation of the World Council of Churches,* p. 33.

13. Ibid.

14. See F.A. Ironmonger, *William Temple, Archbishop of Canterbury: His Life and Letters* (London: Oxford University Press, 1948).

15. Visser 't Hooft, *The Genesis and Formation of the World Council of Churches,* p. 36.

16. "Report of the Committee of Thirty-Five (Westfield College, London)," in *The Genesis and Formation of the World Council of Churches,* Visser 't Hooft, p. 104.

17. Samuel McCrea Cavert, *On the Road to Christian Unity* (New York: Harper and Row, 1961), p. 24.

18. See C.S. McFarland, *Pioneers for Peace through Religion* (New York: Revell, 1946).

19. Visser 't Hooft, *The Genesis and Formation of the World Council of Churches* (Geneva: World Council of Churches, 1982), p. 42.

20. The International Missionary Council did become associated with the WCC in 1949 and was fully integrated in 1961.

21. W.A. Visser 't Hooft, "The Genesis of the World Council of Churches," in *A History of the Ecumenical Movement 1517–1948,* ed. Ruth Rouse and Stephen Charles Neill (Philadelphia: The Westminster Press, 1967), p. 705.

22. "The World Council of Churches: Its Process of Formation, Minutes, and Reports of the Provisional Committee" (Geneva, 1946), p. 175. Cited in Visser 't Hooft, *The Genesis and Formation of the World Council of Churches,* p. 50.

23. Visser 't Hooft, *The Genesis and Formation of the World Council of Churches,* p. 55.

24. Ibid.

25. Ibid.

26. Ibid., pp. 61–62.

27. See W.A. Visser 't Hooft, *The First Assembly of the World Council of Churches* (London: SCM Press, 1949).

28. Ibid., pp. 108–72.

29. "The Message of the Assembly," in *The First Assembly of the World Council of Churches,* ed. W. A Visser 't Hooft, p. 9.

30. "The Church, the Churches, and the World Council of Churches," in *A Documentary History of the Faith and Order Movement, 1927–1963,* ed. Lucas Vischer (St. Louis: The Bethany Press, 1963), pp. 167–76.

31. Oliver S. Tomkins, ed., *The Third World Conference on Faith and Order, Lund, 1952* (London: SCM Press, 1953), pp. 15–16.

32. See W.A. Visser 't Hooft, ed., *The Evanston Report: The Second Assembly of the World Council of Churches* (London: SCM Press, 1955).

33. Limouris, *Orthodox Visions of Ecumenism,* pp. 26–29.

34. See W.A. Visser 't Hooft, ed., *The New Delhi Report: The Third Assembly of the World Council of Churches* (London: SCM Press, 1962).

35. H. Kruger, "The Life and Activities of the World Council of Churches," in *The Ecumenical Advance: A History of the Ecumenical Movement, Volume 2, 1948–1968,* ed. Harold E. Fry (Philadelphia: The Westminster Press, 1970), pp. 51–52.

36. Ibid., pp. 152–59.

37. Visser 't Hooft, ed., *The New Delhi Report*, p. 116.

38. See Norman Goodall, ed., *All Things New: The Fourth Assembly Uppsala 1968* (Geneva: WCC Publications, 1968).

39. Marlin Van Elderin, *Introducing the World Council of Churches* (Geneva: WCC Publications, revised edition, 1992), p. 31.

40. Ibid., p. 33.

41. Günther Gassmann, ed., *Documentary History of Faith and Order, 1963–1993* (Geneva: WCC Publications, 1993), p. 3.

42. Van Elderin, pp. 35–38.

43. See *Baptism, Eucharist, and Ministry* (Geneva: WCC Publications, 1982). See also *Baptism, Eucharist, and Ministry 1982–1990* (Geneva: WCC Publications, 1990).

44. Van Elderin, pp. 39–43.

45. Gassmann, ed., *Documentary History of Faith and Order, 1963–1993*, p. 3.

46. Aram Keshishian, "The Work of the WCC: Past, Present, and Future," in *Together On the Way: Official Report of the Eighth Assembly of the World Council of Churches*, ed. Dianne Kessler (Geneva: WCC Publications, 1999), p. 45.

47. Ibid., p. 363.

48. "Being Together Under the Cross in Africa: The Assembly Message," in *Together On the Way: Official Report of the Eighth Assembly of the World Council of Churches*, ed. Diane Kessler, p. 3.

49. See Ans J. Van der Bent, *Six Hundred Ecumenical Consultations, 1948–1982* (Geneva: WCC Publications, 1982).

50. The outstanding contributions of the late Marlin Van Elderen and the late Jan Kok to the publication department need to be mentioned.

51. W. A. Visser 't Hooft discusses these accusations in his essay "The General Ecumenical Development since 1948," in *The Ecumenical Advance: A History of the Ecumenical Movement, Volume 2, 1948–1968*, ed. Harold E. Fry (Philadelphia: The Westminster Press, 1970), pp. 18–19.

52. H. Kruger, "The Life and Activities of the World Council of Churches," in *The Ecumenical Advance: A History of the Ecumenical Movement, Volume 2, 1948–1968*, ed. Fey, p. 61.

53. Metropolitan John Zizioulas, "Keynote Address," *Programme Unit I: Unity and Renewal, Minutes of the Commission Meeting* (Geneva: Programme Unit I, 1966), pp. 41–47.

54. J. M. R. Tillard, "The World Council of Churches in Quest for Identity," *The Ecumenical Review* 50:3 (1999), pp. 390–98.

55. Van Elderin, p. 144.

56. Günther Gassmann in his "Retrospective of an Ecumenical Century," in *Agapè, Études en l'honneur de Mgr. Pierre Duprey*, ed. Jean-Marie Roger Tillard (Geneva: Centre Orthodoxe de Patriarcat Ecuménique, 2000), p. 86.

57. Metropolitan Chrisostomos Konstantinidis, "Some Thoughts and Proposals for Positive Participation of the Orthodox Churches in the World Council of Churches," in *Agapè, Études en l'honneur de Mgr. Pierre Duprey*, ed. Jean-Marie Roger Tillard (Geneva: Centre Orthodoxe de Patriarcat Ecuménique, 2000), pp. 87–92.

58. This number includes the two families of Orthodox Churches: the Eastern Orthodox and the Oriental Orthodox.

59. "Final Statement of the Orthodox Pre-Assembly Meeting," in *Turn to God, Rejoice in Hope: Orthodox Reflections on the Way to Harare* (Geneva: WCC Orthodox Task Force, 1998), pp. 9–10.

60. S. Mark Heim, "The Next Ecumenical Movement," *The Christian Century* (August 14–21, 1996), p. 783.

61. Visser 't Hooft, "The General Ecumenical Development since 1948," in *The Ecumenical Advance: A History of the Ecumenical Movement, Volume 2, 1948–1968*, ed. Harold E. Fey, pp. 24–25.

62. W.A. Visser 't Hooft, *Memoirs* (Geneva: WCC Publications, 1973), p. 210.

CHAPTER 7

The Entrance of the Roman Catholic Church

> The restoration of unity among all Christians is one of the principal concerns of the Second Vatican Council. Christ the Lord founded one Church and one Church only. However, many Christian communions present themselves to men as the true inheritors of Jesus Christ; all indeed profess to be followers of the Lord but differ in mind and go their different ways, as if Christ Himself were divided. Such division openly contradicts the will of Christ, scandalizes the world, and damages the holy cause of preaching the Gospel to every creature.
>
> —Decree on Ecumenism, Second Vatican Council, 1965[1]

INTRODUCTION

The formal entrance of the Roman Catholic Church into the contemporary ecumenical movement came only after over 40 years of dialogue between Protestants, Anglicans, Old Catholics, and Orthodox churches in various settings. Chief among these were the Faith and Order Movement and the Life and Work Movement. It came also after some bold steps by Roman Catholics to become involved in events of common prayer for Christian unity and informal contacts with early ecumenical organizations. While the Roman Catholic Church expressed concern over Christian disunity during the later nineteenth and early twentieth centuries, it formally declined to be involved in the early ecumenical organizations or in the establishment of the World Council of Churches in 1948.

This position of the Roman Catholic Church regarding the challenge of the ecumenical involvement reached a profound turning point under the leadership of Pope John XXIII (1881–1963) and through the decisions of the Second Vatican Council (1962–65). The council's Constitution on the Church and its Decree on Ecumenism provided a more nuanced theological approach to the reality of other Christian churches and ecclesial communities, as well as to the quest for the unity of the churches. Over the course of 30 years, this document was followed by a number of other significant papal encyclicals and other statements, which further articulated the positions of the Roman Catholic Church. Together with these statements, the Roman Catholic Church, under the leadership of Pope Paul VI (1897–1978), agreed to establish formal bilateral dialogues with the Orthodox Church, the Anglican Communion, and a number of Protestant churches. From 1965 onward, it also agreed to cooperate in a number of areas with the World Council of Churches. In more recent years, the Roman Catholic Church has formally joined a number of local and regional Councils of Churches. For the cause of restoring visible unity, it has also encouraged prayer, theological dialogue, and common witness at all levels of church life.

CONFLICTING PERSPECTIVES

Throughout the late nineteenth and early twentieth century there were increased contacts between the Orthodox, Anglican, Old Catholics, and many Protestant churches in Western Europe and the United States. These contacts eventually led to the establishment of the Faith and Order Movement and the Life and Work Movement in the 1920s and 1930s. The Roman Catholic Church formally refused to become involved in these theological dialogues. Indeed, the early efforts to bring together members of separated churches for common prayer for unity in the Association for the Promotion of Christian Unity were eventually rejected by the Church of Rome in 1864.

During the late nineteenth century, a number of formal developments occurred in the Roman Catholic Church that then appeared to strengthen the line of demarcation between it and other Christian churches. Roman Catholic missionaries continued to operate in areas that had been traditionally Orthodox. The establishment and support of Eastern Catholic churches by Rome was viewed by the Orthodox as proselytism. The Roman Catholic Church proclaimed the doctrine of the Immaculate Conception of Mary by Pope Pius IX in 1854. This teaching appeared to be an additional obstacle to relations, especially with many Orthodox and Protestants who found such perspectives to lack a biblical support. The First Vatican Council (1869–70) formally proclaimed the doctrine of the Infallibility of the Pope. Finally, Pope Leo XIII (1878–1903) in 1896 declared that Anglican ordinations were invalid despite differences of opinion in the Roman Catholic Church of the time.

These decisions of the Roman Catholic Church reflected the spirit of the times. There was little or no formal attempt to assess the perspectives of other churches on critical theological issues. The lack of formal contact and dialogue between Rome and the other churches was taken for granted. An ecclesiology that identified the Roman Catholic Church with the one Church of Christ was normative. This view and the official isolation that accompanied it provided a basis for actions and statements that would only solidify the formal estrangement between Rome and Orthodoxy, on the one hand, and between Rome and Anglicanism and Protestantism, on the other.

During most of the nineteenth century, when the issue of Christian unity was formally raised by the popes, Rome took the position that all other Christians were in a state of separation and had to return to the Roman Catholic Church. Here, however, there was an important difference in the approach of Rome to the Orthodox on the one hand and its approach to the Protestants on the other. Rome continued to consider the Orthodox Churches as somehow a part of their same family, though in a state of schism. Despite the division, the Eastern churches retained the ancient faith and authentic sacraments. "Even after the failure of Florence," says Jean-Marie Tillard, "in the minds of a great number of Catholic theologians, bishops, leaders and laypeople, the Orthodox churches continued to be regarded as real churches."[2]

The attitude of Rome toward the Reformation churches was decidedly different. The Reformation continued to be viewed as an attack upon the traditional faith and practice of Catholic Christianity through the ages. Rome refused to recognize their existence as separated churches in its own historical sphere of influence. The Protestants were compared to the prodigal son who repudiated the family. "This is why," says Jean-Marie Tillard, "the only solution for them was to return to the 'House of God' which they had left, to the father whom they had outraged by their departure but who was still waiting for them."[3]

An important development in the story of the Roman Catholic relationship with both Orthodoxy and Protestantism came during the pontificate of Leo XIII (r. 1878–1903). His encyclical *Praeclara gratulationis* in 1894 was the first devoted to the theme of Christian unity.[4] There is no doubt that Leo continued to reflect the official Catholic position, in this and subsequent letters, that the unity of divided Christians necessitated that all return to unity with the See of Rome and accept the authority of the pope. Yet, at the same time, Leo began to affirm that the restoration of Christian unity was so important that Rome had to promote the search. In addition to this, Leo also began to look upon the Orthodox Church and the Protestant communities with greater sympathy. He stressed the distinction between those who broke with Rome in the past and those in the present who are striving to be faithful Christians through their own communities, which are separated from Rome. He used more frequently the term separated or dissidents, rather than heretics and schematics. Although he ultimately spoke against the validity of the sacrament of Holy Orders in Anglicanism, Leo did support the discussion between Roman Catholics and Anglicans. Moreover, in his letter *Provida Matris* of May 5, 1895, Leo proposed that Roman Catholics pray for Christian unity in the period before the Feast of Pentecost.[5]

The unparalleled developments in the ecumenical movement during the late nineteenth century and early twentieth century undoubtedly challenged the Roman Catholic Church and its own sense of what Christian unity required. The spirit of dialogue affecting the Orthodox, Anglican, Old Catholic, and many Protestant churches could not be ignored for long. Despite the important developments that could be found in the writings of Pope Leo, Rome was still unwilling formally to enter into dialogue with either the Orthodox or the Anglicans and Protestants in the early twentieth century.

In reactions to the dramatic ecumenical developments, Pope Pius XI (r. 1922–39) produced the encyclical *Mortalium animos* on January 6, 1928.[6] In the period following the early Faith and Order and Life and Work Conferences, Rome appears to have identified the new ecumenical movement with an indifference or diminishment of the historic Christian faith and with a faulty vision of the Church. With these perspectives, the encyclical states that it is impossible for Roman Catholics to share this conception of Christian unity and to take part in any of the activities of the ecumenical movement. Repeating the Catholic position of the period, the encyclical says that the dissidents must realize the will of Christ by returning to Rome.

The encyclical as a whole expresses the conviction that the Roman Church is concerned with the need to overcome Christian disunity. This cannot be denied. Yet the letter appears to be based upon a faulty understanding of the early ecumenical movement. Moreover, it reverts to the rather formalistic viewpoint that the problem of Christian disunity will be resolved only when the separated believers return to the Church of Rome. Speaking of this encyclical and its historical context, Jean-Marie Tillard says: "This letter surprised those within the Catholic Church who were involved in ecumenical discussions and reflection. For, at the beginning of his pontificate, Pius XI had, by his positive and constructive attitude, made possible a handful of initiatives, whose consequences on the Roman Catholic mind will be enormous." Tillard continues by noting: "But these initiatives were taken neither by the Holy See nor by the local bishops. They all came from what is described today as 'the grassroots.' It is crucial ecclesiologically to stress this short remark. The *sensus fidelium* has been the main agent of the Holy Spirit for the move of the Catholic Church towards a more authentic ecumenism. In this process the *episcopé* of the hierarchy has been more permissive than creative."[7]

ROMAN CATHOLIC PIONEERS

Despite the harsh evaluation of the ecumenical movement by Pope Pius XI, there was already a momentum in parts of the Roman Catholic Church to pray with other Christians for unity and to engage in dialogue and common witness where possible. These initiatives were found primarily in regions where there was a natural opportunity for Roman Catholics to encounter Orthodox, Anglicans, and Protestants. The initiatives were frequently led by pastors and theologians who came to experience personally the tragedy of division and the possibilities for Christian unity. Here the witness of a number of Catholic pioneers is especially significant.

We have spoken already about the important initiatives taken by Abbé Paul Couturier (1881–1953) of Lyons, France. Some would identify him as the father of spiritual ecumenism because of the importance he placed on the necessity of common prayer for Christian unity. He called for a significant modification of the Roman Catholic practice, in effect since 1908: to pray every year during the period before Pentecost for Christian unity. Beginning in 1935, Abbé Paul proposed that Christians of all the churches pray together for Christian unity with the petition that Christ reunite his Church, according to his will and to his mysterious way. This custom became the basis for the present Week of Prayer for Christian Unity.

Abbé Paul also asked that prayer for unity be one of the main themes at the contemplative Trappist women's monastery at Grottaferrata, near Rome. There, Maria Gabrilla Sagheddu (1914–39), a young Sardinian woman, entered the monastery in 1935. From the start, she made the intention of Christian unity a central element of her prayer. Under her leadership, the entire community of nuns became deeply devoted to prayer for Christian unity. During her short life, she also established contact with the Anglican women's Monastery of Nashdom, which followed the Benedictine rule. The Roman Catholic Church beatified her in 1983. Her tomb is found at the monastery, which was transferred to Vitorchiano in 1957 and has become a place of pilgrimage.[8]

Another important initiative by Abbé Paul was to gather every year a group of theologians and pastors from Eastern France and Western Switzerland who were interested in issues of Christian reconciliation and unity. Starting in 1937, this group began to meet at the old Cistercian monastery called Les Dombes, northeast of the city of Lyons, France. Initially, this meeting began as a simple opportunity for Catholic, Protestant, and Orthodox pastors and theologians to meet together for prayer, theological discussion, and friendship. Eventually, the Groupe des Dombes became an important leaven for the ecumenical movement through its prayer, its witness, and its publications.[9]

Many of the initiatives of Abbé Paul were taken up by Fr. Max Metzger (1887–1944) in Meitingen-bei-Augsburg, Germany. Beginning in 1938, he established a movement known as *Una Sancta.* Under his leadership, *Una Sancta* gatherings were organized throughout Germany. In these gatherings, Catholic and Protestant clergy and laity met for prayer and theological discussions. Considered a subversive by the Nazis, Fr. Max was arrested in 1934, 1938, and 1939. He was accused of being a spy because of his organization and his ecumenical contacts with others outside Germany. As his trial, he declared: "I have offered my life for the peace of the world and the unity of Christ's Church."[10] Fr. Max Metzger was executed in Brandenburg Prison on April 17, 1944.[11]

The activities of Abbé Paul, Maria Gabriella Sagheddu, and Fr. Max were important expressions of a concern for Christian unity that was to be found among other Catholic theologians and pastors in various parts of Western Europe. Frequently, the concern for Christian unity was linked with interests in the renewal of liturgical studies and biblical studies. For example, Dom Lambert Beauduin (1873–1960) established in 1925 the Benedictine monastery of Amay-sur-Meuse (now Chevetogne) in Belgium.[12] The monastery had a special commitment to Christian unity and a particular concern for Orthodox Christianity. Dom Lambert was interested in both liturgy and ecumenical dialogue and he emphasized the importance of theological reflection. In 1926, he established the journal *Irenakon.*

Dom Yves Congar (1904–95), a Dominican priest and theologian from Paris, made a profound contribution to Catholic ecumenism in the period leading up to the Second Vatican Council and in the years after it.[13] From the time of his youth, he had direct contact with Protestant Christians and remembered the hospitality offered by the Protestant parish in his village to the Catholics when their church building was destroyed by a fire in 1914. Ordained a priest in 1930, he recognized through his prayers and biblical studies a calling to contribute to the unity of the churches. This was further strengthened by his contacts with Russian Orthodox exiles living in Paris following the Russian Revolution. His subsequent studies in Germany brought him into contact with Lutherans. He also traveled to England and made contacts with Anglicans. He ultimately became associated with a small group who were interested in ecumenism, some of whom were involved in the Malines Conversations between Anglicans and Roman Catholics. This dialogue between Anglican and Roman Catholic theologians began with the blessing of Pope Benedict XI in 1921 and was led by Cardinal Désiré Mercier (1851–1926).[14] Yet the theologians on both sides were not truly representing their churches. Despite the inherent limitation, the conversations, which lasted until 1926, demonstrated that dialogue between Roman Catholic and Anglican theologians was indeed possible.[15]

He published his first major work *Chrétiens disunis (Christian Disunity)* in the year 1937 in French and in 1939 in English. Although he was refused permission by Rome to attend the Oxford life and Work Conference in 1937, his book marked an important turning point for Roman Catholic theology dealing with the ecumenical movement. With the conclusion of the war, Congar resumed his ecumenical activities. His writings and speeches were not well received by the authorities in Rome. In the year 1947, Rome refused to allow him to publish an article on ecumenism in a publication preparing for the Amsterdam Assembly of the World Council of Churches. A few years later in 1952, he was told that all his writings had to be approved by Rome before they could be published. In the same year he became involved in the Catholic Conference for Ecumenical Questions. This group of notable Catholic theologians began to meet regularly in various cities in Western Europe to discuss issues related to ecumenism. Many the participants later became involved in the Second Vatican Council.[16]

After decades of suspicion by the authorities in Rome, Congar was brought into the center Catholic theology by Pope John XIII, who placed him on the preparatory theological commission for the Second Vatican Council. During the council, he assisted in the drafting of a number of critical documents. His many books contributed immensely to developments in Catholic theology. A year prior to his death in 1995, he was made a cardinal of the Roman Catholic Church.

Speaking of his life long concern for the unity of the churches, he said:

> It very soon occurred to me that ecumenism is not a specialty. It presupposes a movement of conversion and reform co-extensive with the whole life of the community, the Church. It seemed to me also that each individual's ecumenical task lay in the first place in the home among his own people. Our business was to rotate the Catholic Church through a few degrees on its own axis in the direction of convergence towards others, and a possible unanimity with them, in accordance with a deeper and closer fidelity to our unique source, our common source.[17]

THE SECOND VATICAN COUNCIL (1962–65)

Angelo Roncalli (1881–1963), the Patriarch of Venice, was elected pope on October 28, 1958, at the age of 78. Observers first thought that this elderly prelate, who had served many years as a church diplomat, would simply be a caretaker pope after the long reign of Pope Pius XII. These initial observations were very wrong. Three months after his election, Pope John XXIII announced on January 25, 1959, his plan to convene an Ecumenical Council for the Universal Church. This dramatic announcement came at the conclusion of the prayer service of the Week of Prayer for Christian Unity. Moreover, he declared that this council would be of service "not only for the spiritual good and joy of the Christian people but also an invitation to the separated communities to seek again that unity for which many souls are longing in these days throughout the world."[18]

While many were excited about the theme of Christian unity, there also was some measure of anxiety with regard to the manner in which the topic would be addressed. Within six months, the pope issued his first encyclical on June 29, 1959, entitled *Ad Petri Cathedram,* in which he clarified the plans for the council. In it he stated that the council would be for bishops of the Catholic Church who would gather to discuss topics related to its internal renewal. "John XXIII, thus shifted attention," says Thomas Stransky, "from a reunion Council to one of renewal, from other Christians joining Catholic leaders for debate and one hopes, eventual consensus, to their watching at a distance the Roman Catholic Church being renewed through its own exclusive gathering."[19] At first, it seemed as though the concern for Christian unity would somehow be lost.

Yet there was to be more. Those involved in Roman Catholic ecumenical contacts urged the pope immediately to establish a formal commission to examine issues of ecumenical dialogue and relations in light of the coming council. A year later on June 5, 1960, Pope John XXIII formally established the Secretariat for Promoting Christian Unity among the twelve bodies that would prepare for the council. It was envisioned that this Secretariat would enable "those who bear the name Christian but are separated from the Apostolic See...to follow the work of the Council and to find more easily the path by which they may arrive at the unity for which Christ prayed."[20] "From now on," says Jean-Marie Tillard, "Roman Catholic ecumenism will go out of its cradle. It will walk steadily, and friendly, on all the main ecumenical roads."[21]

When the council opened on October 11, 1962, more than two thousand Roman Catholic Bishops and their advisors began a monumental process of deliberations that took place in four autumn sessions until December 1965. In addition to these formal sessions, there were hundreds of meetings involving the bishops and theologians from throughout the world. These deliberations were based upon many studies that had been prepared by the conciliar commissions. These themes reflected issues raised by Roman Catholic leaders in formal responses prepared long before the council began. Following the death of Pope John XXIII on June 3, 1963, the deliberations continued under the leadership of Pope Paul IV (1897–1978). The Second Vatican Council is considered by Roman Catholics to be the 21st Ecumenical Council. It produced 16 major statements.

While the council was one of the Roman Catholic Church, a remarkable number of Orthodox, Anglican, and Protestant theologians were invited to be present as observers. By the end of the council nearly 200 had been involved. Indeed, one of the most important tasks of the newly established Council for Christian Unity was to formally invite these observers and to encourage their participation. The invitation to non-Catholics was a very significant ecumenical gesture. Even more important, however, was the fact that these observers were invited to participate in informal discussions with Roman Catholic bishops and theologians on the issues being discussed by the council. "These observers," says Jean-Marie Tillard, "were not passive guests. Moreover they were treated by the Secretariat as real brothers. They were consulted. Sometimes they were asked to criticize the first drafts of the documents. They were invited to speak to the bishops. It is evident that they contributed to the understanding and discussion of the main questions subject to scrutiny. Without this group—which they gradually learned to trust—some bishops would have been afraid to accept, for instance, many affirmations of the *Decree on Ecumenism*, one of the most decisive documents of the Vatican Council."[22]

The *Decree on Ecumenism* became the charter for Roman Catholic involvement in the ecumenical movement. The document both affirmed the importance of the quest for Christian unity and affirmed the participation of the Roman Catholic Church in this movement. "The restoration of unity among all Christians," says the document, "is one of the principal concerns of the Second Vatican Council. Christ the Lord founded one Church and one Church only. However, many Christian communions present themselves to men as the true inheritors of Jesus Christ; all indeed profess to be followers of the Lord but differ in mind and go their different ways, as if Christ Himself were divided. Such division openly contradicts the will of Christ, scandalizes the world, and damages the holy cause of preaching the Gospel to every creature."[23] The document goes on to affirm that baptism "constitutes the sacramental bond of unity existing among all those who through it are reborn."[24] Yet, as the decree also says, disunity among Christians is real. Thus, the obstacles preventing divided Christians from affirming the same faith and sharing in the same Eucharist must be overcome through prayer, dialogue, and acts of common witness.

Ecumenical issues and concerns can also be found either directly or indirectly in a number of other conciliar texts. A number of important insights are to be found especially in the *Dogmatic Constitution on the Church.* There it says that the Roman Catholic Church "subsists in" the Church. The text goes on to say that "many elements of sanctification and of truth are found outside its visible confines. Since these are gifts belonging to the Church of Christ, they are forces impelling towards Catholic unity."[25] Together with the statements in the *Decree on Ecumenism*, these observations, which would require further elaboration, indicated that Catholicism was moving toward a different way of viewing other churches and Christian communities.

Speaking of the change in perspective, William Henn says: "By choosing not to affirm simply that the church of Christ 'is' the Catholic Church, the Council refused to identify the two in an exclusive way. This change was made so that what was affirmed about the Catholic Church would not contradict the recognition that many elements of sanctification and of truth are found outside its visible confines. These elements are 'ecclesial,' which means that the church of Christ is present and active in a Christian community to the degree that these elements are present."[26]

THE PERIOD AFTER THE COUNCIL

During the period of time following the council, the Roman Catholic Church was engaged in a profound process of applying the conciliar directions and insights. All aspects of the Roman Catholic Church would ultimately be affected by the event and the documents of the Second Vatican Council. Indeed, the relationship between the Roman Catholic Church and the Orthodox Church, the Anglican Communion, the Old Catholic Church, and the Protestant churches and communities would also undergo profound change in the decades following the council.

As early as 1965, the Roman Catholic Church also began to cooperate with the World Council of Churches in selected areas. Among these was the Joint Working Group, which brought together representatives of Rome and the council for discussions. Likewise, Roman Catholic theologians became full members of the Commission on Faith and Order. In addition to this, Roman Catholic observers began participating in the Assemblies of the World Council of Churches from 1968. During the 1970s, there were discussions regarding further involvement of the Roman Catholic Church in the council. However, both sides felt that the time was not opportune for such a formal relationship to develop.

The Pontifical Council for Christian Unity continued its work after the council and was chiefly responsible for guiding and coordinating Roman Catholic ecumenical relationships. Based upon the insights of the council, *Directory Concerning Ecumenical Matters* was published in two parts in 1967 and 1969. The first part was concerned chiefly with the establishment of diocesan and national ecumenical commissions as well with guidelines related to ecumenical prayer services. The second part elaborated upon the principles of Catholic ecumenism. The *Directory* was subsequently revised in 1998.

The Pontifical Council also oversaw the establishment of formal, bilateral theological dialogues with the Lutheran World Federation (1965), the Anglican Communion (1966), the Old Catholic Church (1966), the World Methodist Council (1966), the World Alliance of Reformed Churches (1968), the Pentecostals (1972), the Disciples of Christ (1977), the Coptic Orthodox Church (1973), the Orthodox Church (1979), the Malankara Orthodox Church (1989), and the Assyrian Church of the East (1994).

Over the course of decades, these dialogues have brought together theologians to discuss both issues of agreement and disagreement. Each of these dialogues has produced a number of significant statements. Most recently, after 35 years of dialogue, the discussions between the Roman

Catholic Church and the Lutheran World Federation produced an important agreement known as the *Joint Declaration on the Doctrine of Justification* on October 31, 1999. The text affirms a common understanding of the doctrine of Justification by Lutherans and Roman Catholics. This doctrine was considered to be a major point of difference since the Reformation.[27]

Before, during, and after the council, the Roman Catholic Church was very concerned with establishing a positive relationship with the Orthodox Church. Less than two months after Pope John XXIII called for the council, he met on March 17, 1959, with Archbishop Iakovos of America, the representative of Patriarch Athenagoras (1886–1972) of Constantinople. This meeting is believed to be the first between a pope and a representative from Constantinople since 1547.[28] As relations between the two churches improved, Pope Paul VI and Ecumenical Patriarch Athenagoras of Constantinople met in Jerusalem on January 5–6, 1964. On December 7, 1965, the pope and patriarch removed the ancient excommunications of 1054. In the same year, a bilateral theological dialogue between the Orthodox and Roman Catholic Church was inaugurated in the United States. It was the first of its kind. Following the council, Pope Paul VI visited the patriarch in Istanbul in 1967, and the patriarch later traveled to Rome that same year. During this period, both began to speak of the relationship of sister churches between Rome and Constantinople. Finally, in 1979, the International Orthodox-Roman Catholic Theological Dialogue was established.[29] Pope John Paul II (1920–), elected in 1978, visited Istanbul a year later. In more recent years, Ecumenical Patriarch Demetrios visited Rome in 1987, and Ecumenical Patriarch Bartholomew (1940–) did the same in 1995.[30] These pilgrimages were an important part of a series of visits between the representatives of Orthodoxy and Roman Catholicism that are ongoing.

RECENT PAPAL LETTERS ON ECUMENISM

Pope John Paul II issued two significant letters on ecumenism in the year 1985. The first was an apostolic letter entitled *The Light of the East (Orientale Lumen)* written on May 2, 1995. It was written on the 100th anniversary of the apostolic letter *Orientalium Dignitas* by Pope Leo XIII in 1895 to highlight the importance of the Eastern tradition for the entire church. The letter emphasizes the significance of Eastern Christian theology, spirituality, and liturgy for the entire church. At the same time, the letter affirms the historic bonds that exist between Roman Catholicism and Orthodoxy in spite of the schism. Pointing to the substantial amount of belief and practice that the Eastern and Western traditions already share, Pope John Paul II observed that the movement for Christian unity is irreversible. He noted that both the East and the West share the great gifts of the early church councils, the writing of the Fathers, and monasticism. Most importantly, he pointed out that there is the common appreciation of the Eucharist in the life of the church. With this in mind, the pope decried the break in unity between Orthodoxy and Catholicism. He said: "The sin of our separation is very serious: I feel the need to increase our common openness to the Spirit who calls us to conversion, to accept and recognize others with fraternal respect, to make fresh, courageous gestures, able to dispel any temptation to turn back. We feel the need to go beyond the degree of communion we have reached."[31]

The letter was written at a time when serious tension existed between Rome and the Orthodox Church over the restoration of Eastern Catholic churches in Central and Eastern Europe. Noting these difficulties, the pope called all Christians to make greater efforts in overcoming the misunderstandings and divisive issues of the past. The pope also said that the existence of Eastern churches already in full communion with Rome should not impede progress but rather help to foster the continued efforts toward the full union of the churches. Mindful of the common saints and martyrs of the Eastern and Western Church, he said:

> We are painfully aware that we cannot yet share in the same Eucharist. Now that the millennium is drawing to a close and our gaze turns to the rising Sun, with gratitude we find these men and women before our eyes and in our heart.
>
> The echo of the Gospel—the words that do not disappoint—continues to resound with force, weakened only by our separation: Christ cries out but man finds it hard to hear his voice because we fail to speak with one accord. We listen together to the cry of those who want to hear God's entire Word. The words of the West need the words of the East, so that God's word may ever more clearly reveal its unfathomable riches. Our words will meet forever in the heavenly Jerusalem, but we ask and wish that this meeting be anticipated in the holy Church, which is still on her way towards the fullness of the Kingdom.[32]

Pope John Paul II's encyclical *That All May Be One (Ut Unum Sint)*[33] was published on May 25, 1995. It is a forceful reaffirmation of the Catholic Church's commitment to the cause of unity. Building upon the documents of the Second Vatican Council, it looks forward to the dawn of the third millennium. Throughout the early part of the encyclical, the pope reaffirms a number of the principals of Catholic ecumenism dating from the period of the council. He speaks about the importance of the conversion of hearts, of common prayer for unity, and of the necessity of examining together the past issues of division. He acknowledges the importance of confessing past wrongs of church members and the need for the Bishop of Rome to provide leadership in the search for Christian unity. Citing the statement from the council, he said:

> The Lord of ages wisely and patiently follows out the plan of his grace on behalf of us sinners. In recent times, he has begun to bestow more generously upon divided

Christians remorse over their divisions and a longing for unity. Everywhere, large numbers have felt the impulse of this grace, and among our separated brethren also there increases from day to day a movement, fostered by the grace of the Holy Spirit, for the restoration of unity among all Christians. Taking part in this movement, which is called ecumenical, are those who invoke the Triune God and confess Jesus as Lord and Saviour. They join in not merely as individuals but also as members of the corporate groups in which they have heard the Gospel, and which each regards as his Church and, indeed, God's. And yet almost everyone, though in different ways, longs that there may be one visible Church of God, a Church truly universal and sent forth to the whole world that the world may be converted to the Gospel and so be saved, to the glory of God.[34]

To believe in Christ means to desire unity; to desire unity means to desire the church; to desire the church means to desire the communion of grace that corresponds to the Father's plan from all eternity. Such is the meaning of Christ's prayer: "Ut unum sint."[35]

It is in this spirit that the pope emphasizes the importance of prayer for unity as well as the witness of the saints in every church. Pope John Paul II also paid special attention to the witness of the saints who come from all churches. He declared that "those who at the end of a life faithful to grace, are in communion with Christ in glory. These saints come from all the churches and ecclesial communities which save them entrance into the communion of salvation."[36] In paying special attention to the saints of all churches, the pope has pointed to the deep unity in Christian holiness that transcends church divisions.

The pope affirmed the significance of the divided churches in coming together for common witness and dialogue. He spoke of the importance of collaboration among the churches and the spirit of mutual aid in times of difficulties. The Pope paid special attention to the various theological dialogues between the churches, as well as to the work of the Faith and Order Commission of the World Council of Churches. These dialogues are essential to the restoration of unity. Yet the pope also affirmed that they must be concerned with mutual enrichment and based upon a clear-sighted examination of conscience in the quest for truth. "The unity willed by God can be attained only by the adherence of all to the content of revealed faith in its entirety. In matters of faith, compromise is in contradiction with God who is Truth... A 'being together' which betrayed the truth would thus be opposed both to the nature of God who offers his communion and to the need for truth found in the depths of every human heart."[37]

In discussing the nature of the dialogue, the pope reaffirmed three important principles that are inherent in recent Roman Catholic approaches to ecumenical discussions. The first is the concept of a hierarchy of truths in Catholic teaching. This means that there are some teachings that have a greater importance or centrality to the Christian message. The second concept is the principle that a distinction needs to be made between the unchanging deposit of the faith and the expressions of that faith that can change. The understanding and articulation of the essential doctrines of faith can develop over time. Finally, the pope reaffirmed that the quest for unity is an organic part of the Church's life. He said, "It is absolutely clear that ecumenism, the movement promoting Christian unity, is not just some sort of 'appendix' which is added to the Church's traditional activity. Rather, ecumenism is an organic part of her life and work, and consequently must pervade all that she is and does; it must be like the fruit borne by a healthy and flourishing tree, which grows to its full stature."[38]

Toward the end of the text, the pope looked ahead to the future of ecumenism that, he said, demands "patient and courageous efforts"[39] and he warned that "one must not impose any burden beyond that which is strictly necessary"[40] in the continuing journey toward full communion. He identified five areas that need further study by the divided churches. These are: first, the relationship between sacred Scripture, as the highest authority in matters of faith, and sacred tradition, as indispensable to the interpretation of the Word of God; second, the Eucharist, as the Sacrament of the Body and Blood of Christ, an offering of praise to the Father, the sacrificial memorial and Real Presence of Christ, and the sanctifying outpouring of the Holy Spirit; third, ordination, as a Sacrament, to the threefold ministry of the episcopate, presbyterate, and diaconate; fourth, the Magisterium of the Church, entrusted to the pope and the bishops in communion with him, understood as a responsibility and an authority exercised in the name of Christ for teaching and safeguarding the faith; and fifth, the Virgin Mary, as Mother of God and Icon of the Church, the spiritual Mother who intercedes for Christ's disciples and for all humanity.[41]

In identifying these critical areas for investigation, the pope affirmed that the ecumenical movement must be a quest for the full articulation of the ancient faith of the Church. Clearly, the Roman Catholic Church is not in a position to deny elements of the Christian faith that it considers to be essential. As Jean-Marie Tillard says: "the Roman Catholic Church is convinced of being the guardian, the keeper, of essential elements radically required for the Church to be truly the Church of God. The Catholic Church is not ready to renounce these elements because (together with the Eastern churches) she knows that they belong to the authentic nature and mission of the visible unity all the Christian communities are looking for. Let us be frank. She wants the other churches to rediscover the necessity of these elements. She will not agree with a conception of koinonia within which any of these essential elements would be excluded."[42]

At the same time, however, the Roman Catholic Church is committed to theological dialogue that will examine the points of agreement and disagreement in the hope of finding a consensus. This approach "is grounded in the 'recognition' of the action of the Holy Spirit in all the communities of baptized believers. It is because of this 'recognition' that, through the voice of the Bishop of Rome himself in his encyclical letter, the Roman Catholic Church invites the other traditions to study honestly and discuss with the Roman Catholic Church, the divisive issues in order to find together the authentic way of resolving them."[43]

Indeed, one of the most significant observations in the encyclical is related to the position and understanding of the office of the pope. John Paul II called the bishop of Rome "the first servant of unity" and at the same time recognized that the position of the pope is a major challenge for reconciliation and unity. With this in mind, he called other churches and their theologians to enter into a study of the position and role of the bishop of Rome. He said: "Could not the real but imperfect communion existing between us persuade church leaders and their theologians to engage with me in a patient and fraternal dialogue on this subject, a dialogue in which, leaving useless controversies behind, we could listen to one another, keeping before us only the will of Christ for his church and allowing ourselves to be deeply moved by his plea 'that they may all be one…so that the world may believe that you have sent me' (John 17:21)."[44]

The request of the pope is very significant. It reflects the recognition that the position and significance of the bishop of Rome has contributed to the disunity of the churches and has remained a significant obstacle to reconciliation. The request also appears to affirm that discussions among the divided churches regarding the role of the pope can contribute to a new understanding of his ministry for the movement toward visible unity.

When one compares the encyclical of Pope Pius XI *Mortalium Annos* (1928) with the encyclical *Ut Unum Sint* of Pope John Paul II, it is obvious that the Roman Catholic understanding of the quest for Christian unity has gone through a major development, especially since the time of the Second Vatican Council. Two points are especially noteworthy. First, there is a very significant change in the attitude of the Catholic Church to other Christians. Neither Pope John Paul II nor the council asked other Christians to return to the Catholic Church, as had earlier papal statements. The emphasis now appears to be on the process and requirements of reconciliation. "The reason for this," says William Henn, "seems to lie in the realization that it would not be adequate to think of other Christians as having 'left the church.' Indeed, to identify the church of Christ exclusively with the Roman Catholic Church is the view that has turned out to be inadequate."[45] Following the insights of the council, Roman Catholic theologians are now more prone to speak of the one Church being present in churches and communities beyond the canonical boundaries of their church. "The 'one church of Christ is effectively present' in other Christian communities and the decisive proof of this, if any were needed, are the saints and martyrs who have been formed in these communions and who have given their noble testimony before the whole world."[46]

Yet, at the same time, Pope John Paul, following the insights of the council, affirmed that the de facto disunity of churches is not acceptable. Unity does not preclude legitimate diversity. However, the present disunity of Christians and their churches is contrary to the will of the Lord and a scandal to the world. The ecumenical movement, which is now praised by the pope and the Catholic Church, cannot loose sight of the fact that visible unity in the one faith and the one Eucharist must be restored. It is not enough, said the Pope, for divided Christians simply to be together. Their fundamental unity in Christ through Baptism must be made manifest in a manner that overcomes their visible disunity. There must be an agreement in faith. Among the tasks facing the ecumenical movement is the challenge to articulate the essentials of the faith that are necessary for the reconciliation of the churches. Here, the distinction between the faith and the historic articulation of the faith reaffirmed by Pope John Paul II is a critical insight.[47]

Roman Catholic theologians are quick to point out that the dramatic developments of Roman Catholic ecumenism are not the product of ecclesiastical politics. "The resistance, hesitations, and steps backwards of the Roman See," says Jean-Marie Tillard, "show also that it is not the fruit of a capitulation before pressures coming from outside." Rather, the cautious attitude of Rome "is the guarantee that the new official actualization of the Roman Catholic obedience to the *ut sint unum* of Christ is the result of a renewed way of looking at the reality of the Church of God."[48]

CONCLUSIONS

The development of the ecumenical movement was dramatically altered from the time of the Second Vatican Council (1962–65). At this historic gathering, the Roman Catholic Church formally committed itself to ecumenical prayer, dialogue, and cooperation aimed at the restoration of visible unity among the divided churches. While there were writings and activities by a number of Catholic ecumenical pioneers, the Roman Catholic Church had formally avoided involvement in ecumenical dialogues with Orthodox and Protestants throughout the late nineteenth and early twentieth century. Before the council, the Catholic Church saw Christian unity primarily as a return of the separated brethren to its fold.

This perspective dramatically changed with the coming of Pope John XXIII and the council. The council's Constitution on the Church and its Decree on Ecumenism provided a more nuanced theological approach to the reality of other Christian churches and ecclesial communities, as well as to the quest for the unity of the churches. These documents were followed by a number of significant papal encyclicals that further articulated the position of the Roman Catholic Church. Together with these statements, the Roman Catholic Church, under the leadership of Pope Paul VI, agreed to establish formal bilateral dialogues with the Orthodox Church, the Anglican Communion, and a number of Protestant churches. From 1965 onward, it also agreed to cooperate in a number of areas with the World Council of Churches. In more recent years, the Roman Catholic Church formally joined a number of local and regional Councils of Churches. It has also encouraged prayer, theological dialogue, and common witness for unity at all levels of church life. As the twentieth century ended, Pope John Paul II continued to reaffirm the commitment of the Roman Catholic Church to the ecumenical movement and its quest for the visible unity of the churches in the same faith and Eucharist.

NOTES

1. "Decree on Ecumenism," in *Doing the Truth in Charity,* ed. Thomas Stransky and John B. Sheerin (Ramsay, N.J.: Paulist Press, 1982), p. 5.

2. J.-M. R. Tillard, O. P., "The Roman Catholic Church and Ecumenism," in *The Vision of Christian Unity,* ed. Thomas Best and Theodore Nottingham (Indianapolis: Oekoumene Publications, 1977), p. 181.

3. Ibid., p. 185.

4. George H. Tavard, *Two Centuries of Ecumenism* (New York: Mentor-Omega Books, 1962), p. 71.

5. Ibid., p. 70.

6. Ibid., p. 97.

7. Tillard, "The Roman Catholic Church and Ecumenism," in *The Vision of Christian Unity,* ed. Thomas Best and Theodore Nottingham, pp. 186–87.

8. See Pearce Cusack, *Blessed Gabrellia of Unity: A Patron for the Ecumenical Movement* (Ros Cre, Ireland: Cistercian Press, 1995).

9. See Groupe des Dombes, *For the Conversion of the Churches* (Geneva: WCC Publications, 1993).

10. Cited in Michael Putney, "The Roman Catholic Church and the Ecumenical Movement," in *Living Ecumenism,* ed. Denise Sullivan (Melbourne: JBCE, 1995), p. 186.

11. Leonard Swidler, *Blood Witness for Peace and Unity: The Life of M. J. Metzger* (Denville, N.J.: Diminision, 1977).

12. See S. Quitsland, *A Prophet Vindicated* (New York: Paulist Press, 1973).

13. See Yves Congar, *Une passion: L'Unite, Reflections et souvenirs: 1929–1973* (Paris: Éditions du Cerf, 1974); Jean-Pierre Jossua, *Yves Conger: Theology in the Service of God's People* (Chicago: Priory Press, 1968).

14. See John A. Dick, *The Malines Conversations Revisited* (Leuven: Leuven University Press, 1989).

15. Tavard, *Two Centuries of Ecumenism,* pp. 99–107.

16. See Johannes Willebrands, *Oecuménisme et problems actuels* (Paris: Édition du Cerf, 1969).

17. Cited in Putney, "The Roman Catholic Church and the Ecumenical Movement," p. 182.

18. *Acta Apostolicae Sedis* 51 (1959), p. 69. Cited in Thomas Stransky, "An Historical Sketch: The Secretariate for Promoting Christian Unity," in *Doing the Truth*

in Charity, ed. Thomas Stransky and John B. Sheerin (Ramsay, N.J.: Paulist Press, 1982), p. 5.

19. Ibid., p. 6.
20. "*Superno Dei nutu,*" *Acta Apostolicae Sedis* 52 (1960), p. 436.
21. Tillard, "The Roman Catholic Church and Ecumenism," p. 189.
22. Ibid., pp. 189–90.
23. "Decree on Ecumenism," in *Doing the Truth in Charity,* ed. Stransky and Sheerin, p. 5.
24. Ibid., p. 20.
25. "Dogmatic Constitution on the Church," in *Doing the Truth in Charity,* ed. Stransky and Sheerin, p. 33.
26. William Henn, "*Ut Unum Sint* and Catholic Involvement in Ecumenism," *The Ecumenical Review* 52:2 (April, 2000), p. 237.
27. *Joint Declaration on the Doctrine of Justification: The Lutheran World Federation and the Roman Catholic Church* (Grand Rapids, Mich.: Eerdmans Publishing Company, 2000).
28. Thomas Stransky, "An Historical Sketch: The Secretariate for Promoting Christian Unity," in *Doing the Truth in Charity,* ed. Stransky and Sheerin, p. 9.
29. Edward Kilmartin, *Towards Reunion: The Orthodox and Roman Catholic Churches* (New York: Paulist Press, 1979), pp. 40–44.
30. Thomas FitzGerald, *The Ecumenical Patriarchate and Christian Unity* (Brookline, Mass.: Holy Cross Orthodox Press, 1997), pp. 18–26.
31. "The Light of the East," *Origin* 25:1 (1995), pp. 1–13.
32. Ibid.
33. "*Ut Unum Sint,*" *Origins* 25:4 (1995), pp. 50f.
34. Ibid., p. 52.
35. Ibid., p. 53.
36. Ibid., p. 68.
37. Ibid., p. 18.
38. Ibid., p. 20.
39. Ibid., p. 78.
40. Ibid.
41. Ibid., p. 79.
42. Tillard, "Rome and Ecumenism," www.wcc-coe.org/wcc/what/faith/tillard.html.
43. Tillard, "The Roman Catholic Church and Ecumenism," p. 191.
44. *Ut Unum Sint,* p. 70.
45. William Henn, "*Ut Unum Sint* and Catholic Involvement in Ecumenism," p. 244.
46. Ibid.
47. *Ut Unum Sint,* p. 59.
48. Tillard, "The Roman Catholic Church and Ecumenism," p. 191.

CHAPTER 8

Concerns and Contributions of the Orthodox Church

> The Orthodox Church, in her profound conviction and ecclesiastical consciousness of being the bearer of and the witness to the faith and tradition of the One Holy Catholic and Apostolic Church, firmly believes that she occupies a central place in matters relating to the promotion of Christian unity within the contemporary world.
>
> —Decision of the Third Pan-Orthodox Preconciliar Conference, 1986[1]

INTRODUCTION

Representatives of the Orthodox Church have been present in the major ecumenical gatherings from the early twentieth century. Their presence continued the more recent tradition of dialogue, especially with Anglicans and Old Catholics, developed in the late nineteenth century. Because of the distinctive history, theological perspectives and particular concerns of the Orthodox Church, its participation in ecumenical activities has been cautious and not always easy. Orthodox Churches were among the founding members of the World Council of Churches in 1948. In this body, however, the Orthodox have always confronted and troubled with an overwhelming number of Protestant member churches together with their ethos and theological perspectives.

The Pan-Orthodox Conferences between 1961 and 1968 did much to unify Orthodox participation in the WCC. These conferences also sanctioned bilateral dialogue with the Roman Catholic Church, the Anglican Communion, and the Old Catholic Church and opened the way for subsequent dialogues with a number of Protestant Churches. These and later

Pan-Orthodox decisions gave greater encouragement to Orthodox ecumenical engagement at the regional and local levels.

Since the year 1989, however, the Orthodox presence in ecumenical activities has been affected by strained relationships in some places, both with Roman Catholicism and with some Protestants. These difficulties have arisen chiefly over the revival of Eastern Catholic churches in Central and Eastern Europe as well as by Protestant missions that were often perceived as proselytism. At the same time, many Orthodox have called into question the direction, programs, and ethos of the World Council of Churches and some other ecumenical bodies.

Despite these recent tensions, the Orthodox contribution to the theological discussions of the ecumenical movement has been considerable throughout the twentieth century. With theological perspectives that are neither Protestant nor Roman Catholic, the Orthodox have made a major contribution to the specific discussions on church unity and to the broader issues of Christian life and thought today. In responding to the challenge to heal the wounds of Christian divisions, the Orthodox have also provided profound insights into the fundamental affirmations of the Christian faith. The insights of Orthodox theology in some cases have challenged the perspectives of both the Roman Catholic Church and the Protestant churches and communities, which have been influenced by the Reformation and Counter-Reformation debates as well as by the Enlightenment. In other cases, the insights of Orthodox theology have enabled Roman Catholics and Protestants to reappropriate valuable perspectives on the Christian faith that are part of their own heritage, but that had been underappreciated in recent centuries.

EARLY DIALOGUES FOR CHRISTIAN UNITY

Orthodox participation in activities related to Christian reconciliation and unity began well before the twentieth century. In the decades following the Great Schism between the Christian East centered at Constantinople and the Christian West centered in old Rome, there is ample evidence of attempts to heal the division throughout the Middle Ages. The Orthodox considered the Councils of Lyons (1274) and Florence (1438–45) to be failed efforts to heal the division with Roman Catholicism. However, these councils and related contacts with Rome indicate recognition of the tragedy of disunity and a willingness to enter into dialogue.[2]

With dramatic political and cultural changes in the background, new Christian divisions in Western Europe resulted from the Protestant Reformation of the sixteenth century. Following these new divisions between Rome and the Reformation churches and groups, the impetus toward reconciliation, which characterized earlier periods of church life, weakened especially after the religious wars in Western Europe. Yet, even in this difficult period of time after the Reformation, Orthodoxy was willing to respond to overtures from both Lutherans and Anglicans.[3]

Throughout the period between the seventeenth and the nineteenth centuries, there were limited contacts of a positive nature among the various divided churches. Proselytism and a spirit of ecclesiological exclusivism characterized the relations among the divided churches. Orthodoxy often was the victim of Roman Catholic efforts to establish and support Eastern Catholic churches in Eastern Europe and the Middle East. Likewise, Protestant missionaries in such diverse places as Asia Minor, the Middle East, and Alaska often sought to convert the Orthodox to their versions of Reformed Christianity.

Throughout the late nineteenth century and early twentieth century, however, there were significant signs of more positive developments, especially between the Orthodox and the Anglicans and between the Orthodox and the Old Catholics in Western Europe. The Association for the Promotion of the Unity of Christendom was established in 1857. It sought to unite Orthodox, Anglicans, and Roman Catholics in a bond of intercessory prayer for unity. The Eastern Church Association was founded in 1863 in London. Somewhat later in 1906, the Anglican and Eastern Church Union was founded in London with the express intention of restoring communion. Prior to the First World War, these organizations helped to developed significant relations between the Church of England and the Orthodox Church of Russia. Orthodox and Old Catholics in Western Europe developed substantial contacts and dialogues between 1874 and 1919. Moreover, numerous Orthodox participated in the World Student Christian Federation meeting in Constantinople in 1911.[4]

Similar instances of encounter and dialogue could be found in the United States during the same time period. Fr. John (Innocent) Veniaminov (1797–1879), the noted Orthodox missionary in Alaska, met with Roman Catholic Franciscans in California in 1836.[5] In the early decades of the twentieth century, both Metropolitan Meletios Metaxakis (1871–1935) of the Greek Orthodox Archdiocese and Archbishop Tikhon Belavin (1865–1925) of the Russian Orthodox Archdiocese sought to maintain contacts with bishops of the Episcopal Church.[6] The latter subsequently became patriarch of Moscow and the former, patriarch of Constantinople.

More formal expressions of Orthodox concern for dialogue were expressed by the Church of Constantinople in 1904 and in 1920, as well as the Church of Russia in 1918. The Church of Constantinople in 1904 called upon the other Autocephalous Orthodox Churches to consider formally the issue of Christian unity and the possible establishment of dialogues with the Roman Catholic Church, the Old Catholic Church, and the Protestant churches. The more famous Encyclical of 1920 proposed the establishment of a "fellowship of Churches" to address issues related to Christian reconciliation. This was a dramatic and farsighted proposal.[7]

Likewise, the participants in the historic Council of 1917–1918 of the Church of Russia passed a positive resolution regarding dialogue with the Old Catholics and Anglicans. The council bestowed its blessing "on the labors and efforts of those who are seeking the way towards union with the above-mentioned friendly churches. The Council authorizes the Sacred Synod to organize a Permanent Commission with departments in Russia and abroad for further study of Old Catholic and Anglican difficulties in the way of union, and for the furtherance as much as possible of the speedy attainment of the final aim."[8] The tragic Russian Revolution of 1918 and the Civil War prevented the formal organization of the commission at that time.

All of these encounters and theological conversations involving Orthodox clergy and theologians must be seen as significant expressions of a concern for mutual understanding, and even reconciliation, long before the better known events—the early ecumenical gatherings of the 1920s and 1930s. Likewise, the formal declarations of Constantinople and Moscow set a positive perspective on Orthodox dialogue with other churches during the early twentieth century.

RECENT AFFIRMATIONS AND CHALLENGES

The Edinburgh Missionary Conference of 1910 is frequently identified by some as the genesis of the ecumenical movement in the twentieth century. Undoubtedly, this was an important event for many Protestant participants. For them, it marked the beginning of a new concern for Christian unity.[9] Yet the Orthodox, who were not invited to Edinburgh, had already entered into some serious contacts with Anglicans and Old Catholics in the late nineteenth and early twentieth centuries.

The early meetings of the Faith and Order Movement and the Life and Work Movement provided a valuable opportunity for Orthodox theologians to enter into direct contact with Anglican and Protestant theologians. The Orthodox participants included leading theologians from the patriarchate of Constantinople and the Church of Greece.[10] Also participating were a number of notable theologians from Russia who had become part of the exile communities of Western Europe.[11] Following involvement in the early meetings of the Faith and Order Movement and the Life and Work Movement, a number of Orthodox Churches became founding members of the World Council of Churches in 1948. Over the course of the following two decades, all the Autocephalous Eastern Orthodox Churches and Oriental Orthodox Churches became members of the World Council of Churches.[12]

ORTHODOX PIONEERS AND LEADING CONTRIBUTORS

During this critical period, Ecumenical Patriarch Athenagoras (Spyrou) of Constantinople (1886–1972) was one of the most important advocates for Orthodox ecumenical dialogue.[13] Before becoming patriarch in 1948, Athenagoras had served with distinction in Corfu and in America. In both places, he became acquainted with the tragedy of Christian disunity. During his 24 years as the primatial bishop of Orthodox Christianity, Athenagoras fostered a renewal of the conciliar in his own church and encouraged ecumenical engagement even in the face of criticism. In one of his early encyclicals in 1952, Athenagoras declared, "the task of rapprochement and cooperation between all Christian confessions and organizations is a sacred obligation and a holy duty."[14] He fostered full participation in the WCC. He heralded a new relationship with the Roman Catholic Church through his meetings with Pope Paul VI in Jerusalem, Rome, and Istanbul. In addition, he presided over the establishment of the international bilateral dialogues with other churches. Shortly before his death in 1972, he emphasized the significance of Orthodox witness saying: "Our most holy Orthodox Church should not and can not hide away the treasure which is its faith nor the wealth of its traditions; rather, she must offer herself to the world in a spirit of humble service, with a view to the transfiguration of the world in Christ."[15]

Athenagoras was not alone in expressing the Orthodox concern for unity. A number of outstanding Orthodox theologians took part in the early ecumenical meetings during the period between 1920 and 1948 especially. Among the more prominent in this early period were Archbishop Germanos Strenopoulos, Fr. Sergius Bulgakov, Hamilikar Alivisatos, Paul Evdokimov, Nicholas Zernov, and Fr. Georges Florovsky.[16] In more recent times, distinguished theologians as Archbishop Iakovos Coucousis of America, Metropolitan Chrisostomos Konstantinidis, Metropolitan Emilianos Timiadis, Metropolitan John Zizioulas, Metropolitan Maximos Aghiorgoussis, Archbishop Peter L'Huilier, Bishop Kallistos Ware, Fr. John Meyendorff, Fr. Ion Bria, Fr. Vitali Borovoy, Niko Nissiotis, and Nicholas Lossky have continued the tradition of ecumenical witness.

THE PRECONCILIAR CONFERENCES

For the Orthodox Churches, the formal decisions of the Pan-Orthodox Conferences between 1961 and 1968 and the subsequent preconciliar meetings affirmed their involvement in the quest for Christian unity. Under the inspiration of Patriarch Athenagoras, these Pan-Orthodox Conferences were designed to prepare an agenda for a future "Great and Holy Council of the Orthodox Church."[17] Closely related to this task was the topic of Orthodox involvement in the ecumenical movement, which received much attention. These Conferences endorsed Orthodox participation in the WCC. The Conferences also endorsed the establishment of bilateral dialogues with the Roman Catholic Church, the Anglican Communion, the Old Catholic Church, and the Oriental Orthodox Churches.[18]

The First Preconciliar Conference in 1976 established ten topics to be discussed before a council. Among these was the topic of Orthodox relations with the rest of the Christian world and Orthodoxy in the Ecumenical Movement. This same Conference undertook a thorough review of the relationship of the Orthodox Church with other churches and with the World Council of Churches. It was determined that the theological dialogues with the Anglican Communion, the Old Catholic Church, and the Oriental Orthodox Churches were to be strengthened. Likewise, it was decided to continue preparations for dialogue with the Roman Catholic Church and to establish a dialogue with the Lutheran Church.[19]

At the Third Preconciliar Pan-Orthodox Conference in 1986, the Orthodox Churches reaffirmed their commitment to the quest for Christian reconciliation and the unity of the churches with a very significant statement. A portion of the report says:

> The Orthodox Church, in her profound conviction and ecclesiastical consciousness of being the bearer of and the witness to the faith and tradition of the One, Holy Catholic and Apostolic Church, firmly believes that she occupies a central place in matters relating to the promotion of Christian unity within the contemporary world.
>
> The Orthodox Church notes that in the course of history, for a variety of reasons and in diverse ways, there have been numerous and important deviations from the tradition of the undivided Church. Thus, arose in the Christian world divergent conceptions about the unity and the very essence of the Church. The Orthodox Church grounds the unity of the Church on the fact that she was founded by our Lord Jesus Christ, as well as on the communion in the Holy Trinity and in the Sacraments. This unity is manifested through the apostolic succession and the patristic tradition and to this day is lived within her. It is the mission and duty of the Orthodox Church to transmit, in all its fullness, the truth contained in the Holy Scripture and the Holy Tradition, the truth which gives to the Church her universal character.
>
> The responsibility of the Orthodox Church, as well as her ecumenical mission regarding Church unity were expressed by the Ecumenical Councils. These, in particular, stressed the indissoluble link existing between true faith and the sacramental communion. The Orthodox Church has always sought to draw the different Christian Churches and Confessions into a joint pilgrimage aiming at searching the lost unity of Christians, so that all might reach the unity of faith.
>
> The Orthodox Church, which unceasingly prays "for the union of all," has taken part in the ecumenical movement since its inception and has contributed to its formation and further development. In fact, the Orthodox Church, due to the ecumenical spirit by which she is distinguished, has, throughout the history,

fought for the restoration of Christian unity. Therefore, the Orthodox participation in the ecumenical movement does not run counter to the nature and history of the Orthodox Church. It constitutes the consistent expression of the apostolic faith within new historical conditions, in order to respond to new existential demands.

It is in this spirit that all the local Holy Orthodox Churches actively participate today in the work of the various national, regional and international bodies of the ecumenical movement and take part in different bilateral and multilateral dialogues, despite the difficulties and crises arising occasionally in the normal course of this movement. This many-faceted ecumenical activity derives from the sense of responsibility and from the conviction that coexistence, mutual understanding, cooperation, and common efforts towards Christian unity are essential, so as "not to hinder the Gospel of Christ" (I Cor. 9:12).[20]

RECENT TENSIONS

This statement captures the fundamental approach of the Orthodox Church as a whole to the ecumenical movement. Despite this positive statement affirming the involvement of the Orthodox Church in the ecumenical movement, there have been some serious tensions in recent years. Some of these involve the direction of the World Council of Churches, some involve the practice of proselytism, and some involve the restoration of Eastern Catholic Churches within the Roman Catholic Church.[21]

The Orthodox participation in the WCC has never been entirely comfortable. Yet the Orthodox have certainly benefited from their involvement in the council. While not always easy, encounters between Orthodox and other member churches of the council have assisted the Orthodox in reflecting upon critical theological issues. The council frequently provided opportunities for representatives of Orthodox Churches to meet together to discuss important theological concerns. Moreover, a number of Orthodox Churches have benefited from the material support provided by the council. At the same time, they have made important contributions to its theological discussion.[22] From the beginning of the WCC, however, the Orthodox have had to contend with a body in which Protestant member churches predominate because of their overwhelming numbers. This means that the ethos, methodology, and theology of Protestantism has tended to dominate the council's programs and activities as well as its perspective on ecumenism.

At the heart of the historic tensions between Protestants and Orthodox have been very different understandings of the church and of the essentials of the Christian faith. Orthodox do not share the same view of the church that is held by many Protestants. The Orthodox do not accept the popular Protestant sense of denominationalism. Such a view appears to imply that all the various Protestant bodies, often with very different teachings and organizations, are part of the church. For this reason, Orthodox have reacted against the so-called branch theory, which essentially views all expressions of Christian churches as somewhat complementary.[23] Likewise, Orthodox have been troubled by what appears to be the wide diversity of beliefs within Protestantism as a whole and even within particular Protestant churches. In some cases, the Orthodox have been troubled by what appears to be a movement among some Protestants to diminish the centrality of Christ and the ultimate significance of the Christian gospel. The Orthodox appreciate the concern of many Protestants to struggle against social injustices. Yet, at the same time, the Orthodox believe that all Christian witness must be firmly rooted in the distinctive affirmations of the Christian faith and not primarily in political or social ideologies.[24]

While committed to the goal of visible unity, the Orthodox have firmly affirmed their identity with the Church of Christ and have rejected any attempt to be characterized as simply another denomination. They have professed that they have preserved the apostolic faith of the church free from addition or distortion. Having said this, however, they have also frequently spoken about the tragedy of schism and heresy. Following the example of the early church, the Orthodox have affirmed the obligation to heal the wounds of division. In so doing, most Orthodox would recognize that there are bonds that still unite those who are divided by schism. These bonds, such as faith in the Holy Trinity and the reality of baptism, provide the basis for dialogue.[25] Metropolitan John Zizioulas has recently said: "The Orthodox participate in the Ecumenical Movement out of a conviction that the unity of the Church is an inescapable imperative for all Christians. This unity can not be restored or fulfilled except through the coming together of those who share in the same faith in the Triune God and who are baptized in his name."[26]

The Orthodox concern for the direction and ethos of the World Council of Churches intensified in the period between the Canberra Assembly in 1991 and the Harare Assembly in 1999. At the Canberra Assembly, Orthodox participants issued a significant statement that identified many of their concerns. The Orthodox expressed fears that the council was departing from its fundamental basis and purpose that "must be the restoration of the unity of the Church." The Orthodox also said: "Visible unity, in both the faith and structure of the Church, constitutes a specific goal and must not be taken for granted." They also noted: "We perceive a growing departure from biblically based Christian understanding of (a) the Trinitarian God, (b) salvation, (c) the Good News of the Gospel itself, (d) human beings created in the image and likeness of God, and (d) the Church, among others." The Orthodox concluded their observations with the prayer that the Holy Spirit "helps all Christians to renew their commitment to visible unity."[27] At the Harare Assembly in 1999, in the face of more vocal Orthodox concerns, the assembly agreed to establish a Special Commission to study such features as the ethos, structures, decision-making processes, and worship practices of the council.

The issues that the Orthodox expressed over the WCC also reflected the concern over proselytism by Protestant missionaries. As a result of the political changes in Russia and other parts of Eastern Europe, many Protestant missionaries began to engage in missionary work among Orthodox Christians in these regions. This was often done with little or no regard for the local Orthodox Church or for the profound difficulties experienced by believers and their church under the previous communist regimes. While some of these missionaries were associated with Protestant member churches of the WCC, many were not. At the local level, however, Orthodox clergy and laity were not always in a position to make a distinction between those Protestants who opposed proselytism and those who practiced it. The activities of these Protestant missionary groups seriously damaged ecumenical relationships at the local level and had repercussions at the global level.[28]

At a meeting of the primates of Orthodox Churches in 1992, the bishops repudiated these activities. They said: "The consideration of these countries as 'terra missionis' is unacceptable, since in these countries the Gospel has been preached for many centuries. It is because of their faith in Christ that the faithful in these countries often sacrificed their very lives." In condemning the practice of proselytism, the bishops said that it "poisons the relations among Christians and destroys the road toward their unity."[29]

These concerns have also been reflected in recent relations with the Roman Catholic Church. Since the year 1990, the relationship between the Orthodox Church and the Roman Catholic Church has been deeply troubled, especially in Eastern Europe and Russia. In the wake of great political changes there, there was a resurgence of Eastern Catholic churches. Sometimes known as Uniates, these churches follow the liturgical customs of Eastern Christianity but accept the ultimate authority of the pope.[30] In many places, there were accusations of proselytism and sharp conflicts arose over property rights between Orthodox and Eastern Catholics.[31] Some Orthodox viewed the revival of Eastern Catholic churches as an attempt by Rome to undermine the Orthodox Church in those regions. Some Catholics accused the Orthodox of violating principles of religious freedom.[32] Moreover, the unilateral decision of Rome in 2002 to establish four Latin Rite dioceses in Russia further aggravated the relations between Orthodoxy and Roman Catholicism there. Since 1993, these difficulties greatly hampered the ongoing activities of the International Theological Dialogue between the two churches.

ORTHODOX OPPONENTS TO THE ECUMENICAL MOVEMENT

These recent tensions have greatly troubled those Orthodox who are committed to the quest for unity. The tensions also have contributed to the position of those Orthodox who have consistently opposed the activities of the ecumenical movement. Some of this opposition has come from within a number of the Autocephalous Orthodox Churches. In recent times, for example, this can be found in some quarters of the Church of Greece and the Church of Russia. Because of these tensions, the Orthodox Churches of Georgia and Bulgaria withdrew from membership in the World Council of Churches in 1998. The opposition to Orthodox ecumenical activity has also been expressed in some statements issued from monastic communities on Mount Athos. Following the meeting of Patriarch Athenagoras of Constantinople with Pope Paul in 1964, some monastics began to accuse the patriarch of heresy. In addition, since that time, a number of monastics there have opposed the dialogues with Roman Catholics and Protestants supported by the patriarchate of Constantinople.[33]

Much of the vocal opposition to all forms of Orthodox involvement in the ecumenical movement has emanated from small groups that claim to be Orthodox, but which are not in full communion with the Autocephalous Orthodox Churches. Indeed, at the meeting of the heads of Orthodox Churches in 1992, these groups were identified as "schismatic groups competing with the canonical structure of the Orthodox Church."[34] A number of these groups have sought to distinguish themselves from the Autocephalous Orthodox Churches through their intense opposition to all expressions of Orthodox dialogue with Roman Catholicism and Protestantism. These groups claim that all forms of dialogue are a betrayal of the Orthodox faith. They believe, therefore, that they have preserved the purity of Orthodox faith and practice. Among the small bodies that express these positions are a number of the so-called Old Calendar groups, which separated from the Orthodox Church of Greece beginning in the year 1924.[35] Initially, they opposed the modification of the calendar accepted by a number of Autocephalous Orthodox Churches. They subsequently began to oppose all forms of Orthodox ecumenical dialogue.[36]

Likewise, the Russian Orthodox Church Outside of Russia has also been consistently opposed to Orthodox involvement in the ecumenical movement.[37] From the 1960s onward, this aversion to ecumenism complemented the Synod Abroad's staunch opposition to the activities of the Orthodox Church of Russia, which was viewed as controlled by the communist authorities.[38] The opposition of the Russian Orthodox Synod Abroad to Orthodox participation in ecumenical dialogues became more intense after the Pan-Orthodox Conferences of 1961 and 1963 and especially after the entrance of the Church of Russia into the World Council of Churches in 1961.[39] The Synod Abroad depicted itself as the remnant in which the Orthodox faith is preserved free from all forms of modernism, communism, and ecumenism. While containing only a few thousand members, the Synod Abroad viewed itself as "the only Orthodox Church remaining in America and the entire world whose hierarchy stands fully behind traditional Orthodoxy and against the approaching union."[40] At a meeting of the bishops of the Synod Abroad in 1971 in Montreal, they declared ecumenism to be "a heresy against the dogma of the church."[41]

At the official level, the Autocephalous Orthodox Churches have generally chosen not to respond to the statements of these small groups, which have criticized Orthodox involvement in ecumenical dialogue. As we have already noted, these groups are not in communion with the Autocephalous Orthodox Churches and are, therefore, perceived as being in a state of schism. However, at a meeting of delegates from the Autocephalous Orthodox Churches in Thessaloniki, Greece, in 1998, the perspectives and activities of these groups were noted briefly. In their statement, the Orthodox delegates "denounced those groups of schismatic, as well as certain extremist groups within local Orthodox Churches themselves, that are using the theme of ecumenism in order to criticize the Church leadership and undermine its authority, thus attempting to create divisions and schisms within the Church." The Orthodox delegates also claimed that these groups "use non-factual material and misinformation in order to support their unjust criticism."[42]

THE ORTHODOX THEOLOGICAL CONTRIBUTION TO DIALOGUE AND CHURCH UNITY

The representatives of the Orthodox Church in dialogues have consistently emphasized that the historic Christian faith must be central to the quest for Christian reconciliation and the unity of the churches. Throughout the various phases of the contemporary ecumenical movement, this has been a consistent affirmation by the Orthodox. Unity cannot be found in a minimization of the historic faith. On the contrary, it can only be found through a common affirmation of the faith of the Church throughout the ages.

Through ecumenical meetings and theological dialogues, Western Christian theologians have come into living contact with the Orthodox Church and her theologians.[43] This encounter has enabled many Western Christians to move beyond a distorted perception of Orthodoxy, popularized in the late nineteenth century and early twentieth century.[44] This false perception of Orthodoxy as essentially exotic, decadent, and moribund was rooted especially in the writings of Edward Gibbon (1737–94) and Adolph von Harnack (1851–1930). Their influence can still be found in more recent theological and historical studies that continue to ignore so many of the developments in non-Western Christianity.[45] At the same time, the scholarly writings of Orthodox theologians and historians have done much to provide a more balanced and accurate picture of Eastern Christianity.[46] It is against this backdrop that the Orthodox have made their contribution both to ecumenical witness and to a reaffirmation of Christian perspectives.[47]

The insights of Orthodox theology in some cases have challenged the perspectives both of the Roman Catholic Church and the Protestant churches and communities, which have been so influenced by the Reformation and Counter-Reformation debates as well as by the Enlightenment. In other cases, the insights of Orthodox theology have enabled Roman Catholics and Protestants to reappropriate valuable perspectives on the Christian faith that are part of their own heritage, but which had been underappreciated in recent centuries. Ultimately, the contribution of Orthodox theologians has not sought the victory of one tradition over another. Rather, the Orthodox contribution has been concerned with healing the wounds of division through a deeper understanding of the Christian message. As Orthodox theologians said in 1961:

> The Orthodox Church is willing to participate in this common work as the witness, which has preserved continuously the deposit of the apostolic faith and tradition. No static restoration of old forms is anticipated, but rather a dynamic recovery of a perennial ethos, which can only secure the true agreement 'of the ages.' Nor should there be a rigid uniformity, since the same faith…can be expressed accurately in different manners. The immediate objective of the ecumenical search is, according to the Orthodox understanding, a reintegration of Christian mind, a recovery of Apostolic tradition, a fullness of Christian vision and belief in agreement with all the ages.[48]

Throughout their participation in the activities in the World Council of Churches and in the more recent bilateral dialogues, Orthodox theologians have emphasized a number of themes that have made a valuable contribution to theological discussion on church unity issues and to the witness of Christian faith today. Reflecting a sense of continuity with early Christianity, the following four interrelated perspectives are especially significant.

1. A Perspective on the Triune God

In his classic study, Vladimir Lossky says that the doctrine of the Trinity is "the unshakeable foundation of all religious thought, of all piety, of all spiritual life and of all experience."[49] This affirmation would certainly be taken for granted by all Orthodox theologians. They affirm that, as a consequence of the divine revelation centered upon Christ, Christians have come to know God as Father, Son, and Holy Spirit. In prayers, Christians address and honor each person of the Trinity while affirming the oneness of God. Through Christian living, believers are drawn into a relationship with the persons of the Trinity as well as with one another in the midst of the creation. The mystery of the Holy Trinity provides the very framework for Christian understanding of the human person, the Church, and worship.

Within the context of the ecumenical movement, Orthodox theologians have been forceful advocates of Trinitarian theology. The Orthodox have not only called for an ecumenical recovery of the significance of the Trinity for the Christian faith but also have affirmed that the Trinity provides us with a valuable vision of the meaning of the church and her unity. This advocacy by the Orthodox has directly contributed to a renewed emphasis upon the Trinity both in ecumenical discussions and in the internal theological discussions of many Western churches.[50]

Reflections on the Trinity could barely be found in ecumenical agendas during the early part of the twentieth century. The early ecumenical conferences frequently made a strong affirmation of the significance of Christ. Yet the activity of God the Father and the activity of the Holy Spirit received little attention from most Western Christian theologians. Not long ago, the distinguished Roman Catholic theologian Karl Rahner observed that the doctrine of the Trinity barely occupied a place in the piety and faith of Western Christianity today.[51] His observation confirms the Orthodox suspicion that a "Christomonism" had come to characterize the understanding of God in much of the Christian West. The affirmation of the Trinity became "unintelligible and religiously irrelevant on a wide scale" within many expressions of Western Christianity.[52]

Chiefly because of Orthodox recommendations, the World Council of Churches formally altered its basis at the New Delhi Assembly of 1961. Since that time, the council has described itself as "a fellowship of Churches which accept Our Lord Jesus Christ as God and Saviour to the glory of one God, Father Son and Holy Spirit."[53] This change signaled the renewal of interest in the doctrine of the Trinity not only in the WCC but also in many of the Western churches and in the writings of many of their theologians. Both the Second Vatican Council (1962–65) and the theological discussions within the Faith and Order Commission of the WCC during the1960s and 1970s have reflected this renewed interest in Trinitarian theology.

The fresh emphasis upon the reality and significance of the Holy Trinity can be found in three critical studies from the Faith and Order Commission of the WCC, which reached fruition between 1980 and 1991 and reflected discussions reaching back at least a quarter of a century. These are: *Baptism, Eucharist, and Ministry* (1982), *Church and World: The Unity of the Church and the Renewal of Human Community* (1990), and *Confessing the One Faith: An Ecumenical Explication of the Apostolic Faith as it is Confessed in the Nicene-Constantinopolitan Creed* (1991).[54]

The global bilateral dialogues involving the Orthodox Church in recent years have focused on the doctrine of the Trinity with an eye to its significance for Christian reconciliation and unity. In the work of these dialogues, the Orthodox have affirmed that fundamental agreement on

Trinitarian doctrine is essential to the process of reconciliation as well as to a proper understanding of the Church and her unity. The Joint International Commission of the Orthodox Church and the Roman Catholic Church published, in 1982, its statement on "The Mystery of the Church and of the Eucharist in the Light of the Mystery of the Trinity."[55] The Orthodox-Reformed dialogue published its "Agreed Statement on the Holy Trinity" in 1992.[56] In addition, the International Commission of the Anglican-Orthodox Theological Dialogue circulated its agreed interim statement on "The Trinity and the Church in 1998."[57]

While the full extent of Orthodox influence can never be completely determined, during the past 50 years there has been a resurgence of writings on the Holy Trinity coming from a wide variety of theologians in the Roman Catholic Church, Anglican, Old Catholic, and many Protestant churches. Indeed, one could say that the ecumenical movement has contributed to a genuine cross-fertilization of traditions that are leading to a number of significant common emphases. There is common consensus that the mystery of the Trinity provides the basis for further reflection on such critical topics as the church, worship, salvation, and ministry. There is a preference for a perspective on the Trinity that seeks to balance the emphasis upon both the distinctiveness of the Persons and the unity of the one God. Finally, the understanding of the communion of love of the divine Persons has led to deeper reflection upon the nature of communion between the Triune God and human persons, among persons within creation and among the churches.[58] The icon of the Holy Trinity, which has become so popular in ecumenical gatherings in recent years, has provided a visual basis for meditation on many of these themes.[59]

2. A Perspective on Eucharistic-Trinitarian Ecclesiology

Because of the questions raised by the ecumenical movement, the topic of the Church has received much attention throughout this century from theologians in all the Christian traditions. What is especially significant in the writings of the past three decades is the fact that perspectives on the Church are now being more closely related to the reality of the Holy Trinity. As Metropolitan Maximos Aghiorgoussis has said: "As a reflection of the Trinity, the Church is a unity and community of persons in which unity and diversity are preserved as they are in the three persons of the Holy Trinity. The Holy Trinity is a 'council,' a unity of three diverse persons who live in communion with each other. Thus, conciliarity is inherent in the Church since the Church is also a council, an image and reflection of the 'council' of the Holy Trinity."[60]

An ecclesiology that is expressed through the Holy Eucharist and that reflects the relations of the three Persons of the Holy Trinity has been the hallmark of Orthodox discussions on the Church. Nicholas Afanassieff first expressed the preliminary outline of this ecclesiology.[61] Many Orthodox theologians have taken up the theme of Eucharistic ecclesiology in one form or another in recent years. Chief among these has been Metropolitan John Zizioulas.[62] The proponents of a Eucharistic-Trinitarian ecclesiology advocate a return to an understanding of the Church that is more in harmony with that found in the apostolic and early patristic period. It is an understanding of the Church that is centered upon the activity of the three Persons of the Holy Trinity and highlights the centrality of the Eucharist. It is also an ecclesiology that seeks to overcome the distortions that have emerged due to political and historical contingencies of recent centuries.[63]

Within ecumenical dialogues, the Orthodox have consistently emphasized the importance of the goal of the *visible* unity of the churches.[64] In speaking about visible unity, the Orthodox are certainly not denying the spiritual bonds that exist among Christians and their churches. Indeed, certain bonds continue to exist despite the harsh reality of schism.[65] However, the Orthodox have consistently emphasized that the unity of the divided churches must consist of more than just cooperation and rather vague affirmations of common convictions. In light of the reality of the Incarnation, the Orthodox have affirmed that the unity of the church must find concrete expressions. Chief among these is the celebration of the Eucharist. This involves the profession of the same faith and the recognition of the same sacraments.[66]

The Orthodox emphasis upon the dynamic relationship between the reality of the Holy Trinity and the Church and the Eucharist has influenced ecumenical discussions not only on these topics. The Orthodox perspective has also helped to provide a new framework for ecumenical discussions of the meaning of salvation, the relationship of Scripture and tradition, and the significance of the ordained ministry.[67] These have been especially important topics in ecumenical discussions.

3. A Perspective on the Theocentric Person

The renewed interest in Trinitarian theology has led to a view of the human person that emphasizes the characteristic of relationality. According to the Orthodox perspective, the identity, dignity, and value of the human person are rooted in our fundamental relationship with the Triune God. Human persons have been created by God to live in communion with him both now and throughout all eternity. This relationship with God involves the three divine Persons of the Trinity. It also involves being in positive and healthy relationships with other human persons and with the entire creation.[68]

Within ecumenical dialogue on the topic of the human person, Orthodox theologians begin with orientations quite different from those that developed in the Christian West, which are generally traced to the writings of St. Augustine (354–430). Through the recent encounters with theological anthropologies emanating from the Christian West, the Orthodox have emphasized two critical points. First, the purpose of the divine revelation, which is centered upon the coming of Jesus Christ, is to restore the human person and the entire creation to communion with the Father through the Son and in the Spirit. In the often repeated axiom of the early Church Fathers, "God became human so that human persons may become divine."[69] The Orthodox affirm that God's own revelation is an act of love for his creation.

The Orthodox also affirm that the human person is fundamentally theocentric. It is natural for the human person to live in harmony with God. The human person is not meant to be an autonomous individual. Through a loving relationship with the Triune God and with others, the human person truly grows in the likeness of God. Sin, which can be freely chosen, distorts the relationship but it cannot fully eradicate the fundamental bond of love between God and his sons and daughters. Because of God's love, the human person can never lose the image of God, which is essential to human identity.[70]

With this in mind, the Orthodox view salvation primarily as the process of deification *(theosis)* through which each person responds to the divine initiative and grows in his or her relationship with the Triune God within the life of the believing community, which is the Church.[71] The Church is an integral part of the divine plan of salvation. It is in communion with other believers that each person deepens the communion with God. This communion with God does not destroy the fundamental identity of each person nor does it absorb the human person into the divine. Rather, it is through this relationship of love that the true identity and dignity and destiny of each person are revealed.[72] Orthodox frequently repeat the affirmation of St. Irenaeus of Lyons (ca. 130–ca. 200), who said: "The glory of God is the human person fully alive."[73]

The Orthodox also believe that process of salvation has a cosmic dimension. The human person is not saved from the world but in and through the world. The soul is not saved from the body but in and through the body. Far from rejecting the body and the material world, the Orthodox look upon the physical as the work of God that is fundamentally good and the medium through which the divine is manifest.[74] Thus, the transfiguration of the creation is already prefigured in the lives of the faithful, in the Eucharist, in the icons, and in the relics of the saints.

Within the ecumenical context, the discussion on the human person and the entire creation in the light of the Trinity has only begun to be explored. Yet already some important Orthodox insights based upon the reality of the Trinity can be seen in our approach to a number of contemporary questions.[75] These have to do with moral and ethical issues,[76] with questions of human rights and responsibilities,[77] with questions related to the environment,[78] and with questions related to the relationship of women and men.[79]

4. Perspectives on Worship and Spirituality

From the early decades of this century, movements to renew worship could be found in many of the churches. With the development of greater contacts between the churches through meetings and consultations, questions related to worship, the sacraments, and spirituality began to be examined in an ecumenical manner.[80] Much of this early ecumenical work in the area of liturgics provided the background for the historic text *Baptism, Eucharist, and Ministry (BEM)* by the Faith and Order Commission of the World Council of Churches in 1982.[81] At the time of its publication, the Orthodox theologian Nikos Nissiotis and the Lutheran theologian William Lazareth said that the consensus expressed in the text was "unprecedented in the modern ecumenical movement."[82] *BEM* certainly did not resolve all the differences among the churches related to worship. Yet it clearly marked a breakthrough in the way in which certain topics could be viewed. Indeed, since the time of its publication, *BEM* has become the most popular consensus text to emerge from the contemporary ecumenical movement.[83]

The *BEM* text reflects a number of insights into the nature of worship that have been emphasized by Orthodox theologians in ecumenical meetings for decades.[84] Among these concerns are: the relationship between worship and faith and witness,[85] the significance of worship for the Church and Christian life,[86] the relationship of worship to the activity of the Persons of the Trinity,[87] the centrality of baptism and the Eucharist,[88] as well as the doxological, cosmic, and eschatological dimensions of the Eucharist.[89]

Closely related to the Orthodox contribution to ecumenical discussions on worship has been the contribution to the discussion of spirituality.[90] The Orthodox have sought to express perspectives on spirituality that overcome many of the false dichotomies, such as between the nature and super nature, sacred and the secular, which have afflicted many Western Christian traditions. In so doing, the Orthodox have frequently referred to the insights of the early Christian teachers.[91] Also of special importance has been the emphasis that the Orthodox have placed on the role of Mary the Mother of God (Theotokos), the value of the body and all material creation, the communion of the saints, and the significance of the icon.[92] While these topics are not always prominent in the formal ecumenical agenda, they are frequently expressed in the writings on spirituality by many contemporary Roman Catholics, Anglicans, Old Catholics, and Protestants.[93]

Speaking of the Orthodox witness and contribution to dialogue, Ecumenical Patriarch Bartholomew recently said:

> Disunity is not simply an inconvenience, not simply a hindrance and a scandal, but it is a contradiction of the basic essence of the Church as an icon of God's mutual Trinitarian love. In its quest for unity, the Ecumenical Movement is doing nothing else than reasserting the full practical consequences of our faith in the Trinity.
>
> There is a direct link between the oneness of Christians, after the image of the Trinity, and the missionary dimension of the Church. The Church looks not inward but outward. It exists not for the sake of itself but for the sake of the world's salvation.[94]

CONCLUSIONS

Since the beginning of the twentieth century, the representatives of the Orthodox Church have been present in the major ecumenical initiatives. Their presence continued a tradition of dialogue especially with Anglicans and Old Catholics, which developed in the late nineteenth century. Yet even these dialogues continued a century-old tradition that sought to heal Christian divisions. In recent times, the participation of Orthodox representatives in dialogues has been cautious and not without difficulties. The history and theological perspectives of the Orthodox Church have been different from those of Western Christians. In many early ecumenical gatherings, the Orthodox often encountered a strong emphasis upon Protestant perspectives. Yet Orthodox Churches were among the founding members of the World Council of Churches in 1948. In subsequent years, all Autocephalous Orthodox Churches became members of the WCC.

The Pan-Orthodox Conference between 1961 and 1968 did much to unify and strengthen Orthodox participation in the World Council of Churches. These conferences also sanctioned bilateral dialogue with the Roman Catholic Church, the Anglican Communion, and the Old Catholic Church. They also opened the way for subsequent dialogues with a number of Protestant churches. These and later Pan-Orthodox decisions gave greater encouragement to Orthodox ecumenical engagement at the regional and local levels.

The Orthodox presence in ecumenical activities since 1989 has been affected by strained relationships in some places, both with Roman Catholicism and with some Protestants. These difficulties have arisen chiefly over the revival of Eastern Catholic Churches in Central and Eastern Europe as well as by Protestant missions, which were perceived often as proselytism. At the same time, many Orthodox have called into question the direction, programs, and ethos of the World Council of Churches and some other ecumenical bodies.

Despite these recent tensions, the Orthodox contribution to the theological discussions of the ecumenical movement has been considerable throughout the twentieth century. With distinctive theological perspectives, the Orthodox have made a major contribution to the discussions on church unity as well as to the broader issues of Christian life and thought today. In responding to the challenge to heal the wounds of Christian divisions, the Orthodox have also provided profound insights into the fundamental affirmations of the Christian faith. The insights of Orthodox theology in some cases have challenged the theological perspectives of both the Roman Catholic Church and the Protestant churches, which are so influenced by the Reformation and Counter-Reformation debates as well as by the Enlightenment. In other cases, the insights of Orthodox theology have enabled Roman Catholics and Protestants to reappropriate valuable perspectives on the Christian faith, which are part of their own heritage but were underappreciated in recent centuries.

NOTES

1. "Decision of the Third Pre-Conciliar Pan-Orthodox Conference (November 6, 1986)," in *Orthodox Vision of Ecumenism*, ed. Gennadios Limouris (Geneva: WCC Publication, 1994), p. 112.

2. J.M. Hussey, *The Orthodox Church in the Byzantine Empire* (Oxford: Clarendon Press, 1986), pp. 220–94; John Meyendorff, *Byzantine Theology* (New York: Fordham University Press, 1974), pp. 91–114. Deno Geanakoplos provides a valuable introduction to these attempts at reconciliation in his *Byzantine East and Latin West: Two Worlds of Christendom in Middle Ages and Renaissance* (New York, 1966).

3. Timothy Ware, *The Orthodox Church* (New York: Penguin Books, revised edition, 1976), pp. 102–8.

4. Georges Florovsky, *Ecumenism II A Historical Approach* (Vaduz: Büchervertribsanstalt, 1989), pp. 126–48.

5. Thomas FitzGerald, *The Orthodox Church* (Wesport, Conn.: Greenwood Press, 1995), p. 19.

6. Peter Haskell, "Archbishop Tikhon and Bishop Grafton: An Early Chapter in Anglican-Orthodox Relations in the New World," *St. Vladimir's Theological Quarterly* 11:4 (1967), pp. 193–206 and 12:1 (1969), pp. 2–16.

7. Thomas FitzGerald, "The Patriarchal Encyclicals on Christian Unity," *The Greek Orthodox Theological Review* 22:3 (1977), pp. 300–303.

8. *The Anglican and Eastern Church Association: A Historical Record, 1914–1921* (SPCK: London, 1921), pp. 43–44; Florovsky, p. 148.

9. Stephen Neill, *Brothers of the Faith* (New York: Abingdon Press, 1960), pp. 16–28.

10. Robert Stephanopoulos, *A Study of Recent Greek Orthodox Ecumenical Relations, 1902–1968* (Ann Arbor: University Microfilms, 1970), pp. 56–101.

11. See Nicholas Zernov, "The Significance of the Russian Orthodox Diaspora and its Effect on the Christian West," in *The Orthodox Churches and the West*, ed. Derek Baker (Oxford: Blackwell's, 1976), pp. 307–27.

12. Stephanopoulos, *A Study of Recent Greek Orthodox Ecumenical Relations, 1902–1968*, pp. 102–26; Todor Sabev, *The Orthodox Churches in the World Council of Churches* (Geneva: WCC Publications, 1996), pp. 9–13.

13. See Olivier Clément, *Dialogues avec le Patriarche Athénagoras* (Paris: Fayard, 1976).

14. "Encyclical of the Ecumenical Patriarchate (January 31, 1952)," in *Orthodox Vision of Ecumenism*, ed. Limouris, p. 20.

15. Cited in Oliver Clement, "Athenagoras I: Orthodoxy in the Service of Unity," *The Ecumenical Review* 21 (1969), p. 316.

16. See Andrew Blane, ed., *Georges Florovsky: Russian Intellectual, Orthodox Churchman* (Crestwood, N.Y.: St. Vladimir's Seminary Press, 1993).

17. See *Towards the Great Council: Introductory Reports on the Interorthodox Commission in Preparation for the Next Great and Holy Council of the Orthodox Church* (London: SPCK, 1972).

18. Stephanopoulos, *A Study of Recent Greek Orthodox Ecumenical Relations, 1902–1968*, pp. 214–15.

19. See Stanley S. Harakas, *Something Is Stirring in World Orthodoxy* (Minneapolis: Light and Life Publishing Company, 1978).

20. "Decision of the Third Pre-Conciliar Pan-Orthodox Conference (November 6, 1986)," in *Orthodox Vision of Ecumenism*, ed. Limouris, p. 112.

21. See John Erickson, "A Retreat from Ecumenism in Post-Communist Russia and Eastern Europe," *Ecumenical Trends* 30:9 (2001), pp. 1–10.

22. Sabev, pp. 22–30.

23. Ibid., pp. 37–55.

24. "On the Relationship of the Orthodox Church to the WCC: Statement of the Orthodox Theological Society in America, Boston, June 4–5, 1998," in *Turn to God: Rejoice in Hope*, ed. Thomas FitzGerald and Peter Bouteneff (Geneva: Orthodox Task Force, 1998), pp. 148–49.

25. See *Towards the Great and Holy Council: Introductory Reports of the Interorthodox Commission in Preparation for the Next Great and Holy Council* (London: SPCK, 1972), pp. 39–54.

26. Metropolitan John of Pergamon, "The Self-Understanding of the Orthodox and their Participation in the Ecumenical Movement," p. 46.

27. "Reflections of Orthodox Participants," in *Orthodox Vision of Ecumenism*, ed. Limouris, p. 177.

28. Thomas FitzGerald, *The Ecumenical Patriarchate and Christian Unity* (Brookline, Mass.: Holy Cross Orthodox Press, 1997), pp. 33–34.

29. "Message of the Primates of the Most Holy Orthodox Churches," in *Orthodox Visions of Unity*, ed. Limouris, p. 197.

30. Anton Houtepen, "Uniatism and Models of Unity in the Ecumenical Movement," *Exchange* 25:3 (1996), pp. 207–10.

31. FitzGerald, *The Ecumenical Patriarchate and Christian Unity*, pp. 27–31.

32. See "Uniatism, Method of Union of the Past, and the Present Search for Full Communion," in *The Quest for Unity*, ed. John Borelli and John Erickson (Crestwood, N.Y.: St. Vladimir's Seminary Press, 1966), pp. 175–83.

33. See Alexander Kalomiros, *Against False Union* (Seattle: St. Nectarios Press, 1978).

34. "Message of the Primates of the Most Holy Orthodox Churches," in *Orthodox Visions of Unity,* ed. Gennadios Limouris, p. 195.

35. See Bishop Chrysostomos and Archimandrite Ambrosios, *The Old Catholic Church of Greece* (Etna, Calif.: Center for Traditionalist Orthodox Studies, 1991).

36. Kalomiros, *Against False Union,* pp. 17–28, 81–95.

37. "Pastoral Address of Metropolitan Anastasy, October 18, 1958," *Orthodox Life* 6 (1959), p. 8.

38. For an analysis of the political and religious perspectives of the Russian refugees in Europe, see Robert C. Williams, *Culture in Exile: Russian Emigres in Germany, 1881–1941* (Ithaca, N.Y.: Cornell University Press, 1972).

39. Archimandrite Constantine, "The Spiritual State of the World and the Task of the Orthodox Church Outside of Russia," *Orthodox Life* 4 (1962), p. 4.

40. Eugene Rose, "Witness of Orthodoxy," *The Orthodox Word* 5:6 (1969), p. 268.

41. "On the Heresy of Ecumenism," *The Orthodox Word* 7:6 (1971), p. 297. By the year 2000, there were some signs of a moderation of this extreme position.

42. "Evaluation of New Facts in the Relations of Orthodoxy and the Ecumenical Movement (1998)," in *Turn to God, Rejoice in Hope: Orthodox Reflections on the Way to Harare,* ed. FitzGerald and Bouteneff, p. 136. See Ion Bria, *The Sense of Ecumenical Tradition: The Ecumenical Witness and Vision of the Orthodox* (Geneva: WCC Publications, 1991).

43. Some of the following observations appeared in Thomas FitzGerald, "Orthodox Theology and Ecumenical Witness: An Introduction to Major Themes," *St. Vladimir's Theological Quarterly* 42:3–4 (1998), pp. 339–61.

44. See John Zizioulas, "The Ecumenical Dimension of Orthodox Theological Education," in *Orthodox Theological Education for the Life and Witness of the Church* (Geneva: World Council of Churches, 1978), pp. 3–40.

45. For some further insights into this tendency, see Jaroslav Pelikan, *The Spirit of Eastern Christendom (600–1700)* (Chicago: The University of Chicago Press, 1994), pp. 1–7. Among those Protestant theologians who sought to give a more accurate picture of Orthodoxy, the name of the German Lutheran Professor Ernst Benz should be mentioned. See his *The Eastern Orthodox Church* (New York: Anchor Books, 1963).

46. Among these persons whose writings are readily accessible are John Meyendorff, Anthony-Emil Tachiaos, Deno Geanakoplos, Demetrios Constantelos, Aristeides Papadakis, John Erickson, and Jaraslav Pelikan.

47. It is not possible in this paper to present a complete bibliography of Orthodox contributions. Preference has been shown for those books and articles that reflect Orthodox contributions at particular periods and with regard to particular topics. For additional biographical references, see Todor Sabev, *The Orthodox Churches in the World Council of Churches* (Geneva: World Council of Churches, 1996); Ion Bria, *The Sense of Ecumenical Tradition* (Geneva: World Council of Churches, 1991).

48. "Statement of Orthodox Participants, New Dehli, 1961," in *Orthodox Visions of Ecumenism,* ed. Gennadios Limouris, p. 31.

49. Vladimir Lossky, *The Mystical Theology of the Eastern Church* (Cambridge: James Clarke, 1957), p. 158.

50. Nikos Nissiotis, "The Importance of the Doctrine of the Trinity for Church Life and Theology," in *The Orthodox Ethos,* ed. Angelos Philippou (Oxford: Holy-

well Press, 1964). See also Michael Fahey and John Meyendorff, *Trinitarian Theology East and West: St. Thomas Aquinas-St. Gregory Palamas* (Brookline, Mass.: Holy Cross Orthodox Press, 1977).

51. Karl Rahner, *The Trinity* (New York: Herder and Herder, 1970), pp. 9–21.

52. Elizabeth A. Johnson, "Trinity: To Let the Symbol Sing Again," *Theology Today* (October, 1997), p. 301.

53. See W. A. Visser 't Hooft, "The Basis: Its History and Significance," *The Ecumenical Review,* 38:2 (1985).

54. During his service at the WCC, Gennadios Limouris, now Metropolitan of Sassima, had special responsibility for the Apostolic Faith study. See also Kyriaki FitzGerald, "The Faith and Order Movement: A Time for Assessment," *The Greek Orthodox Theological Review* 37:3–4 (1992), pp. 333–47.

55. See Borelli and Erickson, eds., *The Quest For Unity,* pp. 53–64.

56. Lucas Vischer, ed., *Agreed Statements from the Orthodox-Reformed Dialogue* (Geneva: World Alliance of Reformed Churches, 1998), pp. 12–17.

57. Although not formally published, the text was shared with the bishops at the Lambeth Conference, 1998.

58. The German Lutheran theologian Christoph Schwöbel identifies some of these points of consensus in "The Quest for Communion," in *The Church as Communion* (Geneva: Lutheran World Federation, 1997), p. 244. See John Zizioulas, "The Church as Communion," in *On the Way to Fuller Koinonia,* ed. Thomas Best and Gunther Gassman (Geneva: World Council of Churches, 1994), pp. 103–11. Many of the themes in this essay are elaborated in his major study *Being As Communion* (Crestwood, N.Y.: St. Vladimir's Seminary Press, 1985).

59. Metropolitan Daniel Ciobotea and William Lazareth, "The Triune God: The Supreme Source of Life. Thoughts Inspired by Rublev's Icon of the Trinity," in *Icons: Windows on Eternity,* ed. Genadios Limouris (Geneva: World Council of Churches, 1990), pp. 202–04.

60. Bishop Maximos Aghiorgoussis, "Theological and Historical Aspects of Conciliarity: Some Propositions for Discussion," *The Greek Orthodox Theological Review* 24:1 (1979), p. 5.

61. Nicholas Afanassieff, *L'Eglise du Saint Esprit* (Paris: Cerf, 1975).

62. John Zizioulas, "The Eucharistic Community and the Catholicity of the Church," *One in Christ* 6 (1970), pp. 314–37.

63. Thomas FitzGerald, "Conciliarity, Primacy, and the Episcopacy," *St. Vladimir's Theological Quarterly* 38:1 (1994), p. 18.

64. Stanley Harakas, "The Orthodox Vision of Visible Unity," in *A Communion of Communions,* ed. J. Robert Wright (New York: Seabury, 1979), pp. 168–83; Georges Tsetsis, "The Meaning of the Orthodox Presence," in *Orthodox Visions of Ecumenism,* ed. Limouris, pp. 273–74.

65. Georges Florovsky, "The Boundaries of the Church," *Church Quarterly Review* 117 (1933), p. 131.

66. John Zizioulas, "The Church as Communion," p. 110. The Methodist theologian Geoffrey Wainwright says that the great contribution of the Orthodox to the ecumenical movement "has been their insistence on 'right doctrine,' which is expressed in 'right worship.'... The presence of the Orthodox in the WCC and the National Council of Churches has been particularly important in recent years as a counter to the liberal Protestant tendency, which would minimize the question of

doctrine" in his *The Ecumenical Movement: Crisis and Opportunity for the Church* (Grand Rapids, Mich.: Eerdmans, 1983), p. 3.

67. Christoph Schwöbel says that "the ecumenical encounter with Eastern Orthodoxy in the ecumenical movement has exercised a decisive influence on many Protestant theologians, not least in the area of ecclesiology, over the past twenty years" in "The Quest for Communion," in *The Church as Communion*, p. 236.

68. See Metropolitan John Zizioulas, "On Being a Person: Towards an Ontology of Personhood," in *Persons-Divine and Human*, ed. Christoph Schwöbel and Colin Gunton (Edinburgh, 1991), pp. 33–46.

69. See Maximos Aghiorgoussis, *In the Image of God* (Brookline, Mass.: Holy Cross Orthodox Press, 1999), pp. 131–34.

70. See Georgios I. Mantzaridis, *The Deification of Man* (Crestwood, N.Y.: St. Vladimir's Seminary Press, 1984).

71. See Bishop Kallistos of Diokleia, "Salvation and Theosis in Orthodox Theology," in *Luther et le Réforme allemande dans une perspective oecuménique* (Geneva: Les Etudes théologiques de Chambésy, 1983), pp. 167–83.

72. See Bishop Maximos Aghiorgoussis, "Orthodox Soteriology," in *Salvation in Christ*, ed. John Meyendorff and Robert Tobias (Minneapolis: Augsburg, 1992), pp. 35–57.

73. St. Irenaeus, *Against Heresies*, 4:20:6.

74. Savas Agouridis, "The Social Character of Orthodoxy," in *The Orthodox Ethos*, pp. 209–20.

75. See John Zizioulas, "The Doctrine of God the Trinity Today," in *The Forgotten Trinity 3*, ed. Alasdair Heron (London: BCC-CCBI, 1991), pp. 19–32.

76. Stanley S. Harakas, *Towards Transfigured Life* (Minneapolis: Light and Life Publishing, 1983), pp. 16–39.

77. Stanley S. Harakas, *Living the Faith: The Praxis of Eastern Orthodox Ethics* (Minneapolis: Light and Life Publishing, 1992), pp. 187–224.

78. See John Zizioulas, "Preserving God's Creation," *King's Theological Review* 12 (1989), pp. 1–5, 13, 41–45; (1990), pp. 1–5.

79. Paul Evdokimov, *Woman and the Salvation of the World* (Crestwood, N.Y.: St. Vladimir's Seminary Press, 1994), pp. 137–270. See also Kyriaki FitzGerald, *Women Deacons in the Orthodox Church* (Brookline, Mass.: Holy Cross Orthodox Press, 1998); "The Ministry of Women in the Orthodox Church: Some Theological Presumptions," *Journal of Ecumenical Studies* 20:4 (1983), pp. 558–75.

80. See Teresa Berger, "Worship in the Ecumenical Movement," *Dictionary of the Ecumenical Movement*, ed. Nicholas Lossky et al. (Geneva: World Council of Churches, 1991), pp. 1107–12.

81. Over the years, many Orthodox theologians played a key role in the development of this text. Among them were Metropolitan John Zizioulas, Nikos Nissiotis, Evangelos Theodorou, and Fr. Thomas Hopko.

82. *Baptism, Eucharist, and Ministry* (Geneva: World Council of Churches, 1982), Preface, p. ix.

83. See *Orthodox Perspectives on Baptism, Eucharist, and Ministry*, ed. Gennadios Limouris and Nomikos Michael Vaporis (Brookline, Mass.: Holy Cross Orthodox Press, 1985).

84. See "Confessing Christ through the Liturgical Life of the Church Today, (1975)" in *Orthodox Visions of Ecumenism*, pp. 55–59. The most recent statement by

Orthodox is "Orthodox Liturgical Renewal and Visible Unity, (New Skete, 1998)," in *Turn to God, Rejoice in Hope,* pp. 130–35.

85. Georges Florovsky, "The Elements of Liturgy," in *Ways of Worship,* ed. Pehr Edwall (London: SCM Press, 1951), pp. 52–65.

86. Alexander Schmeman, *For the Life of the World* (New York: National Student Christian Foundation, 1963). Since its first publication, this remarkable book has inspired many to see the relationship between worship and all of life. Certainly, all the publications of Fr. Alexander Schemman could be mentioned here. For a valuable insight into the work of Fr. Alexander, see *Liturgy and Tradition,* ed. Thomas Fisch (Crestwood, N.Y.: St. Vladimir's Seminary Press, 1990), pp. 1–10.

87. See Thomas FitzGerald, "The Holy Eucharist as Theophany," *The Greek Orthodox Theological Review* 28:1 (1982), pp. 27–38.

88. See John Zizioulas, "Some Reflections on Baptism, Confirmation, and Eucharist," *Sobornost* 5:9 (1969), pp. 644–52; "Eucharistic Prayer and Life," *Emmanuel* 81 (1975), pp. 462–70.

89. Kallistos Ware, "The Theology of Worship," *Sobornost* 5:10 (1970), pp. 729–37; Nicholas Apostola, "Theology as Doxology," *Ministerial Formation* 67:4 (1994), pp. 35–45. The Lutheran theologian Gordon Lathrop clearly recognizes the contribution of the Orthodox, specifically the contribution of Fr. Alexander Schmemann, in his *Holy Things, A Theology of Worship* (Minneapolis: Fortress Press, 1993).

90. Kyriaki FitzGerald, "Reflections on Spirituality and Prayer," in *Faith and Order 1985–1989,* ed. Thomas Best (Geneva: World Council of Churches, 1990), pp. 181–83.

91. Kallistos Ware, "Ways of Prayer and Contemplation," in *Christian Spirituality I,* pp. 395–414.

92. See A.M. Allchin, ed., *Sacrament and Image* (London: The Fellowship of St. Alban and Sergius, 1967). For some Roman Catholic and Protestant perspectives on the value of icons, see Gennadios Limouris, ed., *Icons: Windows on Eternity* (Geneva: World Council of Churches, 1990).

93. The insights of early Christianity and Orthodox theology can be seen in such contemporary writers of the Western Christian traditions as Thomas Merton, Henri Nouwen, Kenneth Leech, Richard Forester, Basil Pennington, and John Vanier.

94. "Sermon in the Uppsala Cathedral (August 22, 1993)" cited in FitzGerald, *The Ecumenical Patriarchate and Christian Unity,* pp. 34–35.

CHAPTER 9

Tensions and Accomplishments in the Churches of the Reformation

Division in the life of the Church is a contradiction of its very nature. Christ's reconciling work is one, and members of the Church fail as Christ's ambassadors in reconciling the world to God if they have not been visibly reconciled to one another.

The means by which the good news is preached must be congruous with the content of the good news: a "making whole," a healing of all things in Christ Jesus. The Church, as described in the Bible, is to be a family created by God in Christ out of all tribes and nations and peoples, a family set by God as a sign to the world of the direction in which all creation and history are moving; the summing up of all things in Christ and the coming of the reign of God.

—The COCU Consensus, 1985[1]

INTRODUCTION

Anglican, Old Catholic, and Protestant churches and their representatives have been at the center of the contemporary ecumenical movement from the latter portion of the nineteenth century and the early years of the twentieth century. In both America and Western Europe, a major component of the early steps toward dialogue and the unity of the churches was a process of bringing the divided Anglican, Old Catholic, and Protestant churches and traditions into greater contact and dialogue.

However, as we shall see in this chapter, there have been elements within Protestantism that have had a very different perspective on the ecumenical movement. Some have openly opposed ecumenical efforts.

Others have opted for a cautious involvement in particular ecumenical efforts. These differences often reflect a deeper rift among Protestants over the understanding of the Scriptures going back to the nineteenth century.

We shall also see in this chapter that a number of Anglican and Protestant churches in Europe and America have entered into major agreements in the last quarter of the twentieth century. Accomplished within the broader context of the theological dialogues of the ecumenical movement, these agreements have done much to overcome divisions among Reformation churches dating from the sixteenth century. These agreements have also emphasized the importance of the visible unity of the churches expressed through agreement in faith and manifest in full Eucharistic communion.

POST ENLIGHTENMENT PROTESTANT TENSIONS

From the time of the sixteenth century Reformation, there have been serious divisions within the Protestant world. The Reformation itself led to four clearly discernable traditions. Each shared the essential affirmations of the Reformation. Each affirmed the primacy of divine grace and the gift of salvation. Each affirmed the authority of the Scriptures. Each shared a common reaction to the Roman Catholic Church of the day. Yet there were also serious differences from the start. Not all Lutherans, Reformed, Anabaptists, and Anglicans agreed on issues related to baptism, the Eucharist, church government, and church-state relations. These differences reflected themselves in the teachings, worship, and mission of these traditions from the sixteenth century onward.

These divisions among the major Protestant churches and traditions were compounded in the wake of the Enlightenment of the eighteenth century. The Enlightenment was a philosophical movement placing great emphasis upon human reason and an appreciation for developments in the sciences. The leaders of the Enlightenment often distrusted traditional church authorities, rejected a belief in revelation, and criticized church divisions. They held that truth could be obtained only through reason, observation, and experimentation. Many sought to use their philosophy in the service of tolerance and social justice. Within some Christian circles, they contributed to a tendency to question church authorities and to deprecate Scriptures, theology, and prayer. Ethics free from doctrine and worship was emphasized. These perspectives were boldly expressed in the philosophical views of the Deists as well as in theological perspectives of Unitarianism, which rejected the historic Christian understanding of the Trinity.

The influence of the spirit of the Enlightenment could be found within many of the Protestant churches in both America and Western Europe by the nineteenth century. In some theological schools, professors were accepting a new approach to the Scriptures known as higher criticism. This method employed a critical approach to texts and sources of the Scriptures. Use was made, for example, of newly discovered manuscripts and advances in archeology. For some, the new criticism often led to a depreciation of historic Christian understanding of the Trinity, the Incarnation, the miracles, and the Resurrection of Christ. At the same time, there was an emphasis upon Christian ethics based upon the example and teachings of the historical Jesus. "Protestantism in the nineteenth century in the Lutheran and Reformed Churches of the continent of Europe," says Ruth Rouse, "was profoundly affected by the spirit of the Enlightenment." In many Protestant quarters, "influenced the rational and rationalistic canon of the Enlightenment, the ideas of the supernatural, of grace and redemption, were almost wholly eliminated from Christian preaching and thought."[2] Speaking of the affect of the Enlightenment on Protestantism in Western Europe and America, other authors have said: "The result of the Enlightenment, then, was the mortal wounding of traditional Christian culture. The supernatural authoritative, clerical world to which biblical faith had given rise lay fractured and tattered. Like Humpty Dumpty, traditional Christian faith seemed broken beyond recognition."[3]

By the end of the nineteenth century, a serious theological debate rooted in the significance and interpretation of Scriptures began to divide Protestants and their churches in America and in Western Europe. This debate, which was especially prominent in America, was affected by the development in the sciences and their popular interpretations. The publication of Darwin's *The Origin of the Species* in 1859 and his *The Descent of Man* in 1871 led to new questions about evolution and the biblical description of creation. The debate among Protestants frequently centered about the Bible and whether or not it was to be taken as the inspired Word of God and always interpreted in a literal manner. This frequently led to questions regarding the meaning of the Trinity and divinity of Christ. Eventually these debates led to Protestant church divisions between evangelicals or fundamentalists on the one hand and liberals or modernists on the other. The former emphasized the literal approach to the text of the Scriptures. The latter accepted the insights of what was called the "higher criticism of the Bible. In America especially, they were also more concerned with the response of the churches to critical issues facing the society.[4]

Throughout Western Europe, the theological tensions in the Protestant world generally expressed themselves in the distinction between the Lutheran, Reformed, and Anglican churches on the one hand, and the newly developed Christian groups and organizations on the other. The historic Anglican and Protestant churches often were enmeshed in their own internal theological debates flowing from the Enlightenment periods. These debates generally centered upon the interpretation of Scriptures. Among the important European teachers in this regard were the German theologians Friedrich Schleiermacher (1768–1834), Albert Ritchel (1822–89), and Adolph von Harnack (1851–1930). Many of the followers of these theologians, became supporters of the higher criticism of the Bible and questioned much of the classical understanding of the person and work of Christ. Much emphasis was placed by them upon the importance of Jesus' ethical teachings and, therefore, Christian ethics and the responsibilities of Christians in the society.

In reaction to these tendencies, new Christian groups and organizations were often organized as separate and distinct bodies from the established churches and their congregations. These groups in America and Western Europe frequently emphasized the importance of personal faith and devotions as well as the centrality of the Scriptures interpreted in a literal manner. Often, these groups gathered together persons from a wide variety of church backgrounds who were disturbed by the tensions or theological directions found in their own congregations or church body. These organizations also contributed to the establishment of a number of missionary societies gathering members from a number of church backgrounds in support of foreign missions.

During the late nineteenth century and early twentieth century, the Evangelical Alliance was one of the most prominent organizations of this kind in Western Europe. Subsequently known as the World Evangelical Alliance, it was formally established in London in 1846. More than 800 Christian leaders from more than 52 Protestant churches in Western Europe and America attended its first meeting. The Alliance saw itself from the start as a voluntary association of Christians who accepted its basis. Within a few decades, the Alliance established branches throughout Europe and in the United States. The Basis of the Alliance declared that members accept the "divine inspiration, authority and sufficiency of the Holy Scriptures." Among a number of other points, the basis also affirmed belief in "the unity of the Godhead and the Trinity of Person," the "incarnation of the Son of God," and "justification by faith alone."[5]

THE FUNDAMENTALIST-MODERNIST DEBATE IN THE UNITED STATES

The situation in the United States revealed a similar rift among Protestants during the early decades of the twentieth century. The Social Gospel Movement in the United States during the middle of the nineteenth century sought to encourage the churches and their members to become more sensitive to their social obligations. The opposition to slavery, especially among Northern Protestants in the United States during the mid-1800s, led many to begin to address issues of alcoholism, poverty, labor abuse, and the plight of new immigrants. Based upon their understanding of the ethical teachings of Christ, a number of leading clergy and theologians encouraged their churches to support programs of social welfare. Indeed, many local congregations and their larger church bodies worked to establish hospitals, inner-city missions, soup kitchens, homes for the elderly, and orphanages. While not necessarily neglecting the importance of doctrine, personal faith, and worship, Protestant leaders in a number of churches became very concerned with the reform of the society.

Among the leaders of the American Social Gospel Movement was Walter Rauschenbuch (1861–1918), a Baptist pastor in New York City who subsequently became a Professor at Colgate-Rochester Theological Seminary. The perspectives and writings on social issues of Rauschenbuch and others eventually became aligned with views from other Protestants theologians in Europe and America who questioned the literal interpretation of the Scriptures as well as the significance of classical Christian creedal statements. The ethical teachings of Jesus were highlighted.[6]

During the early twentieth century, these perspectives stood behind what came to be referred to as Liberal Protestantism. This viewpoint was expressed in many Protestant church families, in local parishes and theological schools in the United States. The Protestant Liberals claimed that they were simply teaching Christian faith with the assistance of the advances in biblical studies and the sciences. Rejecting biblical literalism, they placed emphasis upon the immanence of God, the goodness of the human person, and religious experience. Ethics generally replaced doctrine as the centerpiece of their view of Christianity. At the same time, they called into question many of the divisions that had afflicted Protestant churches since the Reformation. Thirty-three Protestant churches in the United States, for example, banded together to establish the Federal Council of Churches in 1908.[7] Six years earlier, four Protestant churches founded the Massachusetts Federation of Churches in 1902. By 1908 the number of members rose to 12.[8] Both groups were especially concerned with cultivating a cooperative spirit among the Protestant churches and with providing a united witness in opposition to the ills of society.

Their perspectives, however, set the stage for a forceful reaction that divided much of Protestantism in the United States. The initial response to the Liberals was led by a number of Protestant scholar and theologians such as Charles Hodge (1820–78) of Princeton. Regarded as the most prominent American Presbyterian theologian of the nineteenth century, he defended his understanding of Protestant Christianity and opposed the influence of the Protestant Liberals, together with their views of Scriptures and Christian doctrine.[9]

However, the more thoughtful and nuanced positions of Hodges and his followers were frequently overlooked in favor of a more simplistic viewpoint. Such views generally aggravated the rift and prevented genuine dialogue. A number of Fundamentalists were intent upon identifying nonnegotiable beliefs and establishing a greater sense of identity. Coming out of the Niagara Bible Conference of 1898, the participants issued the Niagara Creed, for example, which listed 14 fundamentals of the faith. Eventually this number was reduced to the following: the inerrancy of Scripture, the divinity of Christ, his virgin birth, his substitutionary atonement, his bodily resurrection and miracles, and his Second Coming.[10] The strict Fundamentalists left little room for discussion on the subtle points of these affirmations. Between 1910 and 1915, American and European theologians published a series of twelve books known as *The Fundamentals.* These essays sought to identify what was wrong with modern Christianity and society from the perspective of Fundamentalists. They claimed that the "Liberals" had rejected the divine inspiration of the Bible and the biblical basis of Christianity. They also attacked "Romanism" (the Roman Catholic Church), Atheism, Christian Science, Mormonism, spiritualism, and socialism.[11]

During the 1920s and 1930s the controversy between the Fundamentalists and the Liberals afflicted many of the major Protestant churches in the United States. This included the Methodists, the Episcopalians, the Disciples of Christ, the Northern and Southern Presbyterians, and the Baptists.[12] The controversy could be found in the administrative offices of these churches as well as in their local parishes and theological schools. This debate in the United States took place at the same time that many Americans and Europeans were becoming involved in the new Faith and Order and Life and Work Movements.

When the Fundamentalists failed to gain dominance over a church family, parish, or theological school, they generally formed separate bodies. The Fundamentalist tradition gave rise to a number of independent church families, congregations, colleges, and theological schools in the United States. They also established their own publishing houses and mission agencies. The Fundamentalists generally avoided contact with most of the more historic Protestant church families and their parishes, which they saw to be under the sway of Modernism. Throughout the twentieth century, the religious views of the Fundamentalists frequently supported a politically conservative agenda that opposed developments in American society related to immigration, public education, and social welfare programs.

Some Fundamentalists staunchly opposed the developments of the ecumenical movement. A number of Fundamentalists established the American Council of Christian Churches in 1941. This organization was designed to counter the activities of the Federal Council of Churches, which became the National Council of Church of Christ in 1950. Likewise, the International Council of Christian Churches was established in 1948 to oppose the activities of the World Council of Churches.[13] Both the National Council of Churches and the World Council of Churches were frequently accused by Fundamentalists of being theologically liberal and supportive of liberal political causes. Likewise, many of the Fundamentalist church bodies and congregations began to support both domestic and foreign missions that often openly challenged the activities of other Christian churches, be they Protestant, Catholic, or Orthodox. In the period between 1970 and 2004, aspects of the theological and political perspectives of the Fundamentalists have emerged in the views of a number of televangelists and representatives of the so-called Christian Right.

The opposition to the activities of the ecumenical movement by Fundamentalists often led to a new distinction in Protestant Christianity in America. This was the distinction between ecumenical and evangelical. Here, the term ecumenical referred to those Protestant churches and their leaders who were involved in dialogues and cooperative efforts. Among other things, the term evangelical referred to those Protestant churches and leaders who avoided dialogues on issues of Christian unity. They viewed the ecumenical movement as an expression of a watered-down Christianity that was not faithful to the Scriptures. This unfortunate distinction further solidified a sense of American Protestantism being divided into two parties that had very little in common. This dichotomy, however, has begun to break down in recent years.[14]

Within many Protestant churches and theological traditions, the strong emphasis upon the Social Gospel has been complemented in recent years by a renewed concern for worship, spirituality, and mission, as well as a more comprehensive appreciation of the historic Christian faith. This significant development undoubtedly reflects two interrelated factors. First, the writings of Karl Barth (1886–1968), Dietrich Bonhoeffer (1906–45), and Emil Bruner (1889–1966) had a profound impact upon the theological perspectives of recent Protestantism through their reassertion of classical affirmation of Christian faith. The thought of these European theologians was complemented in America by Reinhold Neibuhr (1892–1971) and H. Richard Niebuhr (1894–1962). In addition to this, ecumenical dialogues, especially within the context of the Faith and Order Movement, also helped deepen a consciousness of classical Christian affirmations within many Protestant church bodies and among their theologians. As a result of these developments, a number of Protestant churches and leaders, who were ecumenically committed, also became increasingly open to some of the concerns raised by the Evangelicals.

THE NEO-EVANGELICAL TRADITION IN THE UNITED STATES

Among many American Protestant Christians, who view themselves as theological conservative, the extreme theological and political positions of much of Fundamentalism became less and less appealing in the aftermath of the controversies of the 1920s and 1930s. Beginning in the 1940s, a number of key leaders such as Harold John Ockenga (1905–85) and Carl F. H.

Henry (1913–2003) began to question Fundamentalism's tendency to justify Christian divisions, its lack of social responsibility, and its anti-intellectualism. Fundamentalism "had come to stand for dogma and judgmentalism. It was the reaction against this narrowness in the 1940s and 1950s that prompted the formation of a new evangelical identity, one that was more open than fundamentalism."[15]

An important distinction began to develop between the Fundamentalists and the Evangelical or Neo-Evangelicals. The Fundamentalist tradition in Protestantism, especially in the United States, continued to exist within some church bodies and local congregations. These Fundamentalist bodies generally avoided contact with other Protestant churches and institutions. Likewise, they had little regard for issues of Christian unity and especially dialogue with Roman Catholicism.[16]

The term Evangelical has a rich history within Protestantism. From the time of the sixteenth century, it was often used to describe those who accepted the Reformation principles. In many cases, the term was incorporated into the formal titles on a number of Protestant churches in Western Europe. Through greater use of the term Evangelical from the 1940s onward, many theologically conservative Protestants in the United States were both referring to the Reformation heritage while at the same time distancing themselves from the more extreme aspects of Fundamentalism. While Evangelicals continued to emphasize the centrality of the Scriptures, personal piety, and evangelization, many also began to become more involved in social witness and in ecumenical dialogue. A growing number of Protestant church families and their leaders, who considered themselves to be Evangelicals, became increasingly interested and involved in issues and discussions dealing with Christian unity.

Founded in 1943, the National Association of Evangelicals (NAE) brought together many theologically conservative Protestant Christian church families in the United States who disavowed the extremes of Fundamentalism. Throughout much of its earlier history, the NAE provided an alternative to the National Council of Churches of Christ (NCCC). Smaller church bodies frequently tended to join the NAE both because of its evangelical principles and because of fears over the identity and programs of the NCCC. The NCCC, which included both the so-called Protestant mainline denominations and Orthodox churches, was viewed as being a bastion of Liberal Protestant theology and concerned primarily with social witness.[17]

Presently, the NAE describes itself as a voluntary association of "individuals, denominations, churches, schools, and organizations comprised of approximately 43,000 congregations nationwide from 50 member denominations and individual congregations from an additional 27 denominations, as well as several hundred independent churches." In addition to this, the NAE "includes 250 parachurch ministries and educational institutions. Through the cooperative ministry of these members, NAE directly and indirectly benefits over 27 million people" in the United States.[18] Among the diverse Protestant churches and church bodies that are members of the NAE, for example, are the Assemblies of God, a sizeable Pentecostal body, and the Salvation Army.

The boundaries of contemporary Evangelicalism in the United States are not easy to identify. One can find local congregations, denominations, movements, colleges, and theological schools that affirm their specific Evangelical character. At the same time, however, within the so-called mainline Protestant churches and congregations, one can find Christians and movements that also affirm an Evangelical character.

The diverse membership in the NAE is held together by a Statement of Faith that expresses broadly the concerns of Evangelicals. The Statement says:

1. We believe the Bible to be the inspired, the only infallible, authoritative Word of God.
2. We believe that there is one God, eternally existent in three persons: Father, Son and Holy Spirit.
3. We believe in the deity of our Lord Jesus Christ, in His virgin birth, in His sinless life, in His miracles, in His vicarious and atoning death through His shed blood, in His bodily resurrection, in His ascension to the right hand of the Father, and in His personal return in power and glory.
4. We believe that for the salvation of lost and sinful people, regeneration by the Holy Spirit is absolutely essential
5. We believe in the present ministry of the Holy Spirit by whose indwelling the Christian is enabled to live a godly life.
6. We believe in the resurrection of both the saved and the lost; they that are saved unto the resurrection of life and they that are lost unto the resurrection of damnation.
7. We believe in the spiritual unity of believers in our Lord Jesus Christ.[19]

At the global level, a new Evangelical organization came into existence in 1951 similar to the NAE in the United States. The World Evangelical Fellowship (WEF) was founded in Woudschoten, Netherlands with 91 participants from 21 countries. The basis for this association was similar to the earlier Evangelical Alliance of 1846. It referred, however, to the infallible character of the Scriptures. With a strong emphasis on evangelism, the WEF has grown to an association of over sixty national evangelical associations and has sponsored significant consultations on missions. While tensions continue to exist regarding the interpretation of Scripture and the nature of mission, the WEF has assisted with theological dialogues with representatives of the World Council of Churches and the Roman Catholic Church, especially since 1977.[20]

Some would claim that the most popular exponent of this new evangelicalism is Billy Graham (1918–). While Graham structures his crusades in the style of earlier revival meetings, he has gained the admiration of many beyond the realm of contemporary evangelicalism. Since the 1950s, he has proposed that his crusades have wide ecumenical support in the city he visits. This led many Fundamentalists to disavow his work in 1957. Since the 1960s, he has maintained cordial relations with leaders of the Orthodox Church and the Roman Catholic Church as well as the World Council of Churches.[21] While Graham's ecumenical spirit is not always reflected in all his supporters, his personal convictions have contributed to bridging the gap between old divisions within Protestantism.

In the area of missionary work and ecumenical activity, there continues to be a diversity of opinions among Evangelicals. Most have a strong conviction about the importance of mission and evangelism. And, at the same time, many have a deep-rooted suspicion of the ecumenical movement. Some Evangelicals support missions in the United States and throughout the world that appear in conflict with the presence of other Christian churches. In parts of Eastern Europe and South America, Evangelical missions, supported from the United States, have been very active. In these places, Evangelicals appear to present their Christian teachings in opposition to the Orthodox Church and the Roman Catholic Church as well as to established Protestant churches. Among Orthodox and Roman Catholics especially, this practice has led to a distrust of many Evangelicals and to accusations of proselytism. At the same time, however, other Evangelicals are involved in various aspects of the ecumenical movement and have renounced proselytism. Some have become involved in certain activities of the work of the World Council of Churches and the National Council of Churches in the United States.

THE CONCERNS OF EVANGELICALS OVER ECUMENISM

The quest for Christian unity and the reconciliation of the churches is a process. As the churches and theological traditions have overcome historic isolations, come into contact, and initiated dialogues, new perspectives have been opened on old points of difference. There have been opportunities to engage together the issues that have been divisive. While the theological rift between some Protestants continues to divide conservatives and liberals, the activities of the ecumenical movement have often cast new light on old divisions. The ecumenical movement has provided opportunities for representatives of these traditions to meet and to discuss their perspectives. Over the course of decades, the ecumenical movement has had an impact upon both the Protestant liberals and the Protestant conservatives. This has come about not only through dialogue between these two parties of Protestantism. It has also come about through Protestantism's dialogue with Orthodox Christianity and more recently with Roman Catholicism.[22]

For those churches with a long history of involvement in ecumenism, there is a new interest in listening to the concerns of the Evangelicals. The first critical issue that many Evangelicals have raised is an ecclesiological one. The Evangelical tradition has placed emphasis upon the importance of the personal Christian faith of every believer. This has led Evangelicals to emphasize the spiritual or invisible unity of believers. As a consequence, some Evangelicals have been suspicious of the emphasis on the visible unity of churches that has been so strongly emphasized throughout the history of the ecumenical movement. This has led also to a suspicion that an organization such as the World Council of Churches is intent upon creating some type of superchurch.

Evangelicals have often expressed the fear that ecumenism implies a theological relativism or syncretism that would diminish the centrality of Jesus Christ and his teachings. At the same time, there has been concern that the Scriptures do not receive sufficient prominence and attention in the deliberations and statements of ecumenical bodies such as the World Council of Churches. "This fear," says W. A. Visser 't Hooft, "is not wholly uninformed since there are a certain number of people in several member churches of the WCC whose 'ecumenism' takes the form of theological indifferentism or of a general embracing of all religions."[23]

Evangelicals have questioned whether the ecumenical movement generally is not devoting enough attention to issues of mission and evangelization. For some Evangelicals this is a sign that some ecumenists do not place sufficient emphasis upon Christ and the universality of his message. At the same time, these Evangelicals question the degree of attention that ecumenical bodies, such as the World Council of Churches and the National Council of Churches of Christ in the USA, give to programs related to social issues and political action. Moreover, some Evangelicals would claim that these initiatives often lack a thorough grounding in Christian faith affirmations.

Clearly, the ecumenical movement generally and the theological dialogues among the churches will benefit from the on-going involvement of Evangelicals. And Evangelical theologians and their churches will benefit from contracts with those of different Christian traditions. In recent decades, the World Council of Churches has become more concerned with the involvement of Evangelicals. The WCC Central committee in 1965 said: "The member churches of the World Council, which have already experienced something of the mutual correction and edification which is made possible by our common membership in the Council, needs also the contribution of these evangelical churches."[24] In more recent years, the WCC has initiated dialogues with Evangelical churches and their theologians. A number of the critical issues raised by Evangelicals have also been raised by the Orthodox in their involvement with the WCC.

At the Harare Assembly of the World Council of Churches in 1998, a Letter from the Evangelical participants expressed both the positive concerns for Christian unity as well as questions about the identity of the council. The Evangelical participants affirmed the councils' greater attention to the perspectives of Evangelicals. At the same time, the Letter noted that "some evangelicals still experience a sense of frustration and even crisis about the future of their participation because of uncertainty over the nature of the WCC commitment to mission and evangelism and biblical theology."[25] With regard to the Harare Assembly, the Letter lamented the fact that serious "theological reflection was largely absent" and that some "major speakers fell outside the boundaries of the creedal basis of the member churches and the Council's own faith basis."[26] The Letter noted that in one plenary commitment, there was no reference to Jesus Christ.[27] Despite these critical observations, the Evangelical participants urged the WCC to make further efforts to involve Evangelicals and Pentecostals for the "mutual enrichment and contribution that this relationship can bring."[28]

MAKING VISIBLE UNITY: SOME ANGLICAN AND PROTESTANT ADVANCES

Within the world of Anglican and Protestant Christianity, there have been significant efforts to bring about greater unity through the healing of those divisions that afflicted Reformation churches from the sixteenth century. As we have noted, at least four major trends developed at the time of the Reformation. From the start, these theological traditions were not easily harmonized and serious divisions within Protestantism were evident, especially over issues related to worship and ministry. Throughout the twentieth century, there were efforts made to heal the major divisions within Protestantism in various ways. This process has been affected by and closely related to the broader efforts to reconcile the Orthodox, Roman Catholic, Old Catholic, and Protestant churches.

COUNCILS AND FEDERATIONS

During the early decades of the twentieth century, there were movements to establish councils of churches that would bring together the major Protestant churches for common witness and cooperative activities. Often, these councils grew out of earlier movements dealing with religious education, mission, or social witness.[29] As early as 1893, the distinguished Protestant church historian Philip Schaff (1819–93) proposed a vision of unity whereby the various churches would recognize each other and come together in the form of a federation in a given place. Similar proposals were expressed in the United States by the Congregationalist Elias B. Sanford (1843–1932) and the Episcopalian William Reed Huntington (1838–1909). The common element among these and similar proposals was the fact that the associations would be comprised of member churches. The councils would not simply be associations of believers who had no formal connection with churches.[30]

The first national council of Protestant churches was the Protestant Federation of France, which was established in 1905.[31] From that time onward, a number of national councils comprised of Protestant churches came into existence. The Federal Council of Churches in the United States began in 1908 and had a profound influence upon similar associations in other parts of the world.[32] It was followed by similar associations in Switzerland in 1920, in Germany in 1922, in China in 1922, in Britain in 1937, in the Netherlands in 1935, in New Zealand in 1941, and in Australia in 1946.[33] These early Protestant national councils did much to narrow the gap between a number of Protestant church traditions rooted in the sixteenth century Reformation. At the same time they often contributed to the healing of divisions within particular Reformation traditions. Moreover, these early Protestant conciliar associations at the national level frequently gave rise to others at a regional or local level.

Many of these councils eventually went trough their own significant transformation, reflecting developments in the ecumenical movement. As Orthodox churches began to be more involved in the ecumenical movement, a number of national and regional councils became Protestant and Orthodox bodies. This began in the United States in 1950 when the Federal Council became the National Council and received Orthodox churches as full members. A further development occurred after the 1960s when the Roman Catholic Church began to become more involved in ecumenical activities. This has also led to the development of Councils of Churches in a number of places, such as Canada and Britain, which also have Roman Catholic participation. While the Roman Catholic Church has not joined the World Council of Churches, it is now a full member of about sixty national councils and the regional councils in the Middle East, the Pacific, and Caribbean.[34]

UNITED PROTESTANT CHURCHES

The desire for a unified Protestant church in a number of places was not satisfied simply through a federation or a council of member churches.[35] Some proposed that a form of organic union take place among various existing Protestant churches so that a single church results. This process has proven to be more difficult. It involved not only the reconciliation of Reformation theological and ecclesiological traditions but also some form or genuine structural union. Older church bodies ceased to exist and a new united Protestant church body was established. The various denominational designations were eliminated. These new churches have sometimes been referred to as transconfessional unions because they normally represent a union of Reformation churches from very different historical and theological traditions.[36]

Because each of these new church bodies have their own history and characteristics, it is not possible to easily catalogue all of them. It has been estimated that there are as many as eighteen united churches in various parts of the world and several of these have gone through various stages of development.[37] Among these, the following examples should be noted. The United Church of Canada began in 1925 through a local union of the Presbyterian, Congregational, and Methodist churches. The Anglican Church did not become a member.[38] The Church of Christ in China in 1927 brought together eight major Protestant churches.[39] The Church of Christ in Japan united a number of small Protestant churches in 1941.[40] The Church of South India began in 1947 through a local union of Anglican, Methodist, Reformed, and Congregational churches.[41] The Evangelical Church in Germany came into being in 1948 as a union of regional Lutheran and Reformed churches.[42]

Each of these examples reflects the variety of unions of Reformation churches that can be found today in various countries or regions. While there is diversity in the degree of union expressed in these bodies, there is a common concern. As Stephen Neill says: "All such efforts spring from the conviction that unity among Christians for which Christ prayed was intended to be a unity of faith, worship, administration, and of witness; that it should be in fact a unity which is not merely spiritually experienced by believers, but a manifest reality, apprehensible even by those who are not Christians at all."[43]

EFFORTS TO UNIFY REFORMATION CHURCHES IN THE UNITED STATES

An attempt to unite the major Reformation churches in the United States dates back at least to 1918. In that year representatives of 19 Protestant churches attended a Conference on Organic Union. A plan was drawn up by 1920 that envisioned "The United Churches of Christ in America." The association of Protestant churches was meant to be something less than full organic union. At that time, much emphasis was being place upon practical cooperation and little on issues of "faith and order." As a consequence, the plan faltered primarily because of a lack of consensus on issues related to the mutual recognition of ministry and sacraments.[44]

Serious discussions of a union plan were revived in 1960 by Eugene Carson Blake (1906–85), a leader in the Presbyterian Church. Blake, who later became the General Secretary of the WCC between 1966 and 1972, proposed the union of four American Protestant churches. These were the Episcopal, the Presbyterian, the Methodist, and the United Church of Christ. Blake's plan reflected the developments of the United Church of Canada and the United Church of South India. It also was offered at a time when a number of Reformation church families in the United States were involved in healing internal divisions. Blake spoke of a church "truly catholic and truly reformed." By the year 1962, the Consultation on Church Union was established with nine Protestant churches. In addition to those already mentioned were: the African Methodist Episcopal, the African Methodist Episcopal Zion, the Christian Methodist Episcopal, the Southern Presbyterian, and the Disciples of Christ. While a formal plan of union was in place by 1968, it experienced a setback in 1972 when the Presbyterian Church withdrew support. A new proposal, The COCU Consensus, was submitted to the churches in 1984.[45] As a result of further questions, a new approach based upon the concept of covenanting was proposed in 1989. This approach further diminished the vision of an organic union and emphasized mutual recognition of members, sacraments, and ministries. The plan was called Churches in Covenanting Communion: The Church of Christ Uniting.

Churches Uniting in Christ, a new association of nine Protestant churches in the United States, came into being on January 20, 2002. The association is based upon the plans of the Consultation on Church Union, but the emphasis is somewhat different from the proposal of 1960 and subsequent developments. In this new association, each church "retains its own identity and decision-making structures, but they also have pledged before God to draw closer in sacred things—including regular sharing of the Lord's Supper and common mission, especially a mission to combat racism together. Each church also committed itself to undertake an intensive dialogue toward the day when ministers are authorized to serve and lead worship, when invited, in each of the communions."[46]

Churches Uniting in Christ does not present itself as a new structure. Rather, "it is an officially recognized invitation to live with one another differently. Christians in the pews know that we belong together because we all belong to the same Lord. Churches Uniting in Christ is a framework for showing to the world what we truly are—the one Body of Jesus Christ."[47] Churches Uniting in Christ presently has nine members. These are: the African Methodist Episcopal Church, the African Methodist Episcopal Zion Church, the Christian Church (Disciples of Christ), the Christian Methodist Episcopal Church, the Episcopal Church, the International Council of Community Churches, the Presbyterian Church (USA), the United Church of Christ, and the United Methodist Church.

Churches Uniting in Christ includes nine of the major Reformation churches in the United States. Yet there are a number of large Protestant churches and associations that have been notably absent from the movement toward a more unified Protestant Church in the United States. These include many Evangelical and Pentecostal Church families. Also absent is the Evangelical Lutheran Church in America. Established in 1988 as a result of the union of three Lutheran churches, this Church generally has been active in ecumenical activities.[48] The Lutheran church that has generally avoided ecumenical associations is the Lutheran Church, Missouri Synod.[49] Finally, neither the American Baptist Churches in the United States or the more conservative Southern Baptist Convention have been active in Protestant union discussions. While the former does engage in ecumenical activities, the latter has generally avoided ecumenical dialogues and associations.[50]

AGREEMENTS ON RESTORING FULL COMMUNION

During the late nineteenth century and early twentieth century, representatives of the Old Catholic Churches were engaged in significant dialogues with both the Orthodox Churches and the Anglican Communion. A Reunion Conference was held in Bonn in 1874 and again in 1875 that brought together Orthodox, Old Catholic, and Anglican theologians. These set the stage for a series of discussions between the Old Catholics and Orthodox and the Old Catholics and Anglicans in the late nineteenth century. While the dialogues with the Orthodox were very important for their day, they did not did not lead to any formal restoration of full communion. The dialogues between the Old Catholics and the Anglicans, on the other hand, led to more formal agreements that were quite significant and provided a basis for an agreement to establish full communion between the two churches.

At the Lambeth Conference of 1920, the bishops of the Anglican Communion expressed the desire to strengthen the relationship between their church and the Old Catholic Churches. Five years later in 1925, the Old Catholic bishops meeting in Bonn, Germany, established a committee to investigate the issue of Anglican Orders. This eventually led the Old Catholics to affirm the validity of the ministerial ordinations in the Anglican Communion. This decision which was contrary to the opinion reached by the Roman Catholic Church in 1896.

The decision of the Old Catholics, however, marked a true turning point in their relationship with the Anglican Communion. Representatives of the Old Catholic Churches and the Anglican Communion met in Bonn in 1931. During this meeting, the historic Agreement of Bonn was reached. This agreement affirmed that each church recognized the catholicity and independence of the other. It affirmed that Anglicans and Old Catholics could receive Holy Communion in each other's churches. Finally, the Bonn Agreement affirmed that Anglicans and Old Catholics believe the essentials of the Christian Faith. Old Catholic Bishops affirmed this agreement in 1931. The Anglican Bishops in England affirmed it in 1932. In the following years, it was received by other provinces of the Anglican Communion. While the Agreement did not provide for an organic union between the Anglican Communion and the Old Catholic Churches, it did lead to the establishment of full communion between the two. This agreement also provided direction for subsequent discussions between Anglicans and the Lutheran and Reformed churches.

The fruits of theological dialogues among the divided churches in general and those between Anglican and Protestant churches in particular have led to a number of dramatic agreements since 1973. Based upon decades of discussions, these theological agreements among Anglican and Protestant churches have affirmed a common Christian faith and have established full communion between particular regional churches. To speak about full communion means that both churches affirm in each other the same Christian faith and, therefore, recognize each other's sacraments and ministry.[51]

THE LEUENBERG AGREEMENT

The Leuenberg Agreement of 1973 is an affirmation of unity among certain Reformation churches. This agreement has established full communion among about one hundred regional Lutheran, Reformed, United, and Methodist churches in Western Europe. This agreement has also served as a basis for agreement among five Reformation churches in Argentina.[52] The agreement begins with these affirmations:

> On the basis of their doctrinal discussions, the churches assenting to this Agreement—namely, Lutheran and Reformed Churches in Europe along with the Union Churches which grew out of them, and the related pre-Reformation Churches, the Waldensian Church and the Church of the Czech Brethren—affirm together the common understanding of the Gospel elaborated below. This common understanding of the Gospel enables them to declare and to realize church fellowship. Thankful that they have been led closer together, they confess at the same time that guilt and suffering have also accompanied and still accompany the struggle for truth and unity in the Church.
>
> The Church is founded upon Jesus Christ alone. It is he who gathers the Church and sends it forth, by the bestowal of his salvation in preaching and the sacraments. In the view of the Reformation it follows that agreement in the right teaching of the Gospel and in the right administration of the sacraments is the necessary and sufficient prerequisite for the true unity of the Church. It is from these Reformation criteria that the participating churches derive their view of church fellowship as set out below.[53]

The Leuenberg Agreement is an important statement that affirms that the historic divisions between the churches coming from the Lutheran tradition and the churches coming from the Reformed tradition have been overcome in certain places and within the context of the wider ecumenical movement.

THE PORVOO COMMON STATEMENT

The second major agreement is the Porvoo Common Statement of 1992. This statement is even more significant than Leuenberg because is an affirmation of common faith between four Anglican churches of Britain and Ireland and eight Lutheran churches of Northern Europe. The Porvoo Statement is similar to Leuenberg in that it affirms a common faith and the establishment of full communion among Reformation churches of different historical traditions. It is somewhat different from Leuenberg because the Porvoo Statement deals with Anglican and Lutheran churches. It also provides a much more detailed description of the shared faith and practices, especially with regard to the ordained ministry. "An agreement on bishops in apostolic succession was required because of the Anglican participation, and it was achieved by presenting an understanding of succession as a sign of the continuity of the apostolic faith, life and mission of the whole church."[54] Viewed with this in mind, Porvoo represents an "ecumenical breakthrough" because the issue of apostolic succession of ministry has been a major point of difference in ecumenical discussions.[55]

A portion of the Porvoo Statement declares:

> The faith, worship and spirituality of all our churches are rooted in the tradition of the apostolic Church. We stand in continuity with the Church of the patristic and medieval periods both directly and through the insights of the Reformation period. We each understand our own church to be part of the One, Holy, Catholic Church of Jesus Christ and truly participating in the one apostolic mission of the whole people of God. We share in the liturgical heritage of Western Christianity and also in the Reformation emphases upon justification by faith and upon word and sacrament as means of grace. All this is embodied in our confessional and liturgical documents and is increasingly recognized both as an essential bond between our churches and as a contribution to the wider ecumenical movement.[56]

The Porvoo Statement is especially significant because it expresses a resolution of very difficult issues, especially related to ordained ministry and the Eucharist. These issues were central to differences between Lutherans and Anglicans from the Reformation period.

AGREEMENTS IN THE UNITED STATES

The Leuenberg Agreement and the discussions surrounding it provided a valuable basis for discussions that eventually led to A Formula of Agreement in 1997 between the Evangelical Lutheran Church in the United States and three churches from the Reformed tradition. These are: the Presbyterian Church, the Reformed Church in America, and the United Church of Christ.[57] The official dialogue between these churches reaches back to 1962.

A portion of A Formula of Agreement dealing with the meaning of full communion states:

That the Evangelical Lutheran Church in America, the Presbyterian Church (USA), the Reformed Church in America (RCA), and the United Church of Christ (UCC) declare that they are in full communion with one another. In the specific terms of full communion as they are developed in our study, this recommendation also requires:

1. that they recognize each other as churches in which the Gospel is rightly preached and the sacraments rightly administered according to the Word of God;
2. that they withdraw any historic condemnation by one side or the other as inappropriate for the faith and life of our churches today;
3. that they continue to recognize each other's Baptism and authorize and encourage the sharing of the Lord's Supper among their members;
4. that they recognize each others' various ministries and make provision for the orderly exchange of ordained ministers of Word and Sacrament;
5. that they establish appropriate channels of consultation and decision-making within the existing structures of the churches;
6. that they commit themselves to an ongoing process of theological dialogue in order to clarify further the common understanding of the faith and foster its common expression in evangelism, witness, and service;
7. that they pledge themselves to living together under the Gospel in such a way that the principle of mutual affirmation and admonition becomes the basis of a trusting relationship in which respect and love for the other will have a chance to grow.[58]

The Porvoo Common Statement and related discussions also contributed to the Lutheran Episcopal discussions in the United States. Dialogue between the representatives of these churches reach back to the year 1935. In more recent decades, the dialogue between the Lutheran Church and the Episcopal Church benefited greatly from similar dialogues in Europe as well as from discussions within the context of the Faith and Order Commission of the World Council of Churches. As in the case in Europe, the major point that needed attention between these churches was a different understanding of the meaning and the significance of the order of bishop in the church, which reached back to the Reformation period.

The agreement in 2000, known as Called to Common Mission, establishes full communion between the Evangelical Lutheran Church and the Episcopal Church. This agreement affirms: "The Evangelical Lutheran Church in America and The Episcopal Church recognize in each other the essentials of the one catholic and apostolic faith as it is witnessed in the unaltered *Augsburg Confession*, the *Small Catechism*, and

The Book of Common Prayer of 1979." The agreement further elaborates upon the elements of the common faith by affirming their acceptance of the authority the Old and New Testaments. They also recognize the importance of the "Nicene-Constantinopolitan and Apostles' Creeds and confess the basic Trinitarian and Christological Dogmas to which these creeds testify. That is, we believe that Jesus of Nazareth is true God and true Man, and that God is authentically identified as Father, Son, and Holy Spirit."[59]

With regard to the issue of the recognition of the order of the bishop in the church, the Called to Common Mission statement says:

> As a result of their agreement in faith and in testimony of their full communion with one another, both churches now make the following commitment to share an episcopal succession that is both evangelical and historic. They promise to include regularly one or more bishops of the other church to participate in the laying-on-of-hands at the ordinations/installations of their own bishops as a sign, though not a guarantee, of the unity and apostolic continuity of the whole church. With the laying-on-of-hands by other bishops, such ordinations/installations will involve prayer for the gift of the Holy Spirit. Both churches value and maintain a ministry of *episkopé* as one of the ways, in the context of ordained ministries and of the whole people of God, in which the apostolic succession of the church is visibly expressed and personally symbolized in fidelity to the gospel through the ages. By such a liturgical statement the churches recognize that the bishop serves the diocese or synod through ties of collegiality and consultation that strengthen its links with the universal church. It is also a liturgical expression of the full communion initiated by this Concordat, calling for mutual planning and common mission in each place. We agree that when persons duly called and elected are ordained/installed in this way, they are understood to join bishops already in this succession and thus to enter the historic episcopate.[60]

SIGNIFICANT AFFIRMATIONS

The agreements to establish full communion among churches of the Reformation traditions in both Western Europe and the United States are very significant developments not only for these churches but also for the entire ecumenical movement. At first glance these agreements affect only certain churches that come out of the Reformation. Yet these agreements are important because they overcome serious differences in doctrinal emphasis, which were part of the history of the sixteenth century Reformation. The various churches of the Reformation could not easily find agreement on issues related to the significance of the Lord's Supper (Eucharist) and ordained ministry. While the bitterness of that period is past, the divisive consequences of that period have lasted in a formal manner for over four hundred years. The formal agreements among certain Anglican, Lutheran, and Reformed churches affirm a common understanding of the essential elements of the Christian faith and indicate agreements on previous points of difference.

The affirmation of full communion is also significant. This is the means through which the churches that have entered into agreement affirm that there are no doctrinal differences separating them. This affirmation also means that the churches recognize fully the faith of the other as well as the sacraments and ministry of the other. The churches that accept the agreement continue to maintain a structural identity and an appreciation of their historic heritage. At the same time, they affirm that there is no difference in faith that prevents them from sharing full in each other's sacramental life. Sharing together in the celebration of Holy Communion (Eucharist) is a visible sign of their unity in faith.

These agreements reflect the work of theological dialogue within the broader ecumenical movement, reaching back to the early decades of this century. As such, these agreements reflect also discussions on topics such as church, baptism, the Eucharist, and ministry that have engaged not only Protestant but also Orthodox and Roman Catholics. They also express a very valuable fruit of those who have prayed and worked for Christian reconciliation and the visible unity of the churches.[61]

CONCLUSIONS

From the latter portion of the nineteenth and early twentieth century, Anglican and Protestant churches and their representatives have been at the center of the contemporary ecumenical movement. A significant component of the early steps toward church unity was a process of bringing the divided Reformation churches and traditions into greater contact, cooperation, and dialogue, especially through councils of churches.

There have been elements within Protestantism that have had a very different perspective on the ecumenical movement. In contrast to the major Protestant churches, Fundamentalists have openly opposed all ecumenical efforts. Some Evangelicals have more recently moved toward a cautious involvement in particular ecumenical efforts. These differences among Protestants reflect a deeper rift over issues of Scripture and its interpretation, going back to the nineteenth century.

A number of regional Anglican and Protestant churches in Western Europe and America have entered into major agreements, which have established full communion among them. These agreements have done much to overcome divisions over worship and ministry, especially within the Reformation churches dating from the sixteenth century. Accomplished within the broader context of the ecumenical dialogues, these agreements have also done much to emphasize the importance of the visible unity of the churches expressed through agreement in faith and manifest in full Eucharistic communion.

NOTES

1. *The COCU Consensus: In Quest of a Church Uniting in Christ* (Consultation on Church Union: Princeton, 1984), p. 11.

2. Ruth Rouse, "Voluntary Movements and Changing Ecumenical Climate," in *A History of the Ecumenical Movement 1517–1948,* ed. Ruth Rouse and Stephen Charles Neill (Philadelphia: The Westminster Press, 1967), p. 325.

3. Denise Lardner Carmondy and John Tully Carmody, *Christianity: An Introduction* (Belmont, Calif.: Wardsworth Publishing Company, 1983), p. 142.

4. Edwin Scott Gaustad, *A Religious History of America* (San Francisco: Harper and Row, revised edition, 1990), pp. 255–58.

5. Ruth Rouse, "Voluntary Movements and the Changing Ecumenical Climate," p. 320.

6. Gaustad, p. 205.

7. Don Herbert Yoder, "Christian Unity in Nineteenth Century America," in *A History of the Ecumenical Movement 1517–1948,* ed. Rouse and Neill, pp. 252–59.

8. Elizabeth C. Nordbeck, *That All May Be One: Celebrating a Century of Ecumenical Witness* (Boston: The Massachusetts Council of Churches, 2002), pp. 14–20.

9. Gaustad, p. 275.

10. L.D. Pettegrew, "The Niagara Bible Conference and American Fundamentalism," *Central Bible Quarterly* 19–20 (winter 1976–winter 1977).

11. G.M. Marsden and B.J. Longfield, "Fundamentalism," in *Dictionary of Christianity in America,* ed. Daniel G. Reid (Downers Grove, Ill.: InterVarsity Press, 1990), pp. 461–65.

12. Ibid., p. 463.

13. Samuel McCrea Cavert, *On the Road to Christian Unity* (New York: Harper and Brothers, 1961), pp. 99–100.

14. Douglas Jacobson and William Vance Trollinger, Jr., "Evangelical and Ecumenical: Reforming the Center," *Christian Century,* July 13–20, 1994, p. 682.

15. Ibid., p. 683.

16. See G. Marsdan, *Fundamentalism and American Culture: The Shaping of Twentieth Century Evangelicalism 1870–1925* (New York: Oxford University Press, 1980).

17. James Murch, *Cooperation without Compromise: A History of the National Association of Evangelicals* (Grand Rapids, Mich.: Eerdmans, 1956).

18. National Association of Evangelicals, http://www.nae.net/index.cfm/method/content.aboutus.

19. National Association of Evangelicals, http://www.nae.net/index.cfm/method/content.A2823A13-ED59-4586-AEB8367CDCA562C4.

20. R.C. Cizik, "World Evangelical Fellowship," in *Dictionary of Christianity in America,* ed. Daniel G. Reid (Downers Grove, Ill.: InterVarsity Press, 1990), p. 1275.

21. Jacobson and Trollinger, "Evangelical and Ecumenical: Reforming the Center," p. 683.

22. See Cecil M. Robeck, "A Pentecostal Looks at the World Council of Churches," *The Ecumenical Review* 47 (1995), pp. 60–75.

23. W.A. Visser 't Hooft, "The General Ecumenical Development since 1948," in *A History of the Ecumenical Movement, Volume 2, 1948–1968,* ed. Harold E. Fry (Philadelphia: The Westminister Press, 1970), p. 19.

24. *Minutes and Reports of the Central Committee* (Geneva: World Council of Churches, 1966), p. 72.

25. "A Jubilee Call: A Letter to the WCC by Evangelical Participants," in *Together On The Way: Official Report of the Eighth Assembly of the World Council of Churches,* ed. Dianne Kessler (Geneva: WCC Publications, 1999), p. 267.

26. Ibid., p. 268.

27. Ibid.

28. Ibid., p. 271.

29. Ruth Rouse, "Other Aspects of the Ecumenical Movement" in *A History of the Ecumenical Movement 1517–1948,* ed. Rouse and Neill, pp. 599–620.

30. Ibid., p. 620.

31. Dianne Kessler and Michael Kinnamon, *Councils of Churches and the Ecumenical Vision* (Geneva: WCC Publications, 2000), p. 14.

32. Rouse, "Other Aspects of the Ecumenical Movement," pp. 621–24.

33. Ibid., 624–30.

34. Kessler and Kinnamon, *Councils of Churches and the Ecumenical Vision,* pp. 16–17.

35. Stephen Charles Neill, "Plans of Union and Reunion," in *A History of the Ecumenical Movement 1517–1948,* ed. Rouse and Neill, pp. 445–48.

36. Ibid., p. 454.

37. Michael Kinnamon, "Uniting and United Churches," in *Dictionary of the Ecumenical Movement,* ed. Nicholas Lossky et al. (Geneva: WCC Publications, 1991), p. 1033.

38. Stephen Charles Neill, "Plans of Union and Reunion," in *A History of the Ecumenical Movement 1517–1948,* ed. Rouse and Neill, pp. 454–58.

39. Ibid., pp. 458–60.

40. Ibid., pp. 460–61.

41. Ibid., pp. 473–76.

42. Ibid., pp. 466–68.

43. Ibid., pp. 491–505.

44. Ibid., p. 446.

45. *The COCU Consensus: In Quest of a Church Uniting in Christ* (Princeton: Consultation on Church Union, 1984).

46. Churches Uniting in Christ, http://www.eden.edu/cuic/whatiscuic/whatiscuic.htm.

47. Ibid.

48. See T.W. Nichols, *All These Lutherans: Three Paths towards a New Lutheran Church* (Minneapolis: Augsburg, 1986).

49. See Milton L. Rudnick, *Fundamentalism and the Missouri Synod* (St. Louis: Concordia, 1966).

50. See Robert G. Torbet, *History of the Baptists* (Valley Forge: Judson Press, 1963).

51. Günther Gassmann, "Retrospective of an Ecumenical Century," in *Agapè: Études en l'honneur de Mgr. Pierre Dupre* (Chambésy: Centre Orthodoxe, 2002), p. 79.

52. Ibid., p. 82.

53. "The Leuenberg Agreement," *Lutheran World* 20 (1973), p. 349.

54. Gassmann, "Retrospective of an Ecumenical Century," p. 82.

55. Ibid.

56. *The Porvoo Common Statement,* (London: Council for Christian Unity, 1993), pp. 7–8.

57. K. F. Nickle and T. F. Lull, eds., *A Common Calling: The Witness of the Reformation Churches in North America Today* (Minneapolis: Fortress, 1993).

58. "A Formula of Agreement," http://www.elca.org/ea/Relationships/presbyterians/formula.html.

59. "A Common Mission," http://www.elca.org/ea/Relationships/episcopalian/index.html.

60. Ibid.

61. Gassmann, p. 85. For further background on these agreements, see *A Common Calling: The Witness of Our Reformation Churches in North America Today* (Minneapolis: Augsburg, 1993).

CHAPTER 10

Theological Dialogues for Reconciliation

> The unity of the Church to which we are called is a koinonia given and expressed in the common confession of apostolic faith, a common sacramental life entered by the one baptism and celebrated together in eucharistic fellowship; a common life in which members and ministries are mutually recognized and reconciled; a common mission witnessing to all people to the gospel of God's grace and serving the whole creation. The goal of full communion is realized when all the churches are able to recognize in one another the one, holy, catholic and apostolic church in its fullness.
>
> —Canberra Assembly Statement, 1991[1]

INTRODUCTION

From the earliest days of the ecumenical movement, there has been a clear recognition that the historic divisions between the churches are rooted primarily in major differences in teachings and doctrinal emphasis. These unresolved differences in teachings generally reach back centuries to the period of time when specific church divisions took place. As time passed, the differences became more solidified and were used as distinguishing features in times of polemics. These theological differences also were compounded by political and cultural factors.

Throughout the past century especially, there has been a dramatic and unrelenting effort by the churches to engage in both formal and informal theological dialogues with each other. These dialogues often began with the desire to deepen mutual understanding and enrichment an atmosphere free from polemics and prejudice. As time went on, these dialogues have moved toward a fresh examination of the root causes of the theological and doctrinal differences among the churches. Many of the dialogues have begun to offer substantial proposals for the overcoming of these differences.

EXPRESSIONS OF THEOLOGICAL DIALOGUES

There are a number of different expressions of theological dialogues within the contemporary ecumenical movement. In many places, there are informal dialogues that bring together theologians from different churches but are not directly under the auspice of the churches. Among the most significant of such dialogues is the Groupe des Dombes, which has brought together Roman Catholic, Protestant, and Orthodox pastors and theologians from Eastern France and Western Switzerland since 1937.[2] The influence of this small association has been profound and has inspired similar local groups in other parts of the world. These less formal dialogues, for example, can be associated with local gatherings of clergy and lay leaders of different churches. They can be associated with gatherings of representatives of theological schools of different Christian traditions. They can even be gatherings open to theologians and pastors who wish to study a particular theological theme in an ecumenical context.

The more formal theological dialogues are those that receive the official sanction of the churches and that bring together theologians who officially represent their church. During the twentieth century, the early meetings of the Faith and Order Movement and the Life and Work Movement in the 1920s and 1930s set this pattern. At the global level, both of these became essential components of the World Council of Churches since its founding in 1948. The theological dialogues within the context of the WCC and other Councils of Churches are usually referred to as multilateral. These multilateral theological dialogues bring together theologians from a number of churches and, as a consequence, from different theological traditions. They generally seek to address specific theological themes and seek to find a consensus.

In the past 40 years especially, there has been a dramatic increase of bilateral theological dialogues at the global and regional levels. Bilateral dialogues are those that are formally established by two churches and that bring together theologians from the two separated churches to study particular issues. Some expressions of bilateral dialogues can be found in the nineteenth century. However, since the 1960s there has been a significant growth of bilateral dialogues between the churches. Either at the regional or global levels, these dialogues involve the Orthodox, Roman Catholic, Anglican, and most Protestant churches. At the present time, there are more than 50 bilateral dialogues throughout the world. Over the past four decades especially, these dialogues have examined a wide variety of topics related to historical divisions and contemporary theological concerns.[3] Nils Ehrenström and Günther Gassmann point to the remarkable accomplishments of these dialogues when they say: "The bilateral conversations around the world form a movement of theological exploration and discovery which indeed has yielded truly remarkable results. The advances and convergences that are taking place appear all the more striking when one considers the fact that in several instances they are bridging agelong chasms within Christendom. And that all this has taken place within the short span of a few years."[4]

There have been a number of factors that have contributed to the dramatic developments of these multilateral and bilateral dialogues in the past four decades especially. For one thing, the churches formally have come to sense the tragic character of divisions and the impact of these divisions on Christian witness in the world. This has led to a new desire to heal old divisions. As a consequence, there has also been a new climate of mutual respect and, to some degree, mutual accountability developing among the churches. There has been a movement away from sterile polemics toward a mutual engagement in theological reflection. Together with this, there has been an increasing recognition of the role that linguistic differences, politics, and culture played in contributing to the theological and doctrinal differences. Finally, the dialogues have contributed to and have expressed a revitalization of theological reflection on the central issues of Christian faith. This has been stimulated by the study together of the Scriptures and the deeper tradition of historic Christianity within a context of prayer.[5]

The multilateral and bilateral theological dialogues have done much to enrich the life of the churches, to bring them closer together, and to advance their reconciliation. A comprehensive review of the fruits of all the multilateral and bilateral theological dialogues, however, would require a separate study. Nonetheless, in order to provide a perspective on the work of these dialogues, we can identify some significant statements both from the multilateral dialogue within the context of the World Council of Churches and from a representative number of bilateral theological dialogues among churches.

I. Multilateral Theological Dialogues

A Vision of Visible Unity

The Faith and Order Movement began formally with a planning meeting in 1920 that gathered together a number of Anglican, Orthodox, Old Catholic, and Protestant theologians. This laid the groundwork for historic conferences in 1927 and 1937. The work of Faith and Order at the global level has been integral to the WCC since its establishment in 1948. The multilateral theological dialogue of Faith and Order took on greater significance with greater participation of the Orthodox from the early 1960s and the formal involvement of Roman Catholic theologians after 1968.

Throughout its history, Faith and Order has been concerned with providing a vision of the visible unity of the churches in one faith and Eucharistic fellowship. This vision has gradually matured over the decades as past issues of division have been studied ecumenically and new perspectives on these have developed. The unfolding vision that Faith and Order presents reflects the creative work of theologians, who have formally represented their churches and have kept before them the vision of reconciliation. Within the broader context of the WCC, the fruits of the major studies of Faith and Order have found notable expression in the council's assemblies. This has been especially true for the unfolding vision of visible unity.

At the New Delhi Assembly in 1961, the concern of Faith and Order for visible unity found its first formal extensive expression. The assembly's Statement on Unity declares:

> We believe that the unity which is both God's will and his gift to his Church, is being made visible as all in each place who are baptized into Jesus Christ and confess him as Lord and Saviour are brought by the Holy Spirit into one fully committed fellowship, holding the one apostolic faith, preaching the one Gospel, breaking the one bread, joining in common prayer, and having a corporate life reaching out in witness and fellowship in all places and all ages in such wise that ministry and members are accepted by all, and that all can act and speak together as occasion requires for the tasks to which God calls his people.[6]

Based upon the work of Faith and Order, the Nairobi Assembly in 1975 continued to emphasize the characteristics of visible unity in its statement on What Unity Requires. A portion of the statement says: "The one Church is to be envisioned as a conciliar fellowship of local churches which are themselves truly united. In this conciliar fellowship, each local church possesses, in communion with the others, the fullness of catholicity, witnesses to the same apostolic faith, and therefore recognizes the others as belonging to the same Church of Christ and guided by the same Spirit." The Statement says that the churches "are bound together because they have received the same baptism and share in the same Eucharist; they recognize each other's members and ministries. They are one in their common commitment to confess the gospel of Christ by proclamation and service to the world. To this end, each church aims at maintaining sustained and sustaining relationships with his sister churches, expressed in conciliar gatherings whenever required for the fulfillment of their common calling."[7]

At the Canberra Assembly of the World Council of Churches in 1991, the work of Faith and Order was expressed most especially in the extensive and powerful statement entitled "The Unity of the Church as Koinonia: Gift and Calling." This historic statement placed the quest for visible unity within the wider context of the purpose of God "to gather the whole creation under the leadership of Christ Jesus in whom, by the power of the Holy Spirit, all are brought into communion with God (Eph. 1)." In this view, the Church is seen as the sign of God's reconciliation and healing of all divisions. Yet, because of sin and misunderstandings, "the churches are painfully divided within themselves and among themselves." Thus, the "scandalous divisions damage the credibility of their witness to the world in worship and service" and "contradict not only the church's witness but also its very name." The statement continues:

> The Unity of the Church to which we are called is a koinonia given and expressed in the common confession of apostolic faith, a common sacramental life entered by the one baptism and celebrated together in eucharistic fellowship; a common life in which members and ministries are mutually recognized and reconciled; a common mission witnessing to all people to the gospel of God's grace and serving the whole creation. The goal of full communion is realized when all the churches are able to recognize in one another the one, holy, catholic and apostolic church in its fullness. This full communion will be expressed on the local and universal levels through conciliar forms of life and action.[8]

The visible unity of the churches that is expressed in this unfolding vision is not simply a matter of cooperation or collaboration of divided ecclesial bodies. It is not simply an invisible unity of those who acknowledge Jesus Christ. It is not a minimalist view of church unity that seeks to ignore serious theological differences. Rather, it is a vision of visible unity that demands thoughtful theological resolution of issues of division. It is a vision that is expressed through a united confession of the Christian faith, through a united celebration of the Eucharist, through a full recognition of baptized members and church ministries, and through united service and witness in the world.[9]

The Relationship of Scripture and Tradition

The relationship between Scripture and Tradition has been a vexing problem since the time of the Reformation. While the problem was not evident in the early church, issues dealing with this relationship have been central to the differences between the Roman Catholic Church and most Protestant churches since the sixteenth century. The Roman Catholic Church generally spoke of the truth of divine revelation as being transmitted not only in written Scripture but also through an oral tradition that also expresses itself in church teachings. Protestants generally appealed to Scripture alone as an infallible and sufficient authority for teaching. The

Orthodox, who closely relate Scripture and Tradition, were not directly involved in the Reformation debates.

The Faith and Order Commission published a very important study of this topic in 1963 entitled "Scripture, Tradition, and Traditions."[10] The statement reflects more recent understandings of the development of Scripture, especially the New Testament, in the life of the early church. The statement also reflects a more nuanced understanding of the interrelationship of Scripture and Tradition, which does not set them in opposition to each other but rather sees their dynamic interrelationship. Both Scripture and Tradition reflect the divine revelation and seek to convey it. As the statement says: "The oral and written tradition of the prophets and apostles under the guidance of the Holy Spirit led to the formation of Scripture and the canonization of the Old and New Testament as the Bible of the Church."[11] It also says that: "Historical studies and not least the encounter of the churches in the ecumenical movement have led us to realize that the proclamation of the Gospel is always inevitably conditioned."[12] This means that the creation of the New Testament canon and its interpretation always takes place in the life of the community of faith that produced it. The Scriptures as the written Word of God cannot be appreciated apart from the life and teachings of the believing community that is the church.

With this in mind, the statement proposes a new way of seeing the relationship between Scripture and Tradition. It says in part:

> Our starting point is that we are all living in a tradition, which goes back to our Lord and has its roots in the Old Testament, and are all indebted to that tradition inasmuch as we have received the revealed truth, the Gospel, through its being transmitted from one generation to another. Thus we can say that we exist as Christians by the Tradition of the Gospel (the *paradosis* of the *kerygma*) testified in Scripture, transmitted in and by the Church through the power of the Holy Spirit. Tradition taken in this sense is actualized in the preaching of the Word, in the administration of the Sacraments and worship, in Christian teaching and theology, and in mission and witness to Christ by the lives of members of the Church.[13]

The statement continues by recognizing an important distinction between Tradition (with an uppercase T) and traditions (with a lowercase t). The statement says that we "can speak of Tradition (with a capital T), whose content is God's revelation and self-giving in Christ, present in the life of the Church." Indeed, the Tradition in its written expression is the Scripture. This Tradition is then also expressed in "traditions" which are "the expressions and manifestation in diverse historical forms of the one truth and reality which is Christ."[14]

While this statement is part of an ongoing discussion of Scripture and Tradition, it does indicate that there need not be a harsh and exclusive distinction between the two for the church. Since 1963, this statement and related studies have provided an important perspective on subsequent discussions of church dividing issues. The insights into the relationship between Scripture and Tradition pointed to the possibility of examining historical differences in a new light that recognized both the importance of Scripture and the significance of its context and historical interpretations.[15]

Closely related to this important study has been the movement to provide new collections and translations of the books of the Bible that do not reflect the patrician polemical perspectives of the past. In the period before the 1960s, it was not uncommon for people to speak about the "Protestant Bible" and the "Roman Catholic Bible." In the wake of the Reformation, two basic factors contributed to these popular designations. First, biblical scholars in each church did the translations with little regard for others. Commentaries that emphasized partisan perspectives often accompanied the translations. And second, there were differences in the numbering the books of the Bible. All churches agreed that there were 27 canonical books of the New Testament. The Church firmly established this consensus by the fourth century, well before the divisions that exist today. However, there were different lists of Old Testament books. These differences existed in the early church and also reflected differences in Judaism. At the time of Christ, there was a collection of Scripture in Hebrew and a collection in Greek, known as the Septuagint, which included more books. Because of this, most Protestant Reformers claimed to follow the Hebrew canon and generally included 39 books in the Old Testament. Mindful as well of the Septuagint collection, the Roman Catholics included 46 books and the Orthodox counted 49 books. There were also some differences in the arrangement and some slight differences in the text of some books. Roman Catholics and Orthodox generally spoke of these books as being *deuterocanonical*—that is, a part of the "second canon."

Because of recent ecumenical dialogues, most new translations of the Scriptures from Hebrew and Greek into vernacular languages are usually undertaken in an ecumenical manner by teams of biblical scholars from a variety of churches. This has done much to prevent translations and interpretations that reflect narrow, partisan positions. This fact, of course, has not eliminated the possibilities of legitimate differences in the interpretation of scriptural texts. It has also led to the production of new translations of the Bible that are more sensitive to recent advances in biblical studies and to the changing character of living languages. Moreover, many new editions of the Bible now contain the deuterocanonical books, which are generally referred to a the Apocrypha. The inclusion of these books in many newer versions of the Christian Scriptures means that Protestants, Catholics, and Orthodox increasingly use the same editions of the Bible in their study, worship, and theological dialogues.

Baptism, Eucharist, and Ministry

Among the significant issues that have contributed to divisions among the church have been questions related to Baptism, the Eucharist or Lord's Supper, and the ordained ministry. These questions became especially prominent in the Reformation period. Marked differences in perspectives developed not only between Protestantism and Roman Catholicism, but also among the various Anglican and Protestant churches.

The Faith and Order Commission published its historic consensus statement on Baptism, Eucharist, and Ministry in 1982.[16] The text was the fruit of studies reaching back to the first Faith and Order Conference in 1927. The completed document was commended to the churches as an expression of "significant theological convergence"[17] on these themes. This text has been seen as unprecedented in the contemporary ecumenical movement. "The agreed text purposely concentrates on those aspects of the theme that have been directly or indirectly related to the problem of mutual recognition leading to unity. The main text demonstrates the major areas of theological convergence; the added commentaries either indicate historical differences that have been overcome or identify disputed issues still in need of further research and reconciliation."[18]

A number of critical factors have contributed to the importance of this text. First, it reflects the research and reflections of outstanding theologians from Orthodox, Old Catholic, Roman Catholic, Anglican, and most Protestant churches. Their work reflects ongoing research into the witness of Scripture and Tradition regarding Baptism, the Eucharist, and Ministry, and especially the practices of the early church. Second, the study clearly identifies points of historical differences. Yet, at the same time, the study offers a rich and balanced perspective of the three major topics, which move beyond narrow views of historic polemics. In this sense, the text has helped the churches to recapture some rich perspectives on Baptism, the Eucharist, and Ministry that were often neglected in the past.[19]

The text has produced more than 100 formal responses from churches. At the same time the text and the responses have become basic to all subsequent investigations of the study of Baptism, the Eucharist, and Ministry by theologians and within theological schools. The text and the church responses have also contributed to the process of liturgical renewal within many of the churches.[20] The Faith and Order Commission said in 1989: "No one envisaged the impact which it would have within and among the churches of such diverse historical origins and varying traditions. The fruit of many years of ecumenical discussion has become the most widely distributed, translated, and discussed ecumenical text in modern times."[21]

Church and World

Within the context of the World Council of Churches especially, the contemporary social challenges such as racism, sexism, poverty, apartheid, injustice as well as war and peace have received considerable attention. From the very beginning, the contemporary ecumenical movement has recognized the need for the churches to come together as far as possible in order to address these issues and to speak with a common voice. This has not always been easy, however. While the churches have spoken together on some moral issues, they have been divided over others. The divided churches have often come to different perspectives on some ethical issues. In addition to this, the statements from some ecumenical bodies on social and moral issues have often been criticized because they have not always been firmly rooted in the message of Christ and his Gospel. Political and social ideologies have often had greater influence.

The Faith and Order Commission of the WCC published in 1990 a noteworthy study on *Church and World: The Unity of the Church and the Renewal of the Human Community.*[22] While the study process began formally in 1982, the general theme is one that has accompanied ecumenical discussions for generations. The text seeks to express "what can be said together today about God's call to the church to seek unity and to be signs and instruments of the renewal of the human community." The text claims to be one of "ecumenical convergence on these issues, to be studied and 'tested' by the churches as a help and impetus for their own self-understanding and their common efforts towards unity and renewal."[23]

The text is especially significant in two ways. First, it forcefully affirms that the churches, even in their state of separation, have an obligation to bear witness to the Gospel message in relationship to the critical issues facing the world today. From this perspective, the text affirms that the church exists as a sign and instrument of God's reconciliation offered to all. As the churches struggle to move toward their own unity, they and their members cannot ignore injustice and the abuse of persons in the society. Second, the text relates the concern for the well-being of persons in the society to the quest for church unity and to the worship of the church. Here, the text reaffirms the perspective that Christian worship cannot be separated from Christian service and mission. And these concerns cannot be separated from ecumenical theological reflection and the quest for the reconciliation and unity of the churches today.[24] This text has contributed to more recent studies relating these areas of concern.

Confessing the One Faith

From the very beginning of the ecumenical movement, there has been recognition that the common affirmation or confession of the Christian faith by the churches is an essential requirement for the restoration of their unity. The various divisions among the churches have led to theological and doctrinal particularities that reflect their estrangement and have been aggravated by them. The quest for reconciliation and unity of the churches has sought to overcome these historical divergences in teachings and to find a common understanding of the essential affirmations of the Christian Faith, often referred to as the apostolic faith.

The Faith and Order Commission of the WCC formally began a study process on "Towards the Common Expression of the Apostolic Faith Today" in 1978. The title reflects the "ecumenical commitment to move towards confessing together the one apostolic faith that is attested in the Holy Scriptures and summarized in the creeds of the early Church." The title also reflects the conviction that the "same faith should be expressed together today: it should be witnessed to, confessed, and celebrated in common."[25]

The aim of the project was not to create a new creed for the churches. Rather, the Faith and Order Commission decided to use the historic creed that came out of the Councils of Nicaea (325) and Constantinople (381). This creed received wide acceptance throughout the early church, both in the Christian East and the Christian West. It served as an element in the process of reconciliation in earlier centuries. And it has remained an important creed that has been used in liturgy and instruction by Orthodox, Roman Catholics, Old Catholics, Anglicans and many Protestant churches. As such, this creed has been recognized historically as a valuable expression of the apostolic faith.

Confessing the One Faith: An Ecumenical Explication of the Apostolic Faith as it is Confessed in the Nicene-Constantinopolitan Creed (381) was published and sent to the churches in 1991. Based upon numerous consultations and theological studies, the text uses the historic creed to present an ecumenical explication of the apostolic faith. The purpose of the explication is to provide a basis for a common recognition and confession of the one apostolic faith by the churches. The text reflects the view that the unity of the churches requires that they agree on the essential elements of the Christian faith and find the means of expressing together this agreement. For many, the creed provides both a means of expressing the apostolic faith and a means of confessing that faith together, especially in worship. The use of this creed is also a reminder that the churches, as they seek unity today, are also bearing witness to their unity with the Church and its faith throughout the ages.

Towards a Common Date for Easter

One of the ways in which the divisions of the churches have been manifest is in the yearly observance of the Feast of Easter, considered to be the most important festival of the church. While there were differences in calculating the yearly observance in the early church, by the fourth century there was a recognition that the feast was of such importance that the worldwide church should observe it together on the same Sunday each year. The Council of Nicaea in 325 determined that the regional churches would observe Easter together each year on the first Sunday, after the full moon after the vernal equinox. This formula was followed by all for centuries, although errors in calculation developed. In order to rectify these miscalculations, the Gregorian calendar and the related calculation for Easter were introduced in the Roman Catholic Church in 1582. Since then, Anglican, Old Catholic, Protestant, and some Orthodox churches have accepted the related calculations for Easter. Most Orthodox Churches, however, have continued to calculate the date of Easter with the historic formula, using the old Julian calendar. Occasionally the two dating methods coincide. In most years, however, there is a variation of one to four weeks.[26]

The desire to find a means of having a united observance of Easter has been sought since the early decades of the ecumenical movement. In recent years the topic has been studied by the World Council of Churches as well as by the Orthodox Churches and the Roman Catholic Church. Building upon these discussions, the WCC and the Middle East Council of Churches sponsored a consultation in Aleppo in 1997 that reemphasized the importance of finding an agreement among the churches to establish a unified celebration.

The statement *Towards a Common Date for Easter*[27] affirmed the importance of the paschal celebration for the churches and for all Christians. It is the yearly observance of the Resurrection of Christ, viewed as the very center of Christian faith and worship. The statement recognizes the fact that double observances of this great feast day is a sign of the divisions of the churches and weakens the witness of the churches in the world. The statement proposes that all the churches continue to calculate Easter in accord with the formula established by the Council of Nicaea in 325 but using the most accurate scientific methods to calculate in advance the date each year. The statement and its recommendations were widely received and have led to a renewed interest in moving toward a unified observance of Easter by the churches in coming years.

II. Bilateral Theological Dialogues

The Division Dating from the Council of Ephesus in 431

One of the oldest divisions to afflict churches today is the separation that took place after the Council of Ephesus in 431. At that time, these divisions divided the regional churches of the Roman-Byzantine Empire and the regional churches in the region of the Persian Empire. Today, this church is known as the Assyrian Church of the East. The historic division reflected different interpretations of the person of Christ and the manner of describing the relationship between his humanity and his divinity.

Dialogue involving representatives of the Assyrian Church of the East has been rather recent in its development. A number of important informal dialogues with representatives of the Assyrian Church, the Roman Catholic Church, Eastern Catholic churches, and the Syrian Orthodox Church have taken place under the auspice of the Pro-Oriente Foundation. The so-called Syriac Dialogues were held between 1994 and 2002 in Vienna, Austria. These important theological dialogues led to more formal contacts and theological discussions between the Syrian Orthodox Church and Assyrian Church of the East. Both churches have indicated the desire to establish a formal dialogue.[28]

Important formal theological dialogues have taken place between the Assyrian Church of the East and the Roman Catholic Church. These dialogues began after an historic meeting between Pope John Paul II and Patriarch Mar Dinkha IV 1994. At that time the pope and patriarch declared: "Whatever our Christological divergences have been, we experience ourselves united today in the confession of the same faith in the Son of God who became man so that we might become children of God by his grace. We wish from now on to witness together to this faith in the One who is the Way, the Truth, and the Light proclaiming it in appropriate ways to our contemporaries, so that the world may believe in the Gospel of salvation."[29]

Yearly meetings of the Joint Commission for Theological Dialogue between the Catholic Church and the Assyrian Church of the East have been held since 1994. These discussions have focused upon issues of Christology and on sacramental practices. Most recently, the Roman Catholic Church and the Assyrian Church of the East produced guidelines on the "Admission to the Eucharist in Situations of Pastoral Necessity: Provisions between the Chaldean (Catholic) Church and the Assyrian Church of the East."[30]

The Division Dating from the Council of Chalcedon in 451

The second historical division of ongoing significance dates from the Council of Chalcedon in 451 and relates to different interpretations of the relationship of the divine nature and human nature in Christ. From the fifth century onward, this division separated regional churches of the Roman-Byzantine world, which accepted the council from those churches that were on its periphery or beyond it and rejected the council.[31] Today, the separation is usually described as one between the family of Autocephalous Orthodox Churches and the Autocephalous Oriental Orthodox Churches.[32]

The relationship between these two families of churches has received a great deal of attention, especially since 1961. Between the years 1964 and 1971, theologians from both families met four times. These meetings were held in Aarhus, Denmark, in 1964, in Bristol, England, in 1967, in Geneva, Switzerland, in 1970, and in Addis Ababa, Ethiopia, in 1971. Each of these consultations produced very significant statements that affirmed a common teaching on Christology despite a formal division, lasting about fifteen hundred years. Informal meetings especially in the Middle East accompanied these consultations. The tone for all subsequent meetings was set at the first consultation in Aarhus where the theologians formally affirmed agreement on their understanding of Christology. They said:

> We have spoken to each other in the openness of charity and with the conviction of truth. All of us have learned from each other. Our inherited misunderstandings have begun to clear up. We recognize in each other the one Orthodox Faith of the Church. Fifteen centuries of alienation have not led us astray from the faith of our fathers.
>
> In our common study of the Council of Chalcedon, the well-known phrase used by our common father in Christ, St. Cyril of Alexandria, *mia physis* (or *mia hypostasis*) *tou Theou Logou sesarxomene* (the one *physis* or *hypostasis* (nature) of God's Word Incarnate) with its implications, was at the center of our conversations. On the essence of the Christological dogma we found ourselves in full agreement. Through the different terminologies used by each side, we saw the same truth expressed. Since we agree in rejecting without reservation the teaching of Eutyches as well as of Nestorius, the acceptance or non-acceptance of the Council of Chalcedon does not entail the acceptance of either heresy. Both sides found themselves fundamentally following the Christological teaching of the one undivided church as expressed by St. Cyril.[33]

Based upon this historic statement and the related discussions of the consultations, both the Orthodox Churches and the Oriental Orthodox Churches agreed to establish formal commissions for dialogue. After preliminary meetings, the Joint Commission for Theological Dialogue met in Geneva in 1985. Subsequent meetings were held in Anba Bishoi, Egypt, in 1989 and in Geneva in 1990 and 1993. At the Anba Bishoi meetings the representatives produced an historic statement that also reaffirmed a common teaching on Christology. It said:

> We have inherited from our fathers in Christ the one apostolic faith and tradition, though as Churches we have been separated from each other for centuries. As two families of Orthodox Churches long out of communion with each other, we now pray and trust in God to restore that communion on the basis of the common Apostolic faith of the undivided Church of the first centuries which we confess in our common creed.[34]

More recent meetings of the Joint Commission have built upon the affirmations made at Anba Bishoi. Of particular concern have been issues related to the recognition of Ecumenical Councils and the status of historic anathema dating from the fifth century.

The Orthodox and Oriental Orthodox churches have long regarded the need to heal this schism as the preeminent challenge. While formal dialogues between Orthodox and Western churches often receive more public attention, the ongoing dialogue between the two families of Orthodox Churches is one that could indeed result in the reestablishment of full communion in the near future. Already, there have been expressions of movements to restore full communion between the two patriarchates of Antioch. Likewise, there is an agreement on the recognition of marriages between the Coptic patriarchate of Alexandria and the Greek Orthodox patriarchate in Egypt.

The Division Between the Orthodox Church and the Roman Catholic Church

The Great Schism describes the separation between the Church of Rome and the churches of Constantinople, Alexandria, Antioch, and Jerusalem that took place during the Middle Ages. This was a gradual estrangement that developed at least from the ninth century and was solidified in most places by the fifteenth century. While compounded by cultural and political factors, the schism reflected different understandings of the role of the bishop of Rome and his relationship with other bishops, especially in the Christian East. The division also reflected disagreement about the significance of the addition of the *filioque* to the Nicene-Constantinopolitan Creed in the Christian West. These issues were later compounded especially by the promulgation by the Roman Catholic Church of the doctrine of Papal Infallibility in 1870, as well as the doctrine of the Immaculate Conception of Mary in 1854 and the doctrine of the Assumption of Mary in 1950. Since the sixteenth century, the establishment of Eastern Catholic churches in communion with Rome in parts of Eastern Europe and the Middle East further aggravated the schism.

A new and dramatically different relationship between the Roman Catholic Church and the Orthodox Church began to develop in the wake of both the Second Vatican Council (1962–65) and the Pan-Orthodox Conferences (1961–68.) The new spirit, which was slowly developing between these churches, was also expressed in the historic meetings between Pope Paul IV and Patriarch Athenagoras of Constantinople in Jerusalem in 1964 and in Constantinople and Rome in 1967. Under the leadership of these two great church leaders, the historic Anathemas of 1054 were formally removed in 1965. Since that time, there have been numerous meetings and conferences involving Roman Catholic and Orthodox bishops, theologians, and laity in nearly every part of the world.[35]

The first formal dialogue between the Orthodox and Roman Catholic churches was established in the United States in 1995 by the Standing Conference of Orthodox Bishops and the Conference of Catholic Bishops. This Bilateral Consultation built on informal discussions between Orthodox and Roman Catholic theologians reaching back to the 1950s. Since its establishment, the North American Consultation has produced 22 significant statements dealing with a number of theological issues related to unity. Although operating at the regional level, this Consultation has provided a significant example of the possibilities for serious and thoughtful theological dialogue between Orthodoxy and Roman Catholicism on issues of differences and agreement.[36] As Metropolitan Maximos Aghiorgoussis says: "The spirit which has prevailed in the dialogue all these years has been one of mutual respect and love, kindness and understanding, together with honesty and commitment to truth. Our commitment has been not only to seeking and 'speaking the truth in love' but also to sharing the lives and experiences of our churches."[37]

In a recent statement, the North American Consultation reiterated the importance of the dialogue between the Orthodox Church and the Roman Catholic Church and also spoke about the special relationship that continues to exist despite serious theological differences. The Consultation said:

> As our dialogue completes its thirty-fifth year, the members of the Orthodox-Catholic Consultation in North America take this opportunity to reaffirm the importance of the ecumenical commitment and witness of our churches. We especially reaffirm the significance of theological dialogue between the Orthodox and Catholic churches, which seeks the restoration of full communion based upon the profession of the apostolic faith, and expressed in eucharistic sharing and concelebration.
>
> We are convinced that a unique relationship exists between our churches in spite of our division. This relationship is rooted in the fact that we continue to proclaim and to share the essential elements of the apostolic faith...It is for this very reason that in recent times the Catholic and Orthodox churches have been described as "sister churches."
>
> The bonds that continue to unite our sister churches are powerfully expressed when—together or separately—we worship the Father through Christ in the Spirit, and honor those who are close to God. While we have become separated as churches, our union with Christ and his saints has remained an unbreakable bond of faith, hope, and love. Through the life of both our churches, we share a special bond with Mary, the Virgin Mother of God, and with the other saints who surround us as a "cloud of witnesses" (Heb. 12:1). Among them, both Orthodox and Catholics are especially mindful of the countless martyrs of the twentieth century who have shed their blood in common witness to Christ, the Savior.[38]

In its most recent statement of 2003, the North American Consultation addressed the difficult issue of the *filioque.* This refers to the addition to the Nicene-Constantinopolitan Creed of 381 that was gradually introduced by the Western Church from the sixth century. The Eastern Church from the ninth century vigorously opposed this addition. It continued to use the Creed of 381 in its original form. Indeed, the topic is frequently viewed as one of the major issues leading to the schism.

After over four years of intensive study, the statement by the North American Consultation provides a rich historical and theological analysis of this divisive issue. The consultation also makes a number of significant recommendations to the churches. Among these, the consultation recommends that the Orthodox and Catholic churches commit themselves "to a new and earnest dialogue concerning the origin and person of the Holy Spirit, drawing on the Holy Scriptures and on the full riches of the theological traditions of both our Churches, and to looking for constructive ways of expressing what is central to our faith on this difficult issue." The consultation also recommends that "the Catholic Church, as a consequence of the normative and irrevocable dogmatic value of the Creed of 381, use the original Greek text alone in making translations of that Creed for catechetical and liturgical use." If the Catholic Church accepted this recommendation, it would mean that it would use once again the unaltered text of the Nicene-Constantinopolitan Creed of 381. The historic statement concludes saying:

> We offer these recommendations to our Churches in the conviction, based on our own intense study and discussion that our traditions' different ways of understanding the procession of the Holy Spirit need no longer divide us. We believe, rather, that our profession of the ancient Creed of Constantinople must be allowed to become, by our uniform practice and our new attempts at mutual understanding, the basis for a more conscious unity in the one faith that all theology simply seeks to clarify and to deepen. Although our expression of the truth God reveals about his own Being must always remain limited by the boundaries of human understanding and human words, we believe that it is the very "Spirit of truth," whom Jesus breathes upon his Church, who remains with us still, to "guide us into all truth" (John 16.13). We pray that our Churches' understanding of this Spirit may no longer be a scandal to us, or an obstacle to unity in Christ, but that the one truth towards which he guides us may truly be "a bond of peace" (Eph. 4:3), for us and for all Christians.[39]

The Joint Commission for Theological Dialogue was established at the global level by the Roman Catholic Church and the Orthodox Church in 1979. The establishment of this Commission benefited from the experience of the North American Consultation as well as less formal meetings between Orthodox and Roman Catholic theologians in various parts of the world. Since its establishment, the Commission has produced four significant statements. The first in 1982 deals with the sacramental understanding of the church. The second in 1987 deals with the relationship between faith, sacraments, and the unity of the church. The third in 1988 studies the meaning of ordained ministry. And the fourth in 1993 addresses "Uniatism, Method of Union in the Past, and the Present Search for Full Communion." While not producing a new statement, the most recent meeting of the full Commission took place in Baltimore, Maryland, in 2000.

Since the time of the schism, most Orthodox and Roman Catholic theologians have identified two major points that need resolution in order to move toward the restoration of full communion. These are the understanding of the primacy of the bishop of Rome and his relationship to other bishops and, as has been noted, the meaning of the *filioque* and its addition to the creed in the Christian West. These two topics have not been directly addressed by the International Consultation. However, in its joint statements and related discussions, the International Consultation has touched upon these topics within the broader perspective of discussions of the church, its mission, and its organizational structures.

The first statement of the Joint International Commission in 1982 is titled "The Mystery of the Church and of the Eucharist in the Light of the Mystery of the Trinity."[40] As the title indicates, this statement emphasizes the intimate relationship between an understanding of the Holy Trinity, the Church, and the Eucharist. In discussing aspects of the Trinity, special attention is given to the relationship between the Father, Son, and the Holy Spirit. Referring to this relationship, the statement says in part:

> The incarnation of the Son of God, his death and resurrection were realized from the beginning, according to the Father's will, in the Holy Spirit. This Spirit, which proceeds eternally from the Father and manifests himself through the Son, prepared the Christ event and realized it fully in the resurrection. Christ, who is the sacrament par excellence given by the Father for the world, continues to give himself for the many in the Spirit, who alone gives life (Jn. 6). The sacrament of Christ is also a reality which can only exist in the Spirit.[41]

Within the context of an extensive discussion of the relationship of the Son and the Spirit, the statement makes a significant reference to the issue of the *filioque* by saying:

> Without wishing to resolve yet the difficulties which have arisen between the East and the West concerning the relationship between the Son and the Spirit, we can already say together that this Spirit, which proceeds from the Father (Jn. 15:26) as the sole source of the Trinity and which has become the Spirit of our sonship (Rom. 8:15) since he is already the Spirit of the Son (Gal. 4:6), is communicated to us, particularly in the Eucharist, by this Son upon whom he reposes in time and eternity (Jn. 1:32).[42]

The second statement of the International Commission in 1987 was devoted to the topic "Faith, Sacraments and the Unity of the Church."[43] While the Statement does not make explicit mention of the *filioque,* there is a significant reference to the activity of the Spirit that is certainly relevant to the topic. The statement says:

> The sacraments of the Church are "sacraments of faith" where God the Father hears the epiclesis (invocation) in which the Church expresses its faith by this

prayer for the coming of the Spirit. In them, the Father gives his Holy Spirit, who leads us to the fullness of salvation in Christ. Christ himself constitutes the Church as his body. The Holy Spirit edifies the Church. There is no gift in the Church which cannot be attributed to the Holy Spirit (Basil, PG 30,289). The sacraments are both gift and grace of the Holy Spirit, in Jesus Christ in the Church....

Every sacrament of the Church confers the grace of the Holy Spirit because it is inseparably a sign recalling what God has accomplished in the past, a sign manifesting what he is effecting in the believer and in the Church, and a sign announcing and anticipating the eschatological fulfillment. In the sacramental celebration, the Church thus manifests, illustrates and confesses its faith in the unity of God's design.[44]

Already in these brief references to the activity of the Holy Spirit and to the issue of the *filioque,* there are indications that the representatives of both churches affirm significant areas of agreement, especially in their understanding of the Holy Trinity and the reality of the church. These observations could lead to a more extensive elaboration of a common understanding of the activity of the Holy Spirit in general and the *filioque* issue in particular.[45]

The issue of the papacy has also received some preliminary but significant attention in the work of the two consultations. While the International Commission has not dealt extensively with the topic of the papacy, its statement of 1988 indicates that the issue of primacy in the church cannot be understood apart from conciliarity. There is an interrelationship between both realities in the structure of the church. The text says: "It is in the perspective of communion among local churches that the question could be addressed of primacy in the Church in general and in particular, the primacy of the bishop of Rome, a question which constitutes a serious divergence among us and which will be discussed in the future."[46]

The North American Consultation has also investigated these themes, especially in its statement on "Conciliarity and Primacy in the Church" in 1989.[47] The statement recognizes that conciliarity and primacy are not mutually exclusive principles of church organization. On the contrary, the meeting of bishops in council and the exercise of leadership by designated primatial bishops have been present in a complementary manner within the church since apostolic times. "The two institutions, mutually dependant and mutually limiting, which have exercised the strongest influence on maintaining the ordered communion of the Churches since the apostolic times, have been the gathering of bishops and other appointed leaders in synod, and the primacy or recognized preeminence of one bishop among his Episcopal colleagues."[48] Speaking of the ministry of a primatial bishop, the statement says:

Primacy—whether that of the metropolitan within his province or that of a patriarch or presiding hierarch within a larger region—is a service of leadership that has taken many forms throughout Christian history, but that always should be seen as complementary to the functions of synods. It is the primate *(protos)* who convenes the synod, presides over its activities, and seeks, together with his colleagues, to assure its continuity in faith and discipline with the apostolic church; yet it is the synod which, together with its primate, gives voice and definition to the apostolic tradition. It is also the synod which, in most churches, elects the primate, assists him in his leadership, and holds him to account for his ministry in the name of the whole Church (Apostolic Canons, 34).[49]

The statement recognizes that the "particular form of primacy exercised by the bishops of Rome has been and remains the chief point of dispute between Orthodox Church and the Roman Catholic Church and their chief obstacle to full ecclesial communion with each other."[50] Perspectives differ on the way in which the historic leadership of the apostle Peter among the Twelve has been understood.[51] In identifying some aspects of the different perspectives, the statement notes that the Orthodox "have emphasized that every bishop exercises leadership within his diocese as did Peter among the Twelve. Every bishop expresses a Petrine ministry of leadership in a particular place among the community of believers."[52] The statement notes that the Roman Catholic view emphasizes that the bishop of Rome from at least the fourth century claimed "not only the first place of honor among the Episcopal colleagues but also the 'Petrine' role of proclaiming the Church's apostolic tradition and of ensuring the observation of canonical practices."[53] This perspective is the basis for the universal primacy claimed by the bishop of Rome.

The North American consultation recognizes, however, the ongoing investigation of the relationship between episcopal primacies and conciliarity in the life of the church requires more thorough investigation. Both elements of church organization have been distorted in the past. The statement affirms that there is now a need to rediscover their proper expression and mutual relationship in a manner, which is more clearly consistent with the practice of the early church.

Since the year 1990, the relations between the Orthodox Church and the Roman Catholic Church have been deeply troubled in many places, primarily because of the reestablishment of Eastern Catholic churches in such places as Ukraine and Romania as well as by the establishment of new Roman Catholic dioceses in Russia. Referring to a number of these developments, Patriarch Bartholomew and other Orthodox primates in 1992 said that traditional Orthodox lands had become "missionary territory."[54] The Orthodox bishops lamented the fact that "proselytism is practiced with all the methods which have been condemned and rejected for decades by all Christians."[55]

These critical issues were among those discussed by Pope John Paul II and Patriarch Bartholomew in Rome in 1995. During their historic meeting, they issued a joint statement that called for a renewed commitment to dialogue. They said:

> In this perspective, we urge our faithful, Catholic and Orthodox, to reinforce the spirit of brotherhood which stems from one baptism and from participation in sacramental life. In the course of history, and in the more recent past, there have been attacks and acts of oppression on both sides. As we prepare, on this occasion, to ask the Lord for his great mercy, we invite all to forgive one another and to express a firm will that a new relationship of brotherhood and active collaboration will be established.[56]

DIVISIONS IN WESTERN CHRISTIANITY DATING FROM THE SIXTEENTH CENTURY

The Reformation raised important theological questions about the relationship of Scripture and Tradition, the meaning of salvation, issues of authority, and issues of worship. The different approaches to these issues led to the division between the Reformation churches and Roman Catholicism. At the same time, within Protestantism and Anglicanism there were a variety of approaches to many of these same issues. Protestants were not always in agreement among themselves. This led to the development of four clearly delineated traditions during the sixteenth century alone. These were: the Lutheran, the Reformed or Calvinistic, the Anglican, and the Anabaptist.

The contemporary ecumenical movement has done much to address the historic divisions dividing the traditions of Protestantism from the time of the sixteenth century. In the United States especially, divisions within specific families of Protestant churches, such as the Presbyterian and the Lutheran, have been healed. In other places, such as Canada and India, there have been organic unions that united into one body a number of Protestant churches. In more recent times, there have been significant agreements to restore full communion between churches of different Protestant traditions. In Western Europe, the Leuenberg Agreement of 1973 and the Porvoo Common Statement of 1992 are of particular importance. In the United States, A Formula of Agreement of 1997 has established full communion between Lutheran and Reformed churches. Likewise, the Called to Common Mission Agreement of 1999 has established full communion between the Evangelical Lutheran Church and the Episcopal Church. Also of great significance is the ongoing process now called Church Uniting in Christ, which is bringing nine Protestant and Episcopal churches closer together.

These unions and agreements are very significant because they formally address divisions in the traditions of Western Christianity that reach back to the sixteenth century. At the same time, they reflect the work of theological dialogue within the broader ecumenical movement reaching back to the early decades of this century. While the particular concerns of Protestant and Anglicans are addressed, the agreements also reflect discussions on topics such as church, baptism, the Eucharist, and ministry that have also engaged Orthodox and Roman Catholics. They also express a very valuable fruit of those who have prayed and worked for Christian reconciliation and the visible unity of the churches.[57]

Many of the historic issues that divided Roman Catholics and Protestants in the sixteenth century have also received substantial attention in the many bilateral dialogues within the past three or four decades especially. The Roman Catholic Church at the global level is engaged in formal bilateral dialogues with the Anglican Communion, the Lutheran World Federation, the World Methodist Council, and the Alliance of Reformed Churches. Valuable consultations also have taken place between the Roman Catholics and the Disciples of Christ, the Baptist World Alliance, the Mennonite World Council, and some Pentecostals.[58] In many regions, particularly in the United States, there are similar bilateral dialogues that parallel the global dialogues.[59]

As might be expected, these bilateral dialogues have undertaken the study of many topics related to issues of division and reconciliation. Each bilateral dialogue has explored theological issues that the particular churches deem to be important in their ongoing relationship. For the purposes of this limited study, two particularly significant topics must be noted. These are the issue of Justification by Faith and the issue of the authority of the bishop of Rome, the pope.

The formal agreement entitled "Joint Declaration on the Doctrine on Justification,"[60] which was approved by the Roman Catholic Church and the Lutheran World Federation in 1999, is considered to be an historic breakthrough in the ecumenical movement. The topic Justification by Faith has been an essential affirmation of Protestantism, generally, and Lutheranism, in particular. From the sixteenth century, it was a solemn affirmation that salvation was a divine gift that could not be achieved by human effort. At the time of the Reformation, the emphasis on Justification by Faith was a response to what was perceived as an emphasis on human works necessary to gain salvation in Medieval Roman Catholicism.

When Roman Catholics and Lutherans began their bilateral dialogues both in the United States and at the global level in 1965, the topic of Justification by Faith was clearly seen as a critical issue that stood behind all other topics and would have to be addressed. "For Lutherans," says Günther Gassmann, "the deep differences over the understanding of justification at the time of the Reformation were regarded throughout the centuries as a symbol of the deep chasm that separates Lutherans and Roman Catholics. From the first report of this dialogue on The Gospel and the Church in 1972 up to its most recent one on Justification and the

Church in 1993, a growing agreement on the main aspects of the doctrine of justification has been recorded."[61] The global dialogue between Roman Catholics and Lutherans was supported and complemented by regional dialogues in the United States and Germany.[62]

Supported by these theological discussions and dialogues, the international Lutheran-Roman Catholic Bilateral Dialogue between 1993 and 1997 prepared the statement Joint Declaration on the Doctrine of Justification in 1997. After thorough review by the churches of the Lutheran World Federation and the Roman Catholic Church, the historic statement was formally signed by representatives of the churches on October 31, 1999, in Augsburg, Germany.

The Declaration says in part:

> The understanding of the doctrine of justification set forth in this Declaration shows that a consensus in basic truths on the doctrine of justification exists between Lutherans and Catholics.... Therefore, the Lutheran and Catholic explications of justification are in their differences open to one another and do not destroy the consensus regarding the basic truths. Thus, the doctrinal condemnations of the sixteenth century, in so far as they relate to the doctrine of justification, appear in new light: The teachings of the Lutheran churches presented in this Declaration does not fall under the condemnations of the Council of Trent. The condemnations in the Lutheran Confessions do not apply to the teachings of the Roman Catholic Church presented in this Declaration.[63]

This important Declaration does not resolve all the theological and doctrinal differences among Roman Catholic, Lutheran, or Protestant churches, more generally. However, the background discussions and this significant agreement do strongly indicate that other issues can be addressed and resolved through theological dialogue.

THE MINISTRY AND PRIMACY OF THE BISHOP OF ROME

The issue of the ministry and episcopal primacy of the bishop of Rome is one such issue. Often referred to as the papacy or the Petrine Office, this issue has not only contributed to division between the Orthodox and Roman Catholic. It is an issue that also has contributed to the divisions between the Anglican, Old Catholic, and Protestant churches and Roman Catholicism. Within the context of the contemporary ecumenical movement, this topic has begun to receive attention. Already, we have noted the discussions between Orthodox and Roman Catholics. The topic has also received attention in the bilateral dialogues between Roman Catholics and Anglicans, Lutherans, and Methodists.

The dialogue between the Roman Catholics and the Anglican Communion, however, has taken up the topic in a thorough and thoughtful manner.

The topic of the ministry of the bishop of Rome has been addressed within the broader topic of ministry and authority in the church and the church as communion *(koinonia)*. The Anglican-Orthodox International Commission emphasizes that the exercise of authority in the Church must ultimately be seen as a gift from the Lord, which supports the believers' growth in holiness. "The exercise of authority in the Church is to be recognized and accepted as an instrument of the Spirit of God for the healing of humanity. The exercise of authority must always respect conscience, because the divine work of salvation affirms human freedom."[64] This thoughtful approach has been especially helpful because it places the ecumenical study of the papacy within a broader examination of the interrelationship of a number of factors in church life.

First, the Commission relates authentic authority in the Church to the authority of Christ. "The Spirit of the Risen Lord, who indwells the Christian community, continues to maintain the people of God in obedience to the Father's will. By this action of the Holy Spirit the authority of the Lord is active in the Church...This is Christian authority: when Christians so act and speak, men perceive the authoritative word of Christ." The Commission then says that the Holy Spirit "gives to some individuals and communities special gifts for the benefit of the Church, which entitle them to speak and be heeded (e.g., Eph. 4:11, 12:1, 1 Cor. 12: 4–11)."[65]

Second, the Commission recognizes that there is a mutual interrelationship between the clergy and the laity in the church and this has a bearing also upon the process of decision making "in guarding and developing communion, every member has a part to play. Baptism gives everyone in the Church the right, and consequently the ability, to carry out his particular function in the body." This means that "all members share in the discovery of God's will...that the *sensus fidelium* is a vital element in the comprehension of God's truth...and that all bear witness to God's compassion for mankind and his concern for justice in the world."[66]

Third, the Commission examines the relationship among the bishops of the Church. They "exercise their authority in fulfilling ministerial functions related to 'the apostle's teaching and fellowship, to the breaking of bread and prayers' (Acts 2:42). This pastoral authority belongs primarily to the bishop, who is responsible for preserving and promoting the integrity of *koinonia* in order to further the Church's response to the Lordship of Christ and its commitment to mission. " While certain bishops are gifted with a primacy, this is always in relationship to the entire body of bishops as well as the entire Christian community. Truly, "primacy and conciliarity are complementary elements of *episcopé* (oversight)." The ministry of oversight in the Church is expressed through both primacy and conciliarity. "The *koinonia* of churches require that a proper balance be preserved between the two with the responsible participation of the whole people of God."[67]

Fourth, the Commission recognizes that the "only see which makes any claim to universal primacy and which has exercised and still exercises such *episcopé* is the see of Rome, the city where Peter and Paul died." The consultation further states that it accepts "the need for a universal primacy exercised by the Bishop of Rome as a sign and safeguard of unity within a reunited Church."[68] At the same time, the commission is quick to point out that it does not take on the Roman Catholic understanding of a primacy that is rooted in divine right.[69] Likewise, it envisions a primacy as one that is exercised "in collegial association with his brother bishops" and one that complements and does not supplant the exercise of episcopal oversight in the other local churches.[70]

Finally, the Anglican-Roman Catholic International Commission affirms that human weakness and sin can hamper the proper exercise of authority in the church. These can not only affect particular church leaders but also these realities "can distort the human structuring of authority (cf. Mt. 23). Therefore, loyal criticism and reform are sometimes needed... The consciousness of human frailty in the exercise of authority ensures that Christian ministers remain open to criticism and renewal, and above all to exercising authority according to the example and mind and of Christ."[71]

While affirming the type of ministry that the bishop of Rome could exercise within the unity of the churches, the Commission is also clear in recognizing that this primacy of service must be authentically related both to the rest of the bishops and to the whole body of the church. Thus, the Commission is not necessarily endorsing the present expression of the primacy exercised by the pope. It is pointing toward an understanding of the primacy of the bishop of Rome that could be received by reunited churches. As the Commission says: "What we have written here amounts to a consensus on authority in the Church and, in particular, on the principles of primacy. This consensus is of fundamental importance. While it does not wholly resolve all the problems associated with papal primacy, it provides us with a solid basis from confronting them."[72] Already the Anglican Roman Catholic International Commission (ARCIC) has identified a number of critical observations that cast new perspectives on a topic of grave dispute. The important affirmations that are made in the work of the Commission are significant.

NEW CHALLENGES

These multilateral and bilateral dialogues have focused primarily upon the historic doctrinal and theological issues dividing the churches for centuries. There has been clear recognition that the historic controversies must be addressed. As we have seen, however, they have been addressed in a new spirit. The dialogues have been marked by a quest for truth. Prayer and a spirit of humility have also accompanied them.

Within the ecumenical movement today, some would rightly claim that there are more recent critical issues, which have signaled new tensions between the divided churches. Issues of racism, justice, and peace as well as issues associated with sexual morality and medical ethics often have occasioned different responses from the contemporary Christian churches. Frequently, it appears that the different positions are not easily reconciled.

Likewise, very important theological questions associated with the ordination of women to ministry have led to significant differences of opinion among the divided churches. These differences can be found even within the churches. In seeking to address the issue, churches have examined the Scriptures and tradition. In so doing, questions also have been raised about the influence of cultural mores on the early church. While the investigation is far from complete, churches have come to different conclusions regarding the ordination of women at the present time. This has led to new tensions between certain churches.

At the same time, however, historians and theologians from a number of churches have been engaged in numerous studies that examine the ministries of women in the early church. While recognizing the limited resources available, these studies have made more accessible the writings of early Christian women and the stories of women saints in the early church. They have also examined the important role that early Christian women had in teaching, in preaching, in missionary activity, and in the liturgical life. Of particular interest has been the ministry of women deacons during the early centuries of the church.[73]

A new and unprecedented challenge to the relationships among the churches occurred because of the decision of the Episcopal Church in the United States to ordain as a bishop on November 3, 2003, a person who was an active homosexual. This action aggravated divisions among Episcopalians over this topic and a related question of the blessing of same-sex couples. The ordination was contrary to the general position taken by the Anglican Communion as a whole, which was in the process of studying the question of the legitimacy of ordaining active homosexuals. For many, such ordinations would be contrary to Scripture and Tradition. Because of this, a number of churches in the Anglican Communion, many in Africa and Asia, declared that a state of "impaired communion" existed between them and the Episcopal Church in the United States.

The action of the Episcopal Church also caused serious tensions in ecumenical relationships between the Anglican Communion and other churches. Almost immediately, the scheduled plenary meeting of the Anglican-Roman Catholic Commission on Unity and Mission was canceled. Likewise, the leaders of the Oriental Orthodox Churches also announced that the scheduled meeting of their dialogue with the Anglican Communion was postponed. The Orthodox Church of Russia also announced that it had suspended forms of cooperation with the Episcopal Church.[74]

The decision of the Episcopal Church demonstrated that the actions of one church clearly could have significant repercussions in other churches and in the ecumenical relationships between the churches. The decision of the Episcopal Church could be seen at first as an internal matter. Yet, because it raised serious questions about the interpretation of Scripture and Tradition, the decision was bound to have serious consequences, which immediately affected ecumenical relationships.

More often than not, however, the divided churches have examined these new challenges in isolation from each other. Churches have undertaken their examination of these critical issues and have stated their positions as if they were not involved in ecumenical dialogues on other critical topics. As yet, there have been only few occasions when the valuable experience of ecumenical dialogue and insight has been utilized in a thorough examination of more recent church dividing issues. Clearly, the churches must find the opportunities to let the rich experience of honest dialogue and the sense of reconciliation impact the way they approach together all the contemporary issues of Christian life and witness.

CONCLUSIONS

There have been many remarkable developments in the relationship between divided Christian churches over the past century. One of the most significant of these has been the formal establishment of multilateral and bilateral dialogues bringing together official representatives of the churches. These dialogues often began with the desire to deepen mutual understanding and enrichment in an atmosphere free from polemics and prejudice. As time went on, these dialogues moved toward a fresh examination of the root causes of the theological and doctrinal differences among the churches. Many of the dialogues have begun to offer proposals for the overcoming of these differences. Some have pointed to a fundamental consensus on critical issues.

Many of the most difficult points of differences in teachings among the divided churches reach back centuries. Considering that formal theological dialogues on many of these issues have been in place among the churches for only less than fifty years, the progress made has been remarkable. The churches have willingly been drawn out of their isolation. Theologians from the churches have begun to speak together face to face. Many issues, which once appeared to be irresolvable, have been addressed together. Moreover, in a number of instances, important consensuses have been reached. Referring to a collection of reports on recent bilateral dialogues, Dr. Mary Tanner says: "It is impossible to read these reports without seeing that dialogue can lead to a re-reading together of the history of division, a reconciliation of the bitterest of memories, and even the lifting of the anathemas and condemnations of the past. What is often discovered is that much more is held in common than divides."[75]

NOTES

1. "The Unity of the Church as Koinonia: Gift and Calling (The Canberra Statement)" in *Documentary History of Faith and Order, 1963–1993,* ed. Günther Gassmann (Geneva: WCC Publications, 1993), p. 11.

2. See Groupe des Dombes, *For the Conversion of the Churches* (Geneva: WCC Publications, 1993).

3. See Nils Ehrenström and Günther Gassmann, eds., *Confessions in Dialogue: A Survey of Bilateral Conversations among World Confessional Families* (Geneva: World Council of Churches, 3rd revised edition, 1975).

4. Ibid., p. 237.

5. Ibid., pp. 238–39.

6. W. A. Visser 't Hooft, ed., *The New Delhi Report* (London: SCM Press, 1962), p. 116.

7. Günther Gassmann, ed., *Documentary History of Faith and Order, 1963–1993* (Geneva: WCC Publications, 1993), p. 3.

8. Ibid.

9. See Mary Tanner, "Visible Unity in the Work of the World Council of Churches," in *The Vision of Christian Unity: Essays in Honor of Paul Crow, Jr.,* ed. Thomas F. Best and Theodore J. Nottingham (Indianapolis: Oikoumene Publications, 1997), pp. 149–61.

10. Gassmann, *Documentary History of Faith and Order, 1963–1993,* pp. 10–18.

11. Ibid., p. 11.

12. Ibid.

13. Ibid.

14. Ibid.

15. See Geoffrey Wainwright, "Scripture and Tradition: A Systematic Sketch," *Church Quarterly* 3 (1970–71), pp. 17–28.

16. *Baptism, Eucharist, and Ministry* (Geneva: World Council of Churches, 1982).

17. Ibid., p. ix.

18. Ibid.

19. Max Thurian, "Baptism, Eucharist, and Ministry (the Lima Text)," in *Dictionary of the Ecumenical Movement,* ed. Nicholas Lossky et al. (Geneva: WCC Publications, 1991), pp. 81–83.

20. See Geoffrey Wainwright, *The Ecumenical Moment: Crisis and Opportunity in the Church* (Grand Rapids, Mich.: William B. Eerdmans Publishing Company, 1983).

21. *Baptism, Eucharist, and Ministry 1982–1990: Reports on the Process and Responses* (Geneva: WCC Publications, 1990), p. vii.

22. *Church and World: The Unity of the Church and the Renewal of Human Community* (Geneva: WCC Publications, 1990).

23. Ibid., pp. vii–viii.

24. See Paul A. Crow Jr., *Christian Unity: Matrix for Mission* (New York: Friendship Press, 1982).

25. *Confessing the One Faith: An Ecumenical Explication of the Apostolic Faith as it is Confessed in the Nicene-Constantinopolitan Creed (381)* (Geneva: WCC Publications, 1991), p. viii.

26. See Thomas FitzGerald, "Churches Seek a Common Date for Easter," *Ecumenical Trends* 26:3 (1997), pp. 13–15.

27. *Towards a Common Date for Easter* (Geneva: WCC Programme Unit on Unity and Renewal, 1997).

28. For further information, see "Syriac Orthodox Resources," http://sor.cua.edu/Ecumenism/.

29. Common Christological Declaration, http://www.cired.org/cat/03_Common_Christological_Dec.pdf.

30. Johan Bonny, "Relations with the Ancient Churches of the East," in *The Catholic Church in Ecumenical Dialogue 2002* (Washington: United States Conference of Catholic Bishops, 2002), p. 28.

31. For a comprehensive discussion of the period of the council, see R. V. Sellers, *The Council of Chalcedon: An Historical and Doctrinal Survey* (London: SPCK, 1961); Jaroslav Pelikan, *The Emergence of the Catholic Tradition* (Chicago: University of Chicago Press, 1971), pp. 226–77.

32. Thomas FitzGerald, "Towards the Reestablishment of Full Communion: The Orthodox-Oriental Orthodox Dialogue," *The Greek Orthodox Theological Review* 36:2 (1991), pp. 169–82.

33. "The Aarhus Statement," *The Greek Orthodox Theological Review,* 10:1 (1964–65), p. 14.

34. "The Anba Bishoi Statement," *The Greek Orthodox Theological Review,* 36:2 (1991), p. 394.

35. Thomas FitzGerald, *The Ecumenical Patriarchate and Christian Unity* (Brookline, Mass.: Holy Cross Orthodox Press, 1997), pp. 18–21.

36. See John Borelli and John Erickson, *The Quest for Unity* (Crestwood, N.Y.: St. Vladimir's Seminary Press, 1996).

37. Ibid., p. 3.

38. "Sharing the Ministry of Reconciliation (June 1, 2000)," *Origins* 30:5 (June 15, 2000), pp. 77–80.

39. "The Filioque: A Church Dividing Issue?" www.usccb.org/seia/filioque.htm.

40. "The Mystery of the Church and of the Eucharist in the Light of the Mystery of the Holy Trinity," *The Quest For Unity,* ed. Borelli and Erickson, pp. 53–64.

41. Ibid., p. 54.

42. Ibid., p. 56.

43. "Faith, Sacrament, and the Unity of the Church," in *The Quest For Unity,* ed. Borelli and Erickson, pp. 93–104.

44. Ibid., p. 97.

45. The Roman Catholic Church further addressed the issue of the *filioque* in the document "The Greek and Latin Traditions Regarding the Procession of the Holy Spirit (1995)" as well as in the Catechism of the Catholic Church (1995).

46. "The Sacrament of Orders in the Sacramental Structure of the Church with Particular Reference to the Importance of Apostolic Succession for the Sanctification and Unity of the People of God," in *The Quest For Unity,* ed., Borelli and Erickson, pp. 131–42.

47. "An Agreed Statement on Conciliarity and Primacy in the Church," in *The Quest For Unity,* ed. Borelli and Erickson, pp. 152–55.
48. Ibid., pp. 153–54.
49. Ibid., p. 154.
50. Ibid.
51. Ibid., p. 154.
52. Ibid.
53. Ibid.
54. "Message of the Primates of the Most Holy Orthodox Church," in *Orthodox Visions of Ecumenism,* ed. Gennadios Limouris (Geneva: WCC Publications, 1994), pp. 195–98.
55. Ibid., p. 197.
56. "Common Declaration of Pope John Paul II and Ecumenical Patriarch Bartholomew," June 29, 1995, cited in FitzGerald, *The Ecumenical Patriarch and Christian Unity,* p. 30.
57. Günther Gassmann, "Retrospective of an Ecumenical Century," in *Agapè: Études en l'honneur de Mgr. Pierre Duprey* (Chambésy: Centre Orthodoxe, 2002), p. 85.
58. See *The Catholic Church in Ecumenical Dialogue, 2002* (Washington: United States Conference of Catholic Bishops, 2002).
59. See Joseph A. Burgess and Brother Jeffrey Gros, FSC, eds., *Building Unity: Ecumenical Dialogues with Roman Catholic Participation in the United States*(New York: Paulist Press, 1989); Joseph Burgess and Jeffrey Gros, FSC, eds., *Growing Consensus: Church Dialogues in the United States, 1962–1991* (New York: Paulist Press, 1995).
60. *Joint Declaration on the Doctrine of Justification, The Lutheran World Federation and the Roman Catholic Church* (Grand Rapids, Mich.: William B. Eerdmans Publishing Company, 2000).
61. Ibid., p. 83.
62. Ibid., p. 84.
63. *Joint Declaration on the Doctrine of Justification, The Lutheran World Federation and the Roman Catholic Church,* pp. 25–26.
64. "The Gift of Authority," *Origins* 29:2 (May 27, 1999), p. 27.
65. "Authority in the Church I (Venice Statement), 1976," in *Growth in Agreement: Reports and Statements of Ecumenical Conversations on a World Level,* ed. Harding Meyers and Lukas Vischer (New York: Paulist Press, 1984), pp. 90–91.
66. "Elucidation (1981)," in *Growth in Agreement: Reports and Statements of Ecumenical Conversations on a World Level,* p. 102.
67. "Authority in the Church," p. 97.
68. Ibid.
69. "Authority in the Church II (Windsor Statement) 1981," in *Growth in Agreement: Reports and Statements of Ecumenical Conversations on a World Level,* p. 109.
70. Ibid., p. 111.
71. "The Gift of Authority," *Origins* 29:2 (May 27, 1999), p. 27.
72. "Authority in the Church," p. 97.
73. For a valuable discussion of these issues, see Kyriaki FitzGerald, *Women Deacons in the Orthodox Church* (Brookline: Holy Cross Orthodox Press, revised edition, 1999); Phyllis Zagano, *Holy Saturday: An Argument for the Restoration of the*

Female Diaconate in the Catholic Church (New York: Crossroads Publishing, 2000); Ute E. Eison, *Women Officeholders in Early Christianity* (Collegeville: The Liturgical Press, 2000).

74. "Orthodox Suspend Ties with Episcopalians," *Christian Century* 120:25 (December 13, 2003), pp. 12–13.

75. Mary Tanner, "Growth in Agreement II: Reports of the Agreed Statements of Ecumenical Conversations on a World Level 1982–1998," *International Journal for the Study of the Christian Church* 2:2 (2002), p. 99.

CHAPTER 11

Regional and Local Ecumenism: Perspectives from the United States

Our dream for unity is that the churches will be grounded in the apostolic faith and that they will make this unity visible through eucharistic fellowship and witness. Unity, however, does not mean uniformity. Within the Christian community, we need to celebrate a rich diversity which flourishes. Ecumenism consists not in loosing the distinctive features of our various traditions, but in appreciating them as many ways of proclaiming and demonstrating our common faith rooted in a common baptism. Where differences create barriers to our unity, we trust that the transforming power of the Spirit to work in us and through us.

—Statement on Ecumenical Accountability, 1990
Massachusetts Council of Churches[1]

INTRODUCTION

The ecumenical movement seeks the reconciliation of Christians and the restoration of the visible unity of the churches. By engaging in this process, the churches seek to provide a better witness to the gospel of Jesus Christ and to be a credible agent of reconciliation in the society. This process is characterized by theological dialogue, prayer, and common acts of witness. This process seeks to counter popular misunderstandings and bigotry, reflective of the long history of church divisions. As in many other places, the story of the divisions of churches and their tragic consequences has been a part of the history of the United States. Religious intolerance, bigotry, and misunderstanding have affected and continue to affect people and institutions in this country. Yet the quest for Christian reconciliation and the visible unity of the churches has also begun to affect the life of this country. In the past 50 years especially, new relationships have developed among many of the divided churches and their members that emphasize healing, cooperation, and true reconciliation.

Within many of the churches in the United States, the ecumenical movement began to take root in the 1960s. Before this time, relationships between the churches and their members were not always cordial. In some parts of the country, members of different churches had some contact with each other. In other places, there was limited contact. For the most part, there was limited contact or theological dialogue between the churches. Indeed, formal contacts between Protestant churches and the Catholic Church rarely took place. Indeed, in some places, bigotry and misunderstandings enhanced long-standing differences in teachings and worship. When Senator John F. Kennedy (1917–63) of Massachusetts was running for president in 1960, some Protestants questioned his suitability because he was a member of the Roman Catholic Church. Kennedy's election did not entirely put an end to such questions among some. His election in 1961, however, did coincide with the start of a decade in which there would be remarkable changes in the relationship between the churches and their members throughout the United States. Many of these changes, affecting both the churches and the society, were encouraged by far-sighted church leaders such as Roman Catholic Cardinal Richard J. Cushing (1895–1970), Greek Orthodox Archbishop Iakovos (1911–), and Methodist Bishop James K. Mathews (1913–). Each was a pioneer both in the ecumenical movement and in the civil rights movement.

The civil rights movement in the United States, especially in the 1960s and early 1970s, was a beneficiary of the developing ecumenical movement. The civil rights movement also contributed immeasurably to the development of the ecumenical movement. The Reverend Dr. Martin Luther King Jr. (1929–68), a Baptist minister, led the historic movement that called for the end of discrimination and the recognition of the rights of all citizens. The movement began in 1957 with the establishment of the Southern Christian Leadership Conference. Basing his teachings upon biblical principles, Dr. King affirmed the inherent dignity of every person and challenged the country to be faithful to its deepest commitment to the freedom and equality of its citizens. From all parts of the country, members of a wide variety of churches became associated with the nonviolent activities of Dr. King and the civil rights movement. In their concern for civil rights, the members of different churches found themselves bound together in the quest for justice and equality. Many began to see that church divisions often had contributed to and supported racial divisions within the society. At the same time, many church leaders and church members recognized the need for greater contact and theological dialogue between the churches, which could break down the walls of their division as well as the barriers to justice and racial equality.

PARISHES AND CONGREGATIONS

Christians gather in local churches for prayer, nurture, fellowship, and inspiration to live their faith in the world. Christians believe that these local parish congregations are visible expressions of the Church of Christ. At the same time, however, these local congregations reflect the harsh reality of historic divisions. Most of these parishes identify themselves as being part of a larger church family such as the Protestant Church, the Roman Catholic Church, or the Orthodox Church. The worship and teachings in each of these parishes reflect a particular church tradition. Initially, it would appear that the sheer number of church buildings and congregations in any American city or town expresses the long and difficult history of Christian divisions. And, indeed, some of these Christian communities continue to emphasize their separation from the others. On closer investigation, however, the ecumenical movement has profoundly affected many of these parish congregations. While remaining a particular local community of believers, they have been deeply touched by the global process of Christian reconciliation and the quest for the restoration of visible church unity.

The influence of the ecumenical movement is often reflected in parish worship. In conjunction with the advances in the ecumenical movement, there has been a dramatic renewal of Christian worship in recent decades. This renewal has first of all reemphasized the importance of worship and prayer for Christians and their communities. More specifically, this renewal has reemphasized the Eucharist as the central act of Christian worship. Many Anglican and Protestant parishes have restored the Eucharist as the principal act of worship on Sundays. Many Roman Catholic and Orthodox parishes have reemphasized the importance of the participation of the laity in the Eucharist. There has been something of a Eucharistic revolution in many of the parishes of different churches, bringing them closer together in this central act of Christian worship. In addition, many parishes now make use of hymns, prayers, symbolic gestures, and iconography that come from church traditions other than their own. Many Protestant, Anglican, and Roman Catholic parishes now follow a common lectionary for the readings of Scriptures every Sunday. Because of the ecumenical movement, the appreciation of the Eucharist and worship has been more generally stimulated and enriched by a renewed sense of being part of the world church.[2]

The members of many parishes are also accustomed to the practice of joining in prayer with Christians of other church traditions. This may take place at particular times during the course of a year. The Week of Prayer for Christian Unity often is a time when parishes of a city or region will organize a special prayer service for Christian unity. The World Day of Prayer is another such occasion. Likewise, parishes from different churches often use the seasons of Advent or Lent or the Feast of Pentecost to sponsor special services of common prayer. These acts of common prayer at the local level among Orthodox, Catholics, Anglicans, Old Catholics, and most Protestants were rare as little as 50 years ago.

While these acts of common prayer are now generally accepted, the reality of Christian division is often associated with the celebration of the Eucharist. In the past, divisions among churches and their members were expressed most vividly in prohibitions against receiving Holy Communion in a church other than one's own. Church divisions were expressed as a break in communion. In recent decades, these prohibitions have been removed among most Protestant and Anglican churches. This is especially the case where the churches have formally declared that full communion exists among them as a result of doctrinal agreement. At the present time, however, both the Roman Catholic Church and the Orthodox Church teach that their members cannot receive Holy Communion in another church. Both churches hold that there must be doctrinal agreement among the churches before their members can receive Holy Communion in another church, or members of other churches can receive Holy Communion in their church. While there may be grave circumstances when this teaching is not strictly followed, it does reflect the harsh fact of the ongoing divisions among the churches.[3]

The influence of the ecumenical movement on the local parish is also reflected in the teachings and theological reflection taking place within that community. As the principle teacher in the parish, pastors are profoundly affected by the ecumenical movement either directly or indirectly. They benefit from the translations and interpretations of the Old and New Testaments reflecting the joint work of Protestant, Orthodox, Old Catholic, and Roman Catholic biblical scholars. As guides in Christian nurture and growth, most pastors are influenced by perspectives on spirituality, liturgy, and church history coming from church traditions other than their own. Most pastors are enriched by the theological perspectives and pastoral insights coming from church leader of various Christian traditions and contexts. This means that the sermons, Bible studies, and religious education programs of many parishes often directly reflect the theological dialogues among the churches as well as the encounters of their theologians.[4]

The influence of the ecumenical movement in a local parish is also reflected in its witness and service to the society. Most Christian parishes recognize their obligation to express in concrete ways their concern for the needy and less fortunate, especially in the community around them and throughout the world. From the nineteenth century onward, many churches in America have a distinguished history of reaching out in the name of Christ to the poor, the needy, and those abused because of race, gender, background, or economic condition. Because of the ecumenical movement, many local parishes of different churches have found new opportunities to band together to address issues of poverty, racism, and discrimination at the local level. In some places, this involves the establishment of food banks, food distribution programs, and social service agencies. In other places, parishes of different churches have actually entered into covenants to strengthen both their common prayer for unity and their common witness in the society. This common witness is a powerful expression of the Christian Gospel that was hardly possible a generation ago. As one ecumenical council has said: "In the name of Christ, Christians of various traditions seek to be signs of life, love, and justice in the world. When united in advocacy and service, we can be more effective stewards of creation, more faithful witnesses to the Gospel, and more powerful enablers of social justice."[5]

NEW EXPRESSIONS OF RECONCILIATION AND UNITY

The ecumenical movement touches Christians at the parish level as they become more aware of the changing relationships among the churches. The formal dialogues among the churches have led to a new spirit of dialogue and cooperation at the local level.

Throughout the twentieth century, there were significant movements within many Protestant church families to heal internal divisions. Some of these divisions came to the United States from Europe. Others were the painful consequences of slavery and racism. Theological dialogue and significant acts of reconciliation led, for example, to the establishment of the United Church of Christ in 1957, the United Methodist Church in 1968, the Presbyterian Church (USA) in 1983, and the Evangelical Lutheran Church in 1988.

Many parishes in the Protestant and Anglican traditions have been directly affected by the establishment of full communion between certain churches and the ongoing discussions among others. Dialogues between Lutheran and three churches of the Reformed tradition, reaching back to 1962, led to A Formula of Agreement in 1997. This agreement established a relationship of full communion between the Evangelical Lutheran Church in the United States and the Presbyterian Church, the Reformed Church in America, and the United Church of Christ.[6] Discussion between the Lutheran Churches and the Episcopal Church in the United States reached back to the year 1935. A formal agreement was reached in 1999, known as Called to Common Mission, which establishes full communion between the Evangelical Lutheran Church and the Episcopal Church. To speak about full communion means that both churches affirm in each other the same Christian faith and, therefore, recognize each other's sacraments and ministry.[7]

These developments among Episcopal and Reformed churches in America reflect discussions on unity reaching back to the early decades of the twentieth century. In more recent times, the Consultation on Church Union was established in 1962 as a movement to unite nine Reformed and Episcopal churches. This led to the recent establishment of Churches Uniting in Christ in 2002. In this new association, each church "retains its own identity and decision-making structures, but they also have pledged before God to draw closer in sacred things—including regular sharing of the Lord's Supper and common mission, especially a mission to combat racism together. Each church also committed itself to undertake an intensive dialogue toward the day when ministers are authorized to serve and lead worship, when invited, in each of the communions."[8]

While there are a number of Protestant churches and traditions that are notably absent from these agreements, the positive outcome of dialogues on unity among many of the churches of the Reformation traditions has been remarkable.[9] Divisions among Protestants and Anglicans reaching back to the sixteenth century have been overcome. Some of the more recent church divisions over slavery and racism have been healed with a new commitment to social justice. Clearly, the constant move toward greater unity has both reflected the world wide ecumenical movement and contributed to it in a profound way. Moreover, these dialogues and agreements generally have affected the local parishes and their members in a positive manner.[10]

COUNCILS AND ASSOCIATIONS

A great number of councils of churches and other related associations have been established in the United States, especially in the past 50 years. These bodies have built upon the experiences of cooperative agencies, especially among Protestants that were first established in the nineteenth century. With the growth of the ecumenical movement, especially in the period after the 1960s, many new councils and organizations were developed that included parishes and church bodies of the Protestant, Anglican, Orthodox, Old Catholic, and Roman Catholic traditions.

The National Council of Churches of Christ in the USA (NCCUSA) was established in 1950 and brought together Protestant, Episcopal, and Orthodox churches. Its establishment marked a transformation of the old Protestant Federal Council of Churches, which was founded in 1908. From its beginning, the NCCUSA did much to draw its member churches into greater contact for common witness in the society. While the council did establish its own Faith and Order Commission, discussions of theological themes were not always given prominence in its agenda. A crisis developed in 1991 when the Orthodox temporally suspended their membership for a period as a protest over trends in the council.[11] In more recent times, there have been calls for a new national council that would also include membership from the Roman Catholic Church, as well as Evangelical and Pentecostal churches desiring to be involved in ecumenical discussions.

Throughout the United States there are hundreds of local and regional councils of churches. The oldest of these is the Massachusetts Council of Churches established in 1902.[12] While it began as a Protestant association, it has involved Orthodox and Roman Catholics for decades. Most recently, the Greek Orthodox Metropolis of Boston became a formal member. Throughout the country, many of these councils bring together representatives of the Protestant, Episcopal, Orthodox, Old Catholic, and Roman Catholic parishes or regional church bodies. These councils, therefore, are clearly distinguished from interfaith bodies that include representatives from other religions. The activities of the councils of churches vary from place to place. Most, however, are concerned with providing a common Christian witness within a local setting. Many of these councils also provide opportunities for theological dialogue and common prayer for unity.[13]

Throughout this study, three interrelated aspects of the quest for reconciliation and unity of the churches have been identified as essential. These are: theological dialogue that addresses issues of division and seeks to find new consensus, prayer for unity, and common witness in the society. These three elements find rich expression in the various types of ecumenism in the United States. But, at the same time, it often appears as though the three aspects are not equally appreciated or properly interrelated in all quarters.[14] In many councils of churches and ecumenical organizations, the emphasis is frequently upon the concerns for common witness in the society. This is viewed as the ecumenical cause. It is seen as the principal means and goal that can bring Christians and churches together. In good measure, the difficulties that afflict the National Council of Churches reflect this one-dimensional approach.

One of the most serious challenges, which the ecumenical movement faces in the United States, is to keep the proper and necessary relationship between theological dialogue, prayer for unity, and common witness. Each is necessary to the quest for reconciliation and the restoration of visible unity.[15] It is precisely because of a one-dimensional approach to ecumenism that some councils of churches have failed to attract Orthodox, Roman Catholic, and Evangelical involvement. Indeed, some councils have abandoned the concern for Christian unity altogether and have become interfaith agencies concerned primarily with practical cooperation in social service and advocacy.[16] Yet, as Bishop Lesslie Newbigin says: "The unity that Christ wills for us is something more that cooperation…It is the unity which is described in St. John's Gospel as abiding in him and he in us. It is a unity which comes from the perfect at-one-ment which he has wrought for us in the Cross. Our divisions are a public contradiction of that atonement. Cooperation in common programs of study and action is not a substitute for this unity."[17] This means that councils of churches must be faithful to the mandate for unity rooted in Christian teaching and be servants of the churches in their quest for reconciliation and unity.

Besides the councils of churches, there are numerous associations at the local, regional, and national levels bringing together Christians from different churches for study, prayer, and common witness. Some of these, such as Church Women United, can be found throughout the country. Others, such as clergy associations or meetings of church ecumenical officers, serve local needs. Drawing clergy and laity from throughout the country, the National Workshop for Christian Unity meets yearly to discuss ecumenical concerns. In addition to this, there are also important centers devoted to ecumenical study. Among these are the Graymore Ecumenical and Interreligious Institute in New York and the Institute for Ecumenical and Cultural Research in Collegeville, Minnesota. There are also monastic communities that have a special appreciation of the quest for church unity. Among these are the Community of Jesus in Orleans, Massachusetts, and the Orthodox monastery of New Skete in Cambridge, New York. Countless monasteries and retreat centers provide special opportunities for ecumenical conferences and common prayer. Finally, the remarkable Communities of L'Arche bring together Christians from many churches to serve those with disabilities in the spirit of the Beatitudes.[18]

Related to the churches in the United States, there are a number of significant associations that are devoted to the challenge of the renewal of parish life, of theological reflection, of pastoral leadership, and of worship. While most are these are linked to specific church families, many have developed a strong ecumenical dimension. The organizers have recognized the intimate relationship between renewal, mission, and the unity of the churches that are centered upon Christ and his Gospel.

Among these associations, the following examples are representative. The Orientale Lumen Conference, held each summer at The Catholic University in Washington, addresses themes especially related to relations between Orthodox, Eastern Catholics, and Roman Catholics. Similar issues are explored in conferences organized by the Sheptitsky Institute of Eastern Christian Studies founded in Chicago and now located in Ottawa, Ontario. Related to the United Methodist Church, the Academy of Spiritual Formation organizes extended retreats for leaders from all churches. The Craigville Colloquy, organized by members of the United Church of Christ, meets each summer in Craigville, Massachusetts, to examine theological themes with a strong ecumenical dimension. The Center for Catholic and Evangelical Theology sponsors yearly theological conferences that gathers pastors and theologians from a number of churches. Supported by the Massachusetts Council of Churches, the Envoys for Ecumenism, a group of clergy and laity, meet regularly for retreats and discussions of Christian unity and common witness.

A very notable endeavor, the Valparaiso Project on Education and Formation of People in Faith, has supported a number of projects and publications relating Christian teachings with Christian practices. The project has brought theologians from a number of churches into contact with each other as they explore together the relationship between the Christian faith, expressions of worship, and the disciplines of Christian living.

Each of these associations is significant. Each reflects the positive advances in ecumenical relations between the most of the churches and their members in the United States. While the specific mission of each group may vary, they bring together members of different churches in less formal settings for theological study, prayer, and witness. In so doing, the activities emphasize the centrality of Christ and his Gospel. They express the desire to overcome historic divisions for the sake of renewal and witness.

THEOLOGICAL DIALOGUE

Beginning in the 1960s, there has been a gradual increase in the number of multilateral and bilateral theological dialogues in the United States. These dialogues are distinctive because the churches formally support them. Within the context of the National Council of Churches, the Faith and Order Commission is a multilateral dialogue having Protestant, Episcopal, Orthodox, and Roman Catholic participants. Besides this there are a number of major bilateral dialogues between the churches. These include but are not limited to: the Orthodox-Roman Catholic, the Orthodox-Lutheran, the Orthodox-Episcopal, the Roman Catholic-Lutheran, and the Roman Catholic-Episcopal. As already noted, the Lutheran-Reformed and the Episcopal-Lutheran have led to significant agreements between those churches.[19]

These bilateral dialogues do not avoid the harsh fact of historical differences between the churches. Yet the dialogues honestly approach these differences with the belief that, through theological reflection nurtured by prayer, a common understanding of the Christian faith can emerge. They reflect the fact that, as Georges Florovsky has said, "there are many bonds still not broken, whereby the schisms are held together in a certain unity."[20] The dialogues in the United States have been very productive and have made significant contributions to the ongoing discussions between the churches, not only in this country but also at the global level.

The American dialogues have been especially fruitful because they bring together theologians who share the same cultural context. Moreover, these dialogues frequently reflect relationships that are not encumbered by many of the cultural and religious animosities found, especially in Europe. As a result, the bilateral dialogues in the United States have often been able to address issues in a fresh and creative way, which at times distinguishes them from the international dialogues. For example, the North American Orthodox-Roman Catholic Consultation has continued its meetings at a time when its international counterpart has experienced serious difficulties.[21] Likewise, the Lutheran-Roman Catholic dialogue in the United States came to a valuable consensus in 1983 on the doctrine of Justification long before the more recent agreement was reached at the international level.[22] While these bilateral dialogues generally bring together theologians from the churches, their meetings and their theological statements are discussed in meetings of church leaders and in theological schools and seminaries.

These dialogues have contributed to a renewal of theological reflection. In the various churches, for example, there has been a renewed interest in the reality of the Trinity. The writings of contemporary theologians from Orthodox, Roman Catholic, Anglican, Old Catholic, and most Protestant churches are engaged together in relating the teaching on the Trinity to Christian anthropology, worship, and mission.[23] Speaking of the importance of theological reflection, the Orthodox-Roman Catholic Consultation in North America has said: "The process of reconciliation of the churches, however, is not merely a matter of good will; it requires solid and consistent theological reflection. In order for this theological reflection to bear good fruit, it must be rooted in Scripture and Tradition and nurtured by prayer. It must be oriented toward the needs of God's people today. Our reconciliation requires a theology which is truly life-giving and which serves the Author of life."[24]

ENCOUNTERS THROUGH SPIRITUALITY

The quest for church unity also has connected with the renewed interest in Christian spirituality and Christian nurture, which finds numerous expressions within the churches and their parishes. This interrelationship between ecumenism and spiritual growth has brought divided Christians together through an appreciation of a common literature on spirituality. Orthodox, Roman Catholics, Anglicans, Old Catholics, and many Protestants have rediscovered the important principles of spiritual growth by reading writers from a variety of Christian traditions. These would include Thomas Merton, Kenneth Leech, Bishop Kallistos Ware, Roberta C. Bondi, Basil Pennington, Metropolitan Anthony Bloom, Jean Vanier, Vassula Ryden, Anthony Coniaris, Richard Forester, John Pobee, Kyriaki FitzGerald, and Henri Nouwen. These writers come from a wide variety of Christian churches and traditions.[25]

The themes expressed in their writings reflect the insights of the mystical and spiritual tradition of early Christianity. This means that the readers are gaining an appreciation of aspects of Christian life and history that precede the great divisions. Through the study of the early traditions of Christian thought and worship, contemporary Christians are moving more deeply into a common history and a common heritage. This process is, in a sense, an expression of what has been called "ecumenism in time."[26] It is the affirmation that the quest for reconciliation and visible unity today must also be in harmony with the church before the great divisions.

The deepening appreciation of Christian spirituality and its relationship to ecumenism has led to some to journey on "ecumenical pilgrimages" to the great centers of early Christianity. These journeys have created special bonds among the participants and have led many to a renewed appreciation of the reality of the church that transcends divisions. It has led to a deepened appreciation of the calling of Christians to be persons of reconciliation. "The ecumenical movement," says Diane Kessler, "needs people with a Christlike frame of mind... Attention to the spiritual dimension of our ecumenical vocation fosters this Christlike frame of mind. It widens our vision. It transforms individuals and churches."[27]

HEALING RELATIONSHIPS

The ecumenical movement is not simply changing the way that the divided churches relate to each other. In its best expressions, the ecumenical movement is changing the way in which the Christians from divided churches are relating with each other. Mistrust and bigotry are yielding to mutual respect and understanding. As the many examples from the United States show, Christians from divided churches are coming together for common study, for common prayer, and for common witness in the society. During the past 50 years especially, the ecclesiastical walls that have separated Christians are coming down. Clergy and laity are emerging from their ecclesiastical isolation. Certainly, this process varies from region to region and from place to place in the United States and in other parts of the world. This process may trouble some church leaders who wish to defend an old order. Yet the healing of the wounds of divisions cannot be denied. Ultimately, it is part and parcel of the process of reconciliation and the restoration of the visible unity of the churches.

One expression of these new relationships among Christians from divided churches is the growth of interchurch marriages. This refers to the marriage between persons from different Christian churches. Fifty years ago, the marriage of persons from different churches was rare. While such marriages could be found, they were certainly not the norm. Indeed, church leaders generally discouraged them. In the United States today and in some other parts of the world, interchurch marriage is the norm. No doubt, some persons enter into these marriages with a sense of religious indifference. But this is certainly not always the case. On the contrary, many enter into these marriages with a desire to live their Christian faith with an appreciation of their different church heritages.[28]

These interchurch marriages are bringing Christians of different churches together. At the same time, these marriages may also be bringing the churches themselves closer together. These marriages in themselves do not heal the wounds of church division. Yet the very existence of these marriages and families challenges old animosities and bigotry. One's family member can be a member of another church. These marriages and families are leading the churches to look at their teachings about marriage as well as the sacraments. The marriages are leading church leaders to be more sensitive to the realties of these Christian families. The members of these families truly live within the church and between the boundaries of the churches.[29]

The ecumenical movement has helped to create and foster new relationships among Christians from the still divided churches. In many parts of this country, these relationships are bearing witness to a new spirit of reconciliation characterized by mutual understanding, a desire to heal church divisions, and to heal the divisions of society. There is a growing recognition that the process of reconciliation and the restoration of visible unity cannot simply be the task of church leaders and theologians. Their work is certainly important. Yet the laity within the churches has a very important role to play in receiving and living the theological agreements that are forged by the theologians. It is precisely at the local level of church life that these agreements must ultimately be received in a spirit of prayer and with a desire to give a common witness in the society.[30] "Ecumenical dialogue," says Kyriaki FitzGerald, "is, needless to say, difficult work. This dialogue is not committed by faceless institutions, but by human persons. And while we are still human persons, the goal of our efforts are, indeed, of divine proportions."[31]

CONCLUSIONS

The quest for Christian reconciliation and the visible unity of the churches is very much a part of the life of the Orthodox, Roman Catholic, Episcopal, Old Catholic, and most Protestant churches in the United States at the regional and local levels. While some local Protestant communities have remained opposed to ecumenical encounter and dialogue, most have welcomed it. Within parishes of all Christian traditions, the expressions of the ecumenical movement can be found in worship, in teaching, and in common witness in the society. In addition, numerous councils of churches and other ecumenical bodies serve the churches and their members in the movement toward visible unity. Established by the churches, the multilateral and bilateral dialogues in the United States have made significant contributions to mutual understanding and the resolution of differences in teachings. At the local level, the new relationship between the churches is reflected in new relationships among parishes and the members of those parishes. As exemplified by the many interchurch marriages, the ecumenical movement has not simply changed the churches. It has also changed the way that Christians of different churches relate to each other. The movement for reconciliation and the visible unity of the churches involves all the members of the churches in the ministry of reconciliation.

NOTES

1. *Ecumenical Accountability* (Boston: Massachusetts Council of Churches, 1990), p. 4.

2. Massey H. Shepherd, Jr., "Liturgy and Ecumenism," *Ecumenical Trends* 10 (1981), pp. 65–68.

3. Kallistos Ware, "Communion and Intercommunion," *Sobornost* 7:7 (1978), pp. 550–67.

4. Bernard Marthaler, "Grassroots Ecumenism and Religious Education," *Ecumenical Trends* 16 (1967), pp. 65–68.

5. *Ecumenical Accountability,* p. 10.

6. K.F. Nickle and T.F. Lull, eds., *A Common Calling: The Witness of the Reformation Churches in North America Today* (Minneapolis: Fortress, 1993).

7. Günther Gassmann, "Retrospective of an Ecumenical Century," in *Agapè: Études en l'honneur de Mgr. Pierre Duprey* (Chambésy: Centre Orthodoxe, 2002), p. 79.

8. Churches Uniting in Christ, http://www.eden.edu/cuic/whatiscuic/whatiscuic.htm.

9. Not participating are many Evangelical and Pentecostal church families. Neither the American Baptist Churches in the USA nor the more conservative Southern Baptist Convention have been active in Protestant union discussions. While the former is engaged in ecumenical activities, the latter has generally avoided ecumenical dialogues and associations. Likewise, the Lutheran Church, Missouri Synod has not been fully active in ecumenical dialogues.

10. "Statement of the Consultation," in *A Letter from Christ to the World: An Exploration of the Role of the Laity in the Church Today,* ed. Nicholas Apostola (Geneva: WCC Publications, 1998), pp. 10–11.

11. Leonid Kishkovsky, "Preface," in *Growing Consensus Church Dialogues in the United States, 1962–1991,* ed. Joseph Burgess and Jeffrey Gros (New York: Paulist Press, 1995), p. 2.

12. See Elizabeth Nordbeck, *That All May Be One: Celebrating a Century of Ecumenical Witness* (Boston: Massachusetts Council of Churches, 2002).

13. See Diane Kessler and Michael Kinnamon, *Councils of Churches and the Ecumenical Vision* (Geneva: WCC Publications, 2000).

14. Faith and Order Commission, National Council of Churches, "The Ecclesiological Significance of Council of Churches," in *Growing Consensus Church Dialogues in the United States, 1962–1991,* ed. Burgess and Gros, pp. 585–613.

15. Kessler and Kinnamon, *Councils of Churches and the Ecumenical Vision,* pp. 33–42.

16. Ibid., pp. 43–52.

17. Lesslie Newbigin, *One Body, One Gospel, One World* (London: International Missionary Council, 1958), p. 54.

18. See Jean Vanier, *An Ark for the Poor: The Story of L'Arche* (Ottawa: Novalis, 1995).

19. See Nils Ehrenström and Günther Gassmann, *Confessions in Dialogue* (Geneva: World Council of Churches, 1975).

20. Georges Florovsky, "The Boundaries of the Church," *Church Quarterly Review* 117 (1933), p. 131.

21. See John Borelli and John Erickson, *The Quest for Unity: Orthodox and Catholics in Dialogue* (Crestwood: St. Vladimir's Seminary Press, 1996).

22. See William G. Rusch, "The History and Methodology of the Joint Declaration on Justification: A Case Study in Ecumenical Reception," in *Agapè: Études en l'honneur de Mgr. Pierre Duprey* (Chambésy: Centre Orthodoxe, 2002), pp. 169–84.

23. Gassmann, "Retrospective of an Ecumenical Century," p. 73.

24. "Sharing in the Ministry of Reconciliation," *Origins* 30:5 (2000), p. 80.

25. See Emmanuel Sullivan, "Ecumenical Spirituality," *Crosspoint* 13:4 (2000), pp. 42–44.

26. Georges Florovsky, "The Quest for Christian Unity and the Orthodox Church," *Theology and Life* 4 (1961), p. 202.

27. Diane C. Kessler, "Ecumenical Spirituality: The Quest for Wholeness of Vision," in *The Vision of Christian Unity: Essays in Honor of Paul A. Crow, Jr.*, ed. Thomas F. Best and Theodore J. Nottingham (Indianapolis: Oikoumene Publications, 1997), p. 101.

28. Gerard Kelly, "Local Dialogue on Interchurch Marriages," *Ecumenical Trends* 30:4 (2001), p. 63.

29. "Statement of the Consultation," in *A Letter from Christ to the World: An Exploration of the Role of the Laity in the Church Today,* ed. Apostola, p. 8.

30. Ibid., pp. 10–11.

31. Kyriaki FitzGerald, "The Fifth World Conference and the Walls of the Heart," *Ecumenical Trends* 22:4 (1993), p. 14.

Epilogue

> Never resign yourself to the scandal of the divisions of Christians... Be consumed with a burning zeal for the unity of the body of Christ.
>
> —The Rule of Taizé[1]

Churches are generally not known for their ability to change rapidly. Yet the story of the ecumenical movement points to some remarkable changes in the way that many of the divided Christian churches now relate with each other and relate together to the world.

The Orthodox Church, the Roman Catholic Church, the Old Catholic Church, and most of the churches of the Reformation are actively involved in the quest for reconciliation and the restoration of their visible unity. This quest seeks to overcome the doctrinal differences often dating back centuries. These doctrinal differences were usually compounded by cultural, political, and linguistic factors, as well as by ethnic and racial differences. The churches believe that the quest for reconciliation and unity is rooted in the very gospel that they proclaim. Believing in a God who reconciles and heals in Jesus Christ, the churches have affirmed their obligation to heal their own divisions through prayer, through theological dialogue, and through witness together in the world. This is a dramatic and evolving process of healing and reconciliation.

The process of healing and reconciliation is not always easy. The reconciling activities of the churches always take place within a wider context. In many places, the churches themselves continue to be affected by the animosity, bigotry, and misunderstanding rooted in historic divisions. Moreover, church divisions have often contributed to ethnic, cultural, and racial divisions within societies and nations.

In the churches themselves, there is often a structural indifference to the process of reconciliation. This can prevent the agreements reached in theological dialogues from truly being received. Within councils of churches, there is often a tendency simply to settle for cooperation in social witness while neglecting the importance of prayer and theological dialogue. In some places, there is a strong spirit of secularism, materialism, and religious indifference that challenges the Christian message. In other places, some religious groups engage in acts of proselytism, which challenges the churches' zeal for reconciliation and visible unity. While the advances in the ecumenical movement have been dramatic in recent decades, these difficulties naturally lead some to speak of a crisis in the ecumenical movement.[2]

Despite these difficulties, however, the ecumenical movement has affected the churches and their members in all parts of the world. Depending upon the context, a new relationship among the churches has been growing for decades. Those with no direct knowledge of the preecumenical days may not even be aware of the dramatic changes that have already occurred. While all the churches have not as yet fully restored their unity, there has been recognition of the degrees of unity among the divided churches that already exists. There have been significant changes in the relationships among the churches and their members that reflect and express the process of reconciliation.[3]

There has been a change in the way many churches approach each other. Over the past 100 years, they have come out of the formal isolation from each other, which often characterized their lives for centuries. While divisions still exist, most of the churches no longer see the other as an opponent or competitor. Through meetings, prayer services, dialogues, and acts of compassion, members of the different churches have come to know each other better. They have overcome much hostility, prejudices, and misunderstanding bred through decades or centuries of isolation of the churches.[4]

There has been a change in the way the churches approach their doctrinal differences. No longer are divisive differences in teachings accepted as normative. Through formal theological dialogues, the churches are committed to study the doctrinal differences and to seek together a common articulation of the Christian faith.[5]

There has been a change in the character of theological reflection in the churches and in their theological schools.[6] The encounters and theological dialogues between the churches have not only addressed past issues of division. They have contributed to rich insights into the essential elements of the Christian faith. No topic of Christian teachings or Christian history can now be studied in a narrow manner reflecting only past debates and polemics. On the contrary, theologians of one church or tradition are constantly exposed to the perspectives of their colleagues in other churches, as well as to the results of ecumenical dialogues.[7]

There has been a change in the way the churches pray. Prayer for reconciliation and the restoration of visible unity is a prominent part of petitions of worship service within the churches and within ecumenical gatherings. The Week of Prayer for Christian Unity and the World Day of Prayer continue to be among the special opportunities for Christians from the different churches to come together and to pray for reconciliation and unity.[8]

There has been a change in the way the churches and their members experience the rich treasures of the spirituality, the hymnology, and the art of each other's heritage. This has contributed to a reemphasis upon the centrality of the Eucharist and the significance of baptism in many churches. It has led many to an appreciation of different forms of chant, music, symbolic actions, and icons, coming especially from the Christian East. It has led many in the churches of Europe and the Americas to an appreciation of the insights of African Christian spirituality.[9]

There has been a change in the way the churches express their concern for those in need within the society. The ecumenical movement has encouraged the churches to speak together whenever possible about the issues of race, poverty, hunger, and injustice, which are divisive elements in the society.[10]

There has been a change in the way the churches, especially the local parishes, have responded to those in need. In some places, parishes of different church traditions have banded together to establish food pantries, health clinics, and centers for the elderly or the youth. Churches have come together to speak to governmental agencies about their understanding of the dignity and value of human life, as well as the need to care for the environment.

There has been a change in the way the churches relate to each other through various councils of churches at the global, regional, and local levels. These councils or conferences serve the churches by nurturing the principles of ecumenism. They offer opportunities for encounters and provide occasions for common prayer and theological dialogue, as well as common witness and service to those in need.[11]

The movement toward reconciliation and the visible unity of the churches is a process rooted in the heart of the Christian message. Over the last 100 years especially, it is a dramatic process through which the Orthodox Church, Roman Catholic Church, Old Catholic Church, and most churches of the Reformation have emerged from formal isolation. For the cause of their reconciliation and unity, their members have come together in prayer, in theological reflection, and in witness for the good of the society. The churches believe that these reconciling activities bear witness to the message of Christ and the Christian gospel.[12] The reconciling activities express the conviction that Christians and their churches must "live together in harmony so that together with one voice they may glorify God" (cf. Romans 15:5–6).[13]

NOTES

1. *The Rule of Taizé* (Taizé: Les Presses de Taizé, 1968), p. 21.

2. See Institute for Ecumenical Research, *Crisis and Challenge of the Ecumenical Movement: Integrity and Indivisibility* (Geneva: WCC Publications, 1994).

3. I am indebted to Günther Gassmann for many of these important observations. See his "Retrospective of an Ecumenical Century," in *Agapè: Études en l'honneur de Mgr. Pierre Duprey,* ed. Jean-Marie Roger Tillard (Chambésy: Centre Orthodoxe, 2002), pp. 65–86.

4. Ibid., p. 70.

5. Ibid., pp. 81–82.

6. See John Pobee, ed., *Towards Viable Theological Education* (Geneva: WCC Publications, 1997).

7. "Ecumenical Formation: Ecumenical Reflections and Suggestions," in Joint Working Group Between the Roman Catholic Church and the World Council of Churches, *Seventh Report* (Geneva: WCC Publications, 1998).

8. See Thomas F. Best and Dagmar Heller, eds., *So We Believe, So We Pray: Towards Koinonia in Worship* (Geneva: WCC Publications, 1995).

9. Gassmann, p. 71.

10. Paul A. Crow, Jr., *Christian Unity: Matrix for Mission* (New York: Friendship Press, 1982), pp. 60–76.

11. See Diane Kessler and Michael Kinnamon, *Councils of Churches and the Ecumenical Vision* (Geneva: WCC Publications, 2000).

12. Geoffrey Wainwright, "Ut Unum Sint, ut Mundis Credat: Classic Ecumenism from John R. Mott to John Paul II," in *Agapè: Études en l'honneur de Mgr. Pierre Duprey,* ed. Jean-Marie Roger Tillard (Chambésy: Centre Orthodoxe, 2002), p. 44.

13. Ibid, p. 48.

Appendix I

ESTIMATED WORLDWIDE MEMBERSHIP, MAJOR CHURCH TRADITIONS (2004)

Roman Catholic Church	1,000,000,000
Protestant Churches	316,000,000
Orthodox Church	300,000,000
Anglican Communion	73,000,000
Oriental Orthodox Churches	23,000,000
Old Catholic Churches	1,000,000
Assyrian Church of the East	450,000

These are composite figures based on a number of sources. See: "Religion Statistics," at www.adherents.com; "World Christian Database," at www.worldchristiandatabase.com; and Ion Bria, Martyra and Witness (Geneva: World Council of Churches, 1980).

Appendix II

MAJOR REGIONAL COUNCILS OR CONFERENCES OF CHURCHES

All Africa Conference of Churches
Christian Conference of Asia
Canadian Council of Churches
Caribbean Conference of Churches
Conference of European Churches
Latin American Council of Churches
Middle East Council of Churches
National Council of Churches, USA
Pacific Conference of Churches

Appendix III

MEMBER CHURCHES, NATIONAL COUNCIL OF CHURCHES OF CHRIST, USA (2004)

African Methodist Episcopal Church
African Methodist Episcopal Zion Church
Alliance of Baptists in the U.S.A.
American Baptist Churches in the U.S.A.
Antiochian Orthodox Christian Archdiocese of North America
Armenian Apostolic Church, Diocese of America
Christian Church (Disciples of Christ)
Christian Methodist Episcopal Church
Church of the Brethren
Coptic Orthodox Church
Episcopal Church
Evangelical Lutheran Church in America
Friends United Meeting
Greek Orthodox Archdiocese of America
Hungarian Reformed Church in America
International Council of Community Churches
Korean Presbyterian Church in America
Malankara Orthodox Syrian Church, Diocese of America
Mar Thoma Syrian Church of India

Moravian Church in America (Unitas Fratrum)
National Baptist Convention of America
National Baptist Convention, U.S.A.
National Missionary Baptist Convention of America
Orthodox Church in America
Patriarchal Parishes of the Russian Orthodox Church in the U.S.A.
Philadelphia Yearly Meeting of the Religious Society of Friends
Polish National Catholic Church of America
Presbyterian Church (U.S.A.)
Progressive National Baptist Convention, Inc.
Reformed Church in America
Serbian Orthodox Church in the U.S.A. and Canada
Swedenborgian Church
Syrian (Syriac) Orthodox Church of Antioch
Ukrainian Orthodox Church of the U.S.A.
United Church of Christ
United Methodist Church

The Roman Catholic Church is not a member of the National Council of Churches in the USA. It does appoint participants to the Commission on Faith and Order.

Appendix IV

MEMBER CHURCHES AND ASSOCIATE MEMBER CHURCHES, WORLD COUNCIL OF CHURCHES (2004)

The World Council of Churches in 2004 described itself as a fellowship of 342 churches in 120 countries. The Roman Catholic Church is not a member of the World Council of Churches but it cooperates in some of its activities especially through the Joint Working Group and the Commission on Faith and Order.

AFRICA

Africa Inland Church [Sudan]

African Christian Church and Schools [Kenya]

African Church of the Holy Spirit [Kenya]*

African Israel Church, Nineveh [Kenya]

African Protestant Church [Cameroon]*

Anglican Church of Kenya

Anglican Church of Tanzania

Association of Baptist Churches in Rwanda

Church of Christ—Light of the Holy Spirit [Congo]

Church of Christ in Congo (includes the following)

—Baptist Community of Western Congo
—Community of Disciples of Christ
—Episcopal Baptist Community

—Evangelical Community
—Mennonite Community
—Presbyterian Community
—Presbyterian Community of Kinshasa—Province of the Anglican Church of the Congo

Church of Jesus Christ in Madagascar
Church of Jesus Christ on Earth by his Messenger S. Kimbangu [Congo]
Church of the Brethren in Nigeria
Church of the Lord (Aladura) Worldwide [Nigeria]
Church of Nigeria (Anglican Communion)
Church of the Province of Central Africa [Botswana]
Church of the Province of Southern Africa [South Africa]
Church of the Province of the Indian Ocean [Seychelles]
Church of the Province of Uganda
Church of the Province of West Africa [Ghana]
Episcopal Church of Burundi
Episcopal Church of Rwanda
Episcopal Church of the Sudan
Eritrean Orthodox Tewahdo Church
Ethiopian Evangelical Church Mekane Yesus
Ethiopian Orthodox Tewahedo Church
Evangelical Church of Cameroon
Evangelical Church of Gabon
Evangelical Church of the Congo [Republic of Congo]
Evangelical Congregational Church in Angola
Evangelical Lutheran Church in Congo [Democratic Republic of Congo]
Evangelical Lutheran Church in Namibia
Evangelical Lutheran Church in Southern Africa [South Africa]
Evangelical Lutheran Church in Tanzania
Evangelical Lutheran Church in the Republic of Namibia
Evangelical Lutheran Church in Zimbabwe
Evangelical Lutheran Church of Ghana
Evangelical Pentecostal Mission of Angola
Evangelical Presbyterian Church, Ghana
Evangelical Presbyterian Church in South Africa
Evangelical Presbyterian Church of Togo
Evangelical Reformed Church of Angola
Harrist Church [Côte d'Ivoire]
Kenya Evangelical Lutheran Church*
Lesotho Evangelical Church

Lutheran Church in Liberia
Malagasy Lutheran Church [Madagascar]
Methodist Church, Ghana
Methodist Church in Kenya
Methodist Church in Togo
Methodist Church in Zimbabwe
Methodist Church Nigeria
Methodist Church of Southern Africa [South Africa]
Methodist Church Sierra Leone
Maputo, Mozambique
Moravian Church in Southern Africa [South Africa]
Moravian Church in Tanzania
Native Baptist Church of Cameroon
Nigerian Baptist Convention
Presbyterian Church in Cameroon
Presbyterian Church of Africa [South Africa]
Presbyterian Church of Cameroon
Presbyterian Church of East Africa [Kenya]
Presbyterian Church of Ghana
Presbyterian Church of Mozambique*
Presbyterian Church of Nigeria
Presbyterian Church of Rwanda
Presbyterian Church of the Sudan
Presbytery of Liberia*
Protestant Church of Algeria*
Protestant Methodist Church, Côte d'Ivoire
Protestant Methodist Church of Benin
Reformed Church in Zambia
Reformed Church in Zimbabwe
Reformed Church of Christ in Nigeria
Reformed Presbyterian Church of Equatorial Guinea*
Union of Baptist Churches of Cameroon
United Church of Christ in Zimbabwe
United Church of Zambia
United Congregational Church of Southern Africa [South Africa]
United Evangelical Church "Anglican Communion in Angola"*
Uniting Presbyterian Church in Southern Africa [South Africa]
Uniting Reformed Church in Southern Africa [South Africa]

ASIA

Anglican Church in Aotearoa, New Zealand and Polynesia
Anglican Church of Australia
Anglican Church of Korea
Anglican Communion in Japan (Nippon Seiko Kai)
Associated Churches of Christ in New Zealand
Baptist Union of New Zealand
Batak Christian Community Church [Indonesia]*
Batak Protestant Christian Church [Indonesia]
Bengal-Orissa-Bihar Baptist Convention [India]*
China Christian Council
Christian Church in East Timor
Christian Church of Central Sulawesi [Indonesia]
Christian Church of Sumba [Indonesia]
Christian Evangelical Church in Minahasa [Indonesia]
Christian Evangelical Church in Sangihe Talaud [Indonesia]
Christian Protestant Angkola Church [Indonesia]
Christian Protestant Church in Indonesia
Church of Bangladesh*
Church of Sri Lanka
Church of Christ in Thailand
Church of North India
Church of Pakistan
Church of South India
Church of the Province of Myanmar
Churches of Christ in Australia
Communion of Baptist Churches in Bangladesh
Convention of Philippine Baptist Churches
East Java Christian Church [Indonesia]
Episcopal Church in the Philippines
Evangelical Christian Church in Halmahera [Indonesia]
Evangelical Christian Church in Irian Jaya [Indonesia]
Evangelical Methodist Church in the Philippines
Indonesian Christian Church (GKI)
Indonesian Christian Church (HKI)
Javanese Christian Churches (JKG) [Indonesia]

Kalimantan Evangelical Church [Indonesia]
Karo Batak Protestant Church (GBKP) [Indonesia]
Korean Christian Church in Japan*
Korean Methodist Church
Malankara Orthodox Syrian Church [India]
Mar Thoma Syrian Church of Malabar [India]
Mara Evangelical Church [Myanmar]*
Methodist Church in India
Methodist Church in Malaysia
Methodist Church in Singapore*
Methodist Church of New Zealand
Methodist Church, Sri Lanka
Methodist Church, Upper Myanmar
Myanmar Baptist Convention
Nias Protestant Christian Church [Indonesia]
Orthodox Church in Japan
Pasundan Christian Church (GKP) [Indonesia]
Philippine Independent Church
Presbyterian Church in Taiwan
Presbyterian Church in the Republic of Korea
Presbyterian Church of Aotearoa New Zealand
Presbyterian Church of Korea
Presbyterian Church of Pakistan
Protestant Christian Church in Bali (GKPB) [Indonesia]*
Protestant Church in Indonesia (GPI)
Protestant Church in Sabah [Malaysia]
Protestant Church in South-East Sulawesi [Indonesia]
Protestant Church in the Moluccas (GPM) [Indonesia]
Protestant Church in Western Indonesia (GPIB)
Protestant Evangelical Church in Timor (GMIT) [Indonesia]
Samavesam of Telugu Baptist Churches [India]
Simalungun Protestant Christian Church (GKPS) [Indonesia]
Toraja Church [Indonesia]
United Church of Christ in Japan
United Church of Christ in the Philippines
United Evangelical Lutheran Churches in India
Uniting Church in Australia

CARIBBEAN

Church in the Province of the West Indies [Antigua]
Jamaica Baptist Union
Methodist Church in Cuba*
Methodist Church in the Caribbean and the Americas [Antigua]
Moravian Church, Eastern West Indies Province [Antigua]
Moravian Church in Jamaica
Moravian Church in Surinam
Presbyterian Church in Trinidad & Tobago
Presbyterian Reformed Church in Cuba*
United Church in Jamaica and the Cayman Islands
United Protestant Church [Curaçao]*

EUROPE

Armenian Apostolic Church
Autocephalous Orthodox Church in Poland
Baptist Union of Denmark
Baptist Union of Great Britain
Baptist Union of Hungary
Catholic Diocese of the Old Catholics in Germany
Church in Wales
Church of England
Church of Greece
Church of Ireland
Church of Norway
Church of Scotland
Church of Sweden
Czechoslovak Hussite Church [Czech Republic]
Ecumenical Patriarchate of Constantinople [Turkey]
Estonian Evangelical Lutheran Church
European Continental Province of the Moravian Church [Netherlands]
Evangelical Baptist Union of Italy*
Evangelical Church in Germany (includes the following)
—Church of Lippe
—Evangelical Church in Baden
—Evangelical Church in Berlin-Brandenburg
—Evangelical Church in Hesse and Nassau
—Evangelical Church in Württemberg
—Evangelical Church of Anhalt

—Evangelical Church of Bremen
—Evangelical Church of Hesse Electorate-Waldeck
—Evangelical Church of the Palatinate
—Evangelical Church of the Province of Saxony
—Evangelical Church of the Rhineland
—Evangelical Church of the Silesian Oberlausitz
—Evangelical Church of Westphalia
—Evangelical Lutheran Church in Bavaria
—Evangelical Lutheran Church in Brunswick
—Evangelical Lutheran Church in Oldenburg
—Evangelical Lutheran Church in Thuringia
—Evangelical Lutheran Church of Hanover
—Evangelical Lutheran Church of Mecklenburg
—Evangelical Lutheran Church of Saxony
—Evangelical Lutheran Church of Schaumburg-Lippe
—Evangelical Reformed Church in Bavaria and Northwestern Germany
—North Elbian Evangelical Lutheran Church
—Pomeranian Evangelical Church

Evangelical Church of Czech Brethren [Czech Republic]

Evangelical Church of the Augsburg and Helvetic Confessions in Austria

Evangelical Church of the Augsburg Confession in Poland

Evangelical Church of the Augsburg Confession in Romania

Evangelical Church of the Augsburg Confession in the Slovak Republic

Evangelical Church of the Augsburg Confession of Alsace and Lorraine [France]

Evangelical Lutheran Church in Denmark

Evangelical Lutheran Church in the Kingdom of the Netherlands

Evangelical Lutheran Church of Finland

Evangelical Lutheran Church of France

Evangelical Lutheran Church of Iceland

Evangelical Lutheran Church of Latvia

Evangelical Methodist Church of Italy

Evangelical Presbyterian Church of Portugal*

Evangelical Synodal Presbyterial Church of the Augsburg Confession in Romania

Greek Evangelical Church

Latvian Evangelical Lutheran Church Abroad [Germany]

Lusitanian Church of Portugal*

Lutheran Church in Hungary

Mennonite Church in Germany

Mennonite Church in the Netherlands

Methodist Church [UK]

Methodist Church in Ireland

Mission Covenant Church of Sweden

Moravian Church in Great Britain and Ireland

Netherlands Reformed Church
Old Catholic Church of Austria
Old Catholic Church of Switzerland
Old Catholic Church of the Netherlands
Old Catholic Mariavite Church in Poland
Orthodox Autocephalous Church of Albania
Orthodox Church of Finland
Orthodox Church of the Czech Lands and Slovakia [Czech Republic]
Polish Catholic Church in Poland
Presbyterian Church of Wales
Reformed Christian Church in Slovakia [Slovak Republic]
Reformed Christian Church in Yugoslavia
Reformed Church in Hungary
Reformed Church in Romania [Cluj]
Reformed Church in Romania [Oradea]
Reformed Church of Alsace and Lorraine [France]
Reformed Church of France
Reformed Churches in the Netherlands
Remonstrant Brotherhood [Netherlands]
Romanian Orthodox Church
Russian Orthodox Church
Scottish Episcopal Church
Serbian Orthodox Church [Federal Republic of Yugoslavia]
Silesian Evangelical Church of the Augsburg Confession [Czech Republic]
Slovak Evangelical Church of the Augsburg Confession in Yugoslavia
Spanish Evangelical Church
Spanish Reformed Episcopal Church*
Swiss Protestant Church Federation
Union of Welsh Independents
United Free Church of Scotland
United Protestant Church of Belgium
United Reformed Church [UK]
Waldensian Church [Italy]

LATIN AMERICA

Anglican Church of the Southern Cone of America [Argentina]
Baptist Association of El Salvador*

Baptist Convention of Nicaragua
Bolivian Evangelical Lutheran Church*
Christian Biblical Church [Argentina]*
Christian Reformed Church of Brazil
Church of God [Argentina]*
Church of the Disciples of Christ [Argentina]*
Episcopal Anglican Church of Brazil
Evangelical Church of Lutheran Confession in Brazil
Evangelical Church of the River Plate [Argentina]
Evangelical Lutheran Church in Chile
Evangelical Methodist Church in Bolivia*
Evangelical Methodist Church in Uruguay*
Evangelical Methodist Church of Argentina
Evangelical Methodist Church of Costa Rica*
Free Pentecostal Mission Church of Chile
Methodist Church in Brazil
Methodist Church of Chile*
Methodist Church of Mexico
Methodist Church of Peru*
Moravian Church in Nicaragua
Pentecostal Church of Chile
Pentecostal Mission Church [Chile]
Salvadorean Lutheran Synod*
United Evangelical Lutheran Church [Argentina]*
United Presbyterian Church of Brazil*

MIDDLE EAST

Armenian Apostolic Church [Lebanon]
Church of Cyprus
Coptic Orthodox Church [Egypt]
Episcopal Church in Jerusalem and the Middle East [Egypt]
Greek Orthodox Patriarchate of Alexandria and All Africa [Egypt]
Greek Orthodox Patriarchate of Antioch and All the East [Syria]
Greek Orthodox Patriarchate of Jerusalem [Israel]
Holy Apostolic Catholic Assyrian Church of the East [Iraq]
National Evangelical Synod of Syria and Lebanon [Lebanon]
Synod of the Evangelical Church of Iran

Synod of the Nile of the Evangelical Church [Egypt]
Syrian Orthodox Patriarchate of Antioch and All the East
Union of the Armenian Evangelical Churches in the Near East [Lebanon]

NORTH AMERICA

African Methodist Episcopal Church [USA]
African Methodist Episcopal Zion Church [USA]
American Baptist Churches in the USA
Anglican Church of Canada
Apostolic Catholic Assyrian Church of the East, N.A. Diocese
Canadian Yearly Meeting of the Religious Society of Friends
Christian Church (Disciples of Christ) in Canada
Christian Church (Disciples of Christ)
Christian Methodist Episcopal Church [USA]
Church of the Brethren [USA]
Episcopal Church
Estonian Evangelical Lutheran Church Abroad [Canada]
Evangelical Lutheran Church in America
Evangelical Lutheran Church in Canada
Hungarian Reformed Church in America
International Council of Community Churches [USA]
International Evangelical Church [USA]
Moravian Church in America
National Baptist Convention of America
National Baptist Convention, USA, Inc.
Orthodox Church in America
Polish National Catholic Church
Presbyterian Church in Canada
Presbyterian Church (USA)
Progressive National Baptist Convention, Inc. [USA]
Reformed Church in America [USA]
Religious Society of Friends
United Church of Canada
United Church of Christ [USA]
United Methodist Church [USA]

PACIFIC

Church of the Province of Melanesia [Solomon Islands]
Congregational Christian Church in American Samoa
Congregational Christian Church in Samoa
Cook Islands Christian Church
Ekalesia Niue
Evangelical Church in New Caledonia and the Loyalty Isles [New Caledonia]
Evangelical Church of French Polynesia
Evangelical Lutheran Church of Papua New Guinea
Kiribati Protestant Church
Methodist Church in Fiji
Methodist Church in Samoa
Free Wesleyan Church of Tonga [Methodist Church in Tonga]
Presbyterian Church of Vanuatu
Tuvalu Christian Church
United Church in Papua New Guinea
United Church in the Solomon Islands
United Church of Christ—Congregational in the Marshall Islands

* indicates associate membership.

Bibliography

COLLECTIONS OF DOCUMENTS ON ECUMENICAL THEMES AND ISSUES

Abbott, Walter, ed. *The Documents of Vatican II.* New York: America Press, 1966.

Bell, G. K. A. *Documents on Christian Unity: A Selection from the First and Second Series, 1920–30.* London: Oxford University Press, 1955.

———. *Documents on Christian Unity: Fourth Series, 1948–57.* London: Oxford University Press, 1958.

Bettenson, Henry, and Chris Maunder. *Documents of the Christian Church.* Rev. ed. Oxford: Oxford University Press, 1999.

Borelli, John, and John H. Erickson, eds. *The Quest for Unity: Orthodox and Catholics in Dialogue.* Crestwood, N.Y.: St. Vladimir's Seminary Press, 1996.

Burgess, Joseph A., and Jeffrey Gros, eds. *Building Unity: Ecumenical Dialogues with Roman Catholic Participation in the United States.* New York: Paulist Press, 1989.

———. *Growing Consensus: Church Dialogues in the United States, 1962–1991.* New York: Paulist Press, 1995.

Chaillot, Christine, and Alexander Belopopsky, eds. *Towards Unity: The Theological Dialogue Between the Orthodox Church and the Oriental Orthodox Churches.* Geneva: Inter-Orthodox Dialogue, 1998.

Cope, Brian E., and Michael Kinnamon, eds. *The Ecumenical Movement: An Anthology of Key Texts and Voices.* Geneva: WCC Publications, 1997.

Gassmann, Günther, ed. *Documentary History of Faith and Order 1963–1993.* Geneva: WCC Publications, 1993.

Gros, Jeffrey, et al., eds. *Growth in Agreement 11: Reports and Agreed Statements of Ecumenical Conversations on a World Level, 1982–1998.* Geneva: WCC, 2000.

Joint Working Group of the Roman Catholic Church and the World Council of Churches Seventh Report. Geneva: WCC Publications, 1998.

Limouris, Gennadios, ed. *Orthodox Visions of Ecumenism: Statements, Message and Reports on the Ecumenical Movement 1902–1992.* Geneva: WCC Publications, 1994.

Meyer, Harding, and Lucas Vischer, eds. *Growth in Agreement: Reports and Agreed Statements of Ecumenical Conversations on a World Level.* New York: Paulist Press, 1984.

Patelos, Constantin G., ed. *The Orthodox Church in the Ecumenical Movement: Documents and Statements 1902–1975.* Geneva: World Council of Churches, 1978.

Stormon, E. J., ed. *Towards the Healing of Schism: The Sees of Rome and Constantinople.* New York: Paulist Press, 1987.

Stransky, Thomas F., and John B. Sheerin, eds. *Doing the Truth in Charity: Statements of Pope Paul VI, Popes John Paul I, John Paul II, and the Secretariat for Promoting Christian Unity, 1964–1980.* New York: Paulist Press, 1982.

Vischer, Lukas, ed. *A Documentary History of the Faith and Order Movement 1927–1963.* St. Louis, Mo.: Bethany, 1963.

BIBLIOGRAPHICAL GUIDES

Beffa, Pierre. *Bibliography on the Ecumenical Movement and the World Council of Churches: 1968–1995.* Geneva: WCC Publications, 1995.

———. *Index to the World Council of Churches' Official Statements and Reports, 1948–1994.* Geneva: WCC Publications, 1995.

Crow, A., Jr. *The Ecumenical Movement in Bibliographical Outline.* New York: National Council of the Churches of Christ in the U.S.A., 1965.

Fahey, Michael A. *Ecumenism: A Bibliographical Overview.* Westport: Greenwood Press, 1992.

SELECTED BOOKS ON ECUMENICAL THEMES AND ISSUES

Aghiorgoussis, Maximos. *In the Image of God.* Brookline, Mass.: Holy Cross Orthodox Press, 1999.

Allchin, A. M. *The Abbé Paul Couturier: Apostle of Christian Unity.* Westminster: Faith Press, 1960.

Angel, Charles, and Charles LaFontaine. *Prophet of Reunion: The Life of Fr. Paul of Graymore.* New York: The Seabury Press, 1975.

Apostola, Nicholas. *A Letter from Christ to the World: An Exploration of the Role of the Laity in the Church Today.* Geneva: WCC Publications, 1998.

Ariarajah, S. Wesley. *Gospel and Culture: An Ongoing Discussion Within the Ecumenical Movement.* Geneva: WCC, 1994.

Atiya, Aziz S. *History of Eastern Christianity.* Notre Dame: University of Notre Dame Press, 1968.

Avis, Paul. *Christians in Communion.* London: Geoffrey Chapman, 1990.

Baaten, Carl, and Robert W. Jenson, eds. *In One Body Through the Cross: The Princeton Proposal for Christian Unity.* Grand Rapids, Mich.: Eerdmans, 2003.

Bakare, Sabastian. *The Drumbeat of Life: Jubilee in an African Context.* Geneva: WCC Publications, 1997.

Baker, Dereck, ed. *The Orthodox Churches and the West.* Oxford: Blackwell, 1976.

Balado, J. L. *The Story of Taizé.* London: Mowbray, 1988.*Baptism, Eucharist and Ministry 1982–1990: Report on the Process and Responses.* Geneva: WCC Publications, 1990.

Barrett, D., ed. *World Christian Encyclopedia.* London: Oxford University Press, 1982.

Bass, Dorothy, ed. *Practicing our Faith.* San Francisco: John Wiley and Sons, 1997.

Baum, Gregory. *That They May Be One: A Study of Papal Doctrine (Leo XIII–Pius XII).* Westminster, Md.: Newman Press, 1958.

———. *The Catholic Quest for Christian Unity.* Glen Rock, N.J.: Paulist Press, 1965.

Bea, Augustin. *The Unity of Christians.* New York: Herder and Herder, 1963.

Behr-Sigel, Elizabeth, and Kallistos Ware. *The Ordination of Women in the Orthodox Church.* Geneva: WCC Publications, 2000.

Best, Thomas F., ed. *Instruments of Unity: National Councils of Churches within the One Ecumenical Movement.* Geneva: WCC Publications, 1988.

Best, Thomas F., and Günther Gassman, eds. *On the Way to Fuller Koinonia.* Geneva: World Council of Churches, 1994.

Best, Thomas F., and Dagmar Heller, eds. *So We Believe, So We Pray: Towards Koinonia in Worship.* Geneva: WCC Publications, 1995.

Best, Thomas F., and Theodore J. Nottingham. *The Vision of Christian Unity Essays in Honor of Paul A. Crow, Jr.* Indianapolis: Oekoumene Publications, 1997.

Bilheimer, Robert S. *Ecumenical Breakthrough: The Emergence of the Ecumenical Tradition.* Grand Rapids, Mich.: Eerdmans, 1989.

Birmelé, André. *Local Ecumenism: How Church Unity Is Seen and Practiced by Congregations.* Geneva: WCC Publications, 1984.

Blane, Andrew, ed. *Georges Florovsky: Russian Intellectual, Orthodox Churchman.* Crestwood, N.Y.: St. Vladimir's Seminary Press, 1993.

Bluck, John. *Everyday Ecumenism: Can You Take the World Church Home?* Geneva: WCC Publications, 1987.

Bondi, Roberta C. *To Love as God Loves: Conversations with the Early Church.* Philadelphia: Fortress, 1987.

———. *To Pray and to Love: Conversations on Prayer with the Early Church.* Minneapolis: Fortress, 1981.

Brackney, William H. *Christian Voluntarism in Britain and North America.* Westport, Conn.: Greenwood, 1995.

Bria, Ion. *The Sense of Ecumenical Tradition: The Ecumenical Witness and Vision of the Orthodox.* Geneva: WCC Publications, 1991.

Bria, Ion, and Dagmar Heller, eds. *Ecumenical Pilgrims: Profiles of Pioneers in Christian Reconciliation.* Geneva: WCC Publications, 1995.

Brown, Raymond. *Priest and Bishop: Biblical Reflections.* New York: Paulist Press, 1970.

Brown, Raymond, et al. *Peter in the New Testament.* New York: Paulist Press, 1973.

Campbell, Ted. *Christian Confessions: A Historical Introduction.* Louisville: Westminster John Knox Press, 1996.

Castro, Emilio. *Sent Free: Mission and Unity in the Perspective of the Kingdom.* Grand Rapids, Mich.: Eerdmans, 1985.

———. *When We Pray Together.* Geneva: WCC Publications, 1989.

Cavert, Samuel McCrea. *On the Road to Christian Unity: An Appraisal of the Ecumenical Movement.* New York: Harper and Row, 1961.

———. *Church Cooperation and Unity in America: A Historical Review: 1900–1970.* New York: Association Press, 1970.

Chadwick, Henry. *Early Christian Thought and the Classical Tradition.* New York: Oxford University Press, 1966.

———. *The Early Church.* Baltimore: Penguin Books, 1973.

Chadwick, Owen. *The Mind of the Oxford Movement.* Stanford: Stanford University Press, 1960.

———. *The Reformation.* Baltimore: Penguin Books, 1972.

Chambers, Mortimer, et al. *The Western Experience to 1715.* New York: McGraw-Hill, Inc., 1991.

Charta Oecumenica: Guidelines for Growing Cooperation among the Churches in Europe. Geneva, St. Galen: Conference of European Churches, Council of European Bishops' Conference, 2001.

Church and World: The Unity of the Church and the Renewal of Human Community. Geneva: WCC Publications, 1990.

Clapsis, Emmanuel. *Orthodoxy in Conversation: Orthodox Ecumenical Engagements.* Geneva: WCC Publications, 2000.

Clément, Olivier. *Dialogues avec le Patriarche Athénagoras.* Paris: Fayard, 1976.

———. *Taizé: A Meaning to Life.* Chicago: GIA Publications, 1997.

Clements, Keith. *Faith on the Frontier: A Life of J.H. Oldham.* Edinburgh: T and T Clark, 1999.

Confessing the One Faith: An Ecumenical Explication of the Apostolic Faith as it is Confessed in the Nicene-Constantinopolitan Creed (381). Geneva: WCC Publications, 1991.

Congar, Yves. *Dialogue Between Christians.* London: Chapman, 1966.

———. *Une passion: L'Unite, Reflections et souvenirs: 1929–1973.* Paris: Éditions du Cerf, 1974.

———. *Diversity and Communion.* London: SCM Press, 1985.

———. *Fifty Years of Catholic Theology.* London: SCM Press, 1988.

Coucousis, Iakovos. *Faith for a Lifetime.* New York: Doubleday, 1988.

Crisis and Challenge of the Ecumenical Movement: Integrity and Indivisibility, a Statement of the Institute for Ecumenical Research, Strasbourg. Geneva: WCC Publications, 1994.

Crow, Paul A., Jr. *Christian Unity: Matrix for Mission.* New York: Friendship Press, 1982.

Curtis, Charles J. *Söderblom: Ecumenical Pioneer.* Minneapolis: Augsburg Publishing Company, 1967.

Curtis, Geoffrey. *Paul Couturier and Unity in Christ.* London: SCM Press, 1964.

Cusack, Pearce. *Blessed Gabrellia of Unity: A Patron for the Ecumenical Movement.* Ros Cre, Ireland: Cistercian Press, 1995.

Cushing, Richard. *Pastoral Letter to the Clergy and Laity of the Archdiocese of Boston and to Men of Good Will in Every Tradition.* Boston: Daughters of St. Paul, 1963.

Davey, Colin. *Pioneer for Unity: Metropolitan Kritopoulos 1589–1639 and Relations between the Orthodox, Roman Catholic and Reformed Churches.* London: British Council of Churches, 1987.

Dick, John A. *The Malines Conversations Revisited.* Leuven: Leuven University Press, 1989.

Duffy, Eamon. *The Stripping of the Altars: Tradition Religion in England c. 1400–c. 1580.* New Haven: Yale University Press, 1992.

Dvornik, Francis. *The Photian Schism.* Cambridge: University Press, 1948.

Ellingsen, Mark. *The Cutting Edge: How Churches Speak on Social Issues.* Geneva: WCC Publications, 1993.

Evans, G. R., Lorelei F. Fuchs, and Diane C. Kessler. *Encounters for Unity.* Norwich: The Canterbury Press, 1995.

Every, George. *Misunderstandings Between East and West.* Richmond: John Knox Press, 1966.

Fackre, Gabriel J. *Restoring the Center: Essays Evangelical and Ecumenical.* Downers Grove, Ill.: InterVarsity Press, 1998.

Fackre, Gabriel, and Michael Root. *Affirmations and Admonitions: Lutheran Decisions and Dialogues with Reformed, Episcopal, and Roman Catholic Churches.* Grand Rapids, Mich.: Eerdmans, 1998.

Fahey, Michael A. *Assembly 2000 A.D.: Preparing for a Truly Ecumenical Council.* Regina: Campion College, 1981.

Fahey, Michael A., and John Meyendorff. *Trinitarian Theology East and West: St. Thomas Aquinas–St. Gregory Palamas.* Brookline, Mass.: Holy Cross Orthodox Press, 1977.

Faith and Order Commission. *Baptism Eucharist and Ministry.* Geneva: World Council of Churches, 1982.

———. *Church and World.* Geneva: WCC Publications, 1990.

———. *Confessing the One Faith.* Geneva: WCC Publications, 1992.

Fry, Harold E., ed. *A History of the Ecumenical Movement 1948–1968.* Geneva: WCC, 1970.

FitzGerald, Kyriaki Karidoyanes. Women Deacons in the Orthodox Church. Rev. ed. Brookline, Mass.: Holy Cross Orthodox Press, 1999.

FitzGerald, Kyriaki, and Thomas FitzGerald. *Happy in the Lord: The Beatitudes for Everyday Perspectives from Orthodox Spirituality.* Brookline, Mass.: Holy Cross Orthodox Press, 2000.

FitzGerald, Thomas. *The Orthodox Church.* Westport: Greenwood Press, 1995.

———. *The Ecumenical Patriarchate and Christian Unity.* Brookline, Mass.: Holy Cross Orthodox Press, 1997.

FitzGerald, Thomas, and Peter Bouteneff. *Turn to God, Rejoice in Hope: Orthodox Reflections on the Way to Harare: The Report of the WCC Orthodox Pre-Assembly Meeting and Selected Resource Materials.* Geneva: WCC, Orthodox Task Force, 1998.

Flesseman-Van Leer, Ellen. *The Bible: Its Authority and Interpretation in the Ecumenical Movement.* Geneva: WCC Publications, 1980.

Florovsky, Georges. *Ways of Russian Theology.* Belmont, Mass.: Nordland Publishing Company, 1979.

———. *Ecumenism I: A Doctrinal Approach.* Vaduz, Lichtenstein: Büchervertriebsanstalt, 1989.

———. *Ecumenism II: A Historical Approach.* Vaduz, Lichtenstein: Büchervertriebsanstalt, 1989.

Ford, John T. *Ecumenical Findings: Toward a Conciliar Fellowship.* New York: National Council of Churches of Christ, USA, 1987.

Fouyas, Methodios. *Anglicanism, Orthodoxy, and Roman Catholicism.* Brookline, Mass.: Holy Cross Orthodox Press, 1984.

Gaustad, Edwin Scott. *A Religious History of America.* Rev. ed. San Francisco: Harper and Row, 1990.

Geanakoplos, Deno. *Byzantine East and Latin West: Two Worlds of Christendom in Middle Ages and Renaissance.* Oxford: Blackwell, 1966.

George, K.M. *The Silent Roots: Orthodox Perspectives on Christian Spirituality.* Geneva: WCC Publications, 1994.

———. *The Early Church: Defending the Faith, Witness and Proclamation: Patristic Perspectives.* Geneva: WCC Publications, 1996.

Goodall, Norman, ed. *All Things New: The Fourth Assembly Uppsala 1968.* Geneva: WCC Publications, 1968.

Goosen, Gideon. *Bringing Churches Together: An Introduction to Ecumenism.* Newtown, Australia: Dwyer, 1993.

Granberg-Michaelson, Karen. *Healing Community.* Geneva: WCC Publications, 1991.

Granberg-Michaelson, Wesley. *Redeeming the Creation: the Rio Earth Summit: Challenges for the Churches.* Geneva: WCC Publications, 1992.

Gregorios, Paulos. *The Meaning and Nature of Diakonia.* Geneva: World Council of Churches, 1988.

Groupe des Dombes. *For the Conversion of the Churches.* Geneva: WCC Publications, 1993.

Harakas, Stanley S. *Towards Transfigured Life.* Minneapolis: Light and Life Publishing, 1983.

———. *Living the Faith: The Praxis of Eastern Orthodox Ethics.* Minneapolis: Light and Life Publishing, 1992.

Harling, Per, ed. *Worshipping Ecumenically: Orders of Service from Global Meetings with Suggestions for Local Use.* Geneva: WCC Publications, 1995.

Haugh, Richard. *Photios and the Carolingians: The Trinitarian Controversy.* Belmont: Nordland Publishing Company, 1975.

Henn, William. *The Honor of My Brothers: A Short History of the Relations Between the Pope and the Bishops.* New York: Crossroad, 2000.

———. *One Faith: Biblical and Patristic Contributions Towards Understanding Unity in Faith.* New York: Paulist Press, 1995.

Hodgson, Leonard, ed. *The Second World Conference on Faith and Order.* London: SCM, 1938.

Holze, Heinrich, ed. *The Church as Communion: Lutheran Contributions to Ecclesiology.* Geneva: Lutheran World Federation, 1997.

Horgan, Thaddeus D. *Walking Together: Roman Catholics and Ecumenism Twenty-five Years after Vatican II.* Grand Rapids, Mich.: Eerdmans, 1990.

Hurley, Michael. *Christian Unity: An Ecumenical Second Spring?* Dublin: Veritas, 1998.

Hussey, J.M. *The Orthodox Church in the Byzantine Empire.* Oxford: Clarendon Press, 1986.

Ironmonger, F.A. *William Temple, Archbishop of Canterbury: His Life and Letters.* London: Oxford University Press, 1948.

Istavridis, Vasilios. *Orthodoxy and Anglicanism.* London: SPCK, 1966.

Jossua, Jean-Pierre. *Yves Conger: Theology in the Service of God's People.* Chicago: Priory Press, 1968.

Keshishian, Aram. *Conciliar Fellowship: A Common Goal.* Geneva: WCC Publications, 1992.

Kessler, Diane, ed. *Together on the Way: Official Report of the Eighth Assembly of the World Council of Churches.* Geneva: WCC Publications, 1999.

Kessler, Diane, and Michael Kinnamon. *Councils of Churches and the Ecumenical Vision.* Geneva: WCC Publications, 2000.

Kilmartin, Edward. *Towards Reunion: The Orthodox and Roman Catholic Churches.* New York: Paulist Press, 1979.

Kinnamon, Michael. *Truth and Community: Diversity and Its Limits in the Ecumenical Movement.* Grand Rapids, Mich.: Eerdmans, 1988.

———. *Vision of the Ecumenical Movement and How It Has Been Impoverished by Its Friends.* St. Louis, Mo.: Chalice Press, 2003.

Lash, Nicholas. *Doctrinal Development and Christian Unity.* London: Sheed and Ward, 1967.

Lathrop, Gordon. *Holy Things: A Theology of Worship.* Minneapolis: Fortress Press, 1993.

L'Huillier, Peter. *The Church of the Ancient Councils.* Crestwood, New York: St. Vladimir's Seminary Press, 1996.

Limouris, Gennadios. *Justice, Peace, and the Integrity of Creation: Insights from Orthodoxy.* Geneva: WCC Publications, 1990.

Lossky, Nicholas, et al., eds. *Dictionary of the Ecumenical Movement.* Geneva: WCC Publications, 1991.

Massie, J. W. *The Evangelical Alliance.* London, 1847.

Mathews, James K. *A Church Truly Catholic.* Nashville: Abington, 1969.

May, Melanie A. *Bonds of Unity: Women, Theology, and the Worldwide Church.* Atlanta: Scholars Press, 1989.

McNeill, John T. *The History and Character of Calvinism.* Oxford: Oxford University Press, 1954.

Metzger, Bruce M. *The New Testament: Its Background, Growth, and Content.* Nashville: Abington Press, 1965.

Meyendorff, John. *Byzantine Theology.* New York: Fordham University Press, 1974.

———. *Christ in Eastern Christian Thought.* Washington: Corpus Publications, 1969.

———. *The Orthodox Church.* New York: Pantheon Books, 1962.

Meyendorff, John, and Robert Tobias, eds. *Salvation in Christ.* Minneapolis: Augsburg, 1992.

Meyer, Harding. *That All May Be One: Perceptions and Models of Ecumenicity.* Grand Rapids, Mich.: Eerdmans, 1999.

Neill, Stephen. *A History of Christian Missions.* New York: Penguin Books, 1964.

Neill, Stephen T. *Brothers of the Faith.* New York: Abingdon Press, 1960.

Nelson, J. Robert. *Overcoming Christian Divisions.* New York: Association Press, 1962.

Newbigin, Lesslie. *Is Christ Divided?* Grand Rapids, Mich.: Eerdmans Publishing Company, 1961.

———. *Unfinished Agenda: An Autobiography.* Grand Rapids, Mich.: Eerdmans, 1985.

Nichols, Aidan. *Rome and the Eastern Churches.* Collegeville: The Liturgical Press, 1992.

Nissiotis, Marine, and Mihail P. Grigoris. *Nicco Nissiotis: Religion, Philosophy, and Sport in Dialogue.* Athens: Gregoris, 1994.

Nordbeck, Elizabeth C. *That All May Be One: Celebrating a Century of Ecumenical Witness.* Boston: Massachusetts Council of Churches, 2002.

O'Gara, Margaret. *The Ecumenical Gift Exchange.* Collegeville, Minn.: Liturgical Press, 1998.

Oldham, J.H., ed. *The Oxford Conference: Official Report.* Chicago: Willet, Clark, 1937.

Outler, Albert. *The Christian Tradition and the Unity We Seek.* New York: Oxford University Press, 1957.

Pelikan, Jaroslav. *The Christian Tradition: A History of the Development of Doctrine, Vols. 1–5.* Chicago: The University of Chicago Press, 1971–89.

Philippou, A.J., ed. *The Orthodox Ethos.* Oxford: Holywell, 1964.

Piepkorn, Arthur Cary. *Profiles in Belief: The Religious Bodies in the United States and Canada.* 4 vols. in 3. New York: Harper and Row, 1977–79.

Pobee, J.S. *West Africa: Christ Would Be an African Too.* Geneva: WCC Publications, 1996.

———. *Towards Viable Theological Education: Ecumenical Imperative, Catalyst of Renewal.* Geneva: WCC Publications, 1997.

Pobee, J.S., and Gabriel Ositelu. *African Initiatives in Christianity: The Growth, Gifts and Diversities of Indigenous African Churches: A Challenge to the Ecumenical Movement.* Geneva: WCC Publications, 1998.

Potter, Philip. *Life in All Its Fullness: Reflections on the Central Issues of Ecumenical Agenda.* Geneva: WCC Publications, 1981.

Programme Unit on Unity and Renewal. *Towards a Common Date for Easter.* Geneva: Programme Unit on Unity and Renewal, 1997.

Raiser, Konrad. *Ecumenism in Transition: A Paradigm Shift in the Ecumenical Movement?* Geneva: WCC Publications, 1991.

———. *To Be the Church: Challenges and Hopes for the New Millennium.* Geneva: WCC Publications, 1997.

Rilliet, Jean. *Zwingli: Third Man of the Reformation.* Philadelphia: Westminster Press, 1964.

Roberson, Ronald. *The Eastern Christian Churches: A Brief Survey.* Rome: Orientalia Christiana, 1999.

Root, Michael, and Risto Saainen. *Baptism and Unity of the Church.* Grand Rapids, Mich.: Eerdmans, 1998.

Rouse, Ruth. *The World Student Christian Federation.* London: SCM Press, 1948.

Rouse, Ruth, and Stephen Neill, eds. *A History of the Ecumenical Movement 1517–1948.* Philadelphia: Westminster, 1967.

Rusch, William G. *Reception: An Ecumenical Opportunity.* Philadelphia: Fortress, 1988.

Rusch, William, et al., eds. *Justification and the Future of the Ecumenical Movement.* Collegeville, Minn.: Liturgical Press, 2003.

Ryan, Thomas. *A Survival Guide for Ecumenically-Minded Christians.* Ottawa: Novalis, 1989.

Sabev, Todor. *The Orthodox Churches in the World Council of Churches: Towards the Future.* Geneva: WCC Publications, 1996.

Sagovsky, Nicholas. *Ecumenism, Christian Origins, and the Practice of Communion.* Cambridge: Cambridge University Press, 2000.

Sarkesian, Karekin. *The Council of Chalcedon and the Armenian Church.* London: SPCK, 1965.

Sauca, Ioan. *Orthodoxy and Cultures: Inter-Orthodox Consultation on Gospel and Cultures.* Geneva: WCC Publications, 1996.

Sawyer, Mary R. *Black Ecumenism: Implementing the Demands of Justice.* Valley Forge, Pa.: Trinity Press International, 1994.

Schutz, Roger. *Unity: Man's Tomorrow.* London: Faith Press, 1962.

Sellers, R. V. *The Council of Chalcedon: A Historical and Doctrinal Survey.* London: SPCK, 1953.

Slack, Kenneth, ed. *Hope in the Desert: The Churches' United Response to Human Need 1944–1984.* Geneva: WCC Publications, 1986.

Southern, R. W. *Western Church and Society in the Middle Ages.* New York: Penguin Books, 1970.

Spitz, Lewis W. *The Protestant Reformation.* New York: Harper and Row, 1985.

Stephanopoulos, Robert. *A Study of Recent Greek Orthodox Ecumenical Relations, 1902–1968.* Ann Arbor: University Microfilms, 1970.

Stylianopoulos, Theodore and S. Marr. Heim, eds. *Ecumenical Perspectives on the Holy Spirit.* Brookline, Mass.: Holy Cross Orthodox Press, 1986.

Swidler, Leonard. *Blood Witness for Peace and Unity: The Life of M. J. Metzger.* Denville, New Jersey: Diminision, 1977.

Taft, Robert. *Beyond East and West: Problems of Liturgical Understanding*. Washington, D.C.: The Pastoral Press, 1984.

Tanner, Norman, ed. *Decrees of the Ecumenical Councils.* New York: Sheed and Ward, 1990.

Tavard, George. *Two Centuries of Ecumenism.* New York: Mentor-Omega Book, 1962.

———. *The Church, Community of Salvation: An Ecumenical Ecclesiology.* Collegeville, Minn.: Liturgical Press, 1992.

Taylor, Michael. *Not Angels but Agencies: The Ecumenical Response to Poverty.* Geneva: WCC, 1995.

Thurian, Max, ed. *Churches Respond to BEM, vols. I–VI.* Geneva: WCC Publications, 1983.

Thurian, Max, and Geoffrey Wainwright, eds. *Baptism and Eucharist: Ecumenical Convergence in Celebration.* Geneva: WCC Publications, 1983.

Tillard, Jean-Marie R. *The Bishop of Rome.* Collegeville, Minn.: The Liturgical Press, 1983.

———. *Church and Churches: The Ecclesiology of Communion.* Collegeville, Minn.: The Liturgical Press, 1992.

———, ed. *Agapè, Études en l'honneur de Mgr. Pierre Duprey.* Geneva: Centre Orthodoxe de Patriarcat Ecuménique, 2000.

Tobias, Robert. *Heaven on Earth: A Lutheran-Orthodox Odyssey.* Racine, Wisc.: Tobias-Wells Endowments, 1977.

Tomkins, Oliver. *A Time for Unity.* London: SCM Press, 1964.

Torrance, Thomas Forsyth. *Conflict and Agreement in the Church.* London: Lutterworth Press, 1959.

———. *Theological Dialogue Between Orthodox and Reformed Churches.* Edinburgh: Scottish Academic Press, 1985.

Towards the Great Council: Introductory Reports on the Interorthodox Commission in Preparation for the Next Great and Holy Council of the Orthodox Church. London: SPCK, 1972.

Tsetsis, Georges. *Orthodox Thought: Reports of Orthodox Consultations Organized by the World Council of Churches, 1975–1982.* Geneva: World Council of Churches, 1983.

Van der Bent, A. J. *Historical Dictionary of Ecumenical Christianity,* Metuchen, N.J.: Scarecrow Press, 1994.

———. *Commitment to God's World: A Concise Critical Survey of Ecumenical Social Thought.* Geneva: WCC Publications, 1995.

Van Elderen, Marlin. *Introducing the World Council of Churches.* Geneva: WCC Publications, 1990.

Vassiliadis, Petros. *Eucharist and Witness: Orthodox Perspectives on the Unity and Mission of the Church.* Geneva: WCC Publications, 1998.

Villain, M. *The Life and Work of Abbé Paul Couturier.* Hayward Heath: Holy Cross Convent, 1959.

Vischer, Lucas. *Spirit of God, Spirit of Christ: Ecumenical Reflections on the Filioque Controversy.* London: SPCK, 1981.

Visser 't Hooft, W. A. *The Pressure of Our Common Calling.* Garden City, N.Y.: Doubleday, 1959.

———. *Memoirs.* London: SCM, 1973.

———. *The Genesis and Formation of the World Council of Churches.* Geneva: WCC, 1982.

Volf, Miroslav, and Dorothy C. Bass. *Practicing Theology.* Grand Rapids, Mich.: 2002.

von Arx, Urs, ed. *Koinonia auf Altkirchlicher Basis.* Bern: Internationalen Kirchlichen Zeitschrift, 1989.

Wainwright, Geoffrey. *The Ecumenical Moment: Crisis and Opportunity for the Church.* Grand Rapids, Mich.: William B. Eerdmans Publishing Company, 1983.

———. *Worship with One Accord: Where Liturgy and Ecumenism Embrace.* Oxford: Oxford University Press, 1997.

———. *Lesslie Newbigin: A Theological Life.* Oxford: Oxford University Press, 2000.

Ware, Timothy Kallistos. *Eustratios Argenti: A Study of the Greek Church Under Turkish Rule.* Oxford: Clarendon Press, 1964.

Ware, Timothy (Kallistos). *The Orthodox Church.* Rev. ed. Baltimore: Penguin Books, 1976.

Webb, Pauline, ed. *Faith and Faithfulness: Essays on Contemporary Ecumenical Themes.* Geneva: WCC Publications, 1984.

Wigenbach, Gregory. *Broken, Yet Never Sundered.* Brookline, Mass.: Holy Cross Orthodox Press, 1987.

Willebrands, Johanes. *Oecuménisme et problems actuels.* Paris: Édition du Cerf, 1969.

With All God's People: The New Ecumenical Prayer Cycle. Geneva: WCC Publications, 1989.

Zabriskie, A. *Bishop Brent, Crusader for Christian Unity.* Philadelphia: The Westminster Press, 1948.

Zizioulas, John D. *Being as Communion.* Crestwood, N.Y.: St. Vladimir's Seminary Press, 1985.

———. *Eucharist, Bishop, Church.* Brookline, Mass.: Holy Cross Orthodox Press, 2002.

Index

About the Author

THOMAS E. FITZGERALD is Professor of Church History and Historical Theology at Holy Cross Greek Orthodox School of Theology in Brookline, Massachusetts. He has served as Executive Director of the Program on Unity and Renewal at the World Council of Churches in Geneva, Switzerland. As a theologian in the Orthodox Church, he has participated in theological conferences and ecumenical dialogues in over 30 countries. He is the author of a number of articles and books including *The Orthodox Church* published by Greenwood Press.